I0590081

FREE FALL

Writings on Voice, Desire & Surrender

DUSTIN BEALL SMITH

NOT-TWO PRESS

The following essays first appeared in the publications listed below. They
have been revised and updated from their original form.
"Teacher, Time to Go," *Writing on the Edge* © 2005 Dustin Beall Smith
"One Draft at a Time: The Rewards of Process," *Writing on the Edge* ©
2007 Dustin Beall Smith
"Shade: A Letter from Gettysburg," *The Sun* © 2007 Dustin Beall Smith
"Being [T]here," *You: An Anthology of Essays Devoted to the Second Person* © 2013 Dustin Beall Smith
"At Once," *Gray Love: Stories About Dating and New Relationships After
60* © 2023 Dustin Beall Smith

Not-Two Press
Gettysburg, PA, USA

Library of Congress Control Number: 2025904596

ISBN 979-8-9925552-0-2 (hardcover)
ISBN 979-8-9925552-1-9 (paperback)
ISBN 979-8-9925552-2-6 (e-book)

Also available in audiobook.

Editing by Lynn Slobogian and Julia Grandison
Cover and interior design by Alex Hennig

ADVANCE PRAISE FOR *FREE FALL*

"This book is a marvel of lucidity, grace, and courage. *Free Fall* entrances and delights while imparting an iconoclastic wisdom, one we so desperately need in these times."

—Kim Dana Kupperman, series editor, *The Best American Essays*, and founder, Welcome Table Press

"Smith speaks to us from those liminal spaces—between teaching and learning, writing and reading, loving and leaving, freedom and restraint—where voice finds its footing. But what seems at first to be a limen turns out to be a precipice and if we really want to be alive in our writing, it is not enough to stand on the edge. We must, as *Free Fall* sublimely illustrates, jump."

—Suzanne Maria Menghraj, essayist and Clinical Professor of Writing and Critical Creative Production at New York University

"With a wise and winning authenticity, Smith captures the meaning of a fully lived life. In essays, fiction, and poetry, he revisits his nine-decade journey as truth seeker. We happily go along for the ride. *Free Fall* is a gift of storytelling and late-life reflection on where we've been and what lies ahead."

—Mimi Schwartz, author, *Good Neighbors, Bad Times Revisited: New Echoes of My Father's German Village*

"Whether writing about leading a class of writing students (or being led by them) into a 'place of not knowing,' or a poem to his dead son, or about the clear-cutting of trees from a Gettysburg battlefield as if they were the scab on a wound, time and again Smith underscores with bracing clarity how the things least visible to us—time and death—matter most. He is a writer of rare insight, depth, and beauty."

—Peter Selgin, author, *A Boy's Guide to Outer Space*

"*Free Fall* is the kind of book you want to keep on your bedside table forever. The wise voice weaving through this collection reminds us that it's never too late to change your life. Deeply philosophical and spiritual in surprising ways, Smith's gorgeous writing will inspire you and teach you how and where to find wonder wherever you are."

—Marjory Wentworth, author, *One River, One Boat: Occasional Poems and Other Stories*

FREE FALL

To Elizabeth Dane, the love of my late life,
with endless gratitude,

and

For my wise and wonderful daughter,
Trellan Karr Smith, always.

Old age is deserved by anyone who refuses to abdicate, [. . .]
It presupposes a life dedicated to all those who have
foundered, but also to all those whom we expect not to fail.
I would call that the twin face, the Janus face of old age:
one side is turned toward the defeated, while the other side
is turned toward those who have not yet been defeated and
perhaps never could be.

—Elias Canetti, *The Agony of Flies*

Contents

Preface

Dream last night, 8 August 2024

I'm standing on a street corner, aware that I must cross the avenue carefully. I must look both ways, then both ways again, which is odd because there are no people, no cars, no buses, no taxis or bicycles, no buildings of any kind, and everything seems both inwardly and outwardly lit. I'm totally alone in this place, and I'm struck by the strange seductive beauty of the blue-hued sunlight. Winterish, for sure, but unearthly, too.

I step off the curb onto the ice melt that fills the avenue—onto it, not into it—and my feet don't get wet or cold. The blue-filtered sun has no warmth, yet I feel no chill. I cross atop the watery avenue and walk toward the sea, which is frozen solid, the waves etched and motionless, as if carved into shape. I see the sea, see the stillness ahead, see the quality of cold sunlight and bluish ice.

I turn and look back at the intersection, which seems to have disappeared. Just an avenue of ice water now, motionless, un-flowing. I know I must look both ways again if I am to make it back across the avenue. As I step forward, the water deepens.

I awake from this dream knowing what it portends, or proposes, and I'm infused with awe; I feel grateful for the message it communicates to me. An analyst might guess at its meaning, but that's doubtful, since the analysis of dreams is now considered by those in academia to be a pseudoscience. And they are partly right, of course. Dreams have nothing to do with science.

Neuroscience does. But the value of dreams is precisely that they are *not* subject to scientific investigation or rigorous testing.

My dreams are me communicating with myself subconsciously, perhaps using archetypal imagery mined from the unconscious. In my sleep, I let go. That's what sleep is. I lose control and then the part of me that abhors control takes over. When I awake, I regain control and attempt to make rational sense of whatever it is I've dreamt. Not scientific sense, though; more like intuitive "human" sense, which is achieved in part by investigating the *feeling* associated with the dream.

If you keep journals over a period of many years, you'll likely discover that the dreams you've recorded are more memorable, more sharply resonant, than other journal entries about, say, quotidian doings, relationship struggles, or vacation plans.

I ignore certain dreams; some are nonsensical, some frivolous, some just plain weird. But many others simply must be listened to and made sense of, honored, if you are to lead a multidimensional, creative life, where intuition and reason interact in a balanced way. As with flint and steel, that interaction can produce a spark.

—Dustin Beall Smith, February 2025

Acknowledgments

I am immensely grateful to the sensitive and talented editors that saw merit in this book and helped me shape it: Carra Simpson, Lynn Slobogian, Julia Grandison, and book designer Alex Hennig. As well, to Kim Dana Kupperman for recommending Carra, and to archivist Jessica Cromer, who patiently scanned hundreds of drawings from my notebooks.

Thanks also to my dear friends and colleagues: Will and Anne Lane, Susan and Kerr Thompson, Barbara and Tom Oliver, Jack and Liz Ryan, Jeffrey Williams, Glenn Alan Cheney, Doug Miller, Haddon Hufford, Taylor Pape, Kristina Radha Curtiss, Charles and Cornelia Saltzman, Mark Rudd, Sam Clinton and Rusty Harrington, Sandra Bonk, Jemima James, Katherine Bigham, Noah Lyons, Scott Reinhardt, and Grace Dane Mazur and Barry Mazur.

My gratitude to former students, now friends: Tim Gillham, Emily Cranfill, Sydney Kaplan, Maelina Frattaroli, Laurie Elwin (née de Castro), Allison Caras, Julia Gokalp, Hilary Landfried, Jake A. Hill, Abby Kallin, Caroline Fuestel, Heather Grace Simons, Joyin Shi, Nazli Inal, Erica Uszak, and Michele Zampini.

Special thanks to my daughter, Trellan Karr Smith, and her husband, Dan Taylor; to my siblings, Leslie Borden and Lochlin Smith; and to my ever-caring and generous partner, Elizabeth Dane, who insisted that I compile this selection.

My heartfelt gratitude goes to the doctors and nurses, angels all, who have paved an easy path through some difficult times recently.

SELECTED

PERSONAL ESSAYS

The Secret of Begin

2013

—new moon! [. . .]

teach disappearing also me the keen
illimitable secret of begin

—e. e. cummings

. . . Take that particularly dreary January day in the year 2000, when I decided uncharacteristically to nap in the middle of the afternoon. I was almost sixty. Both my parents had died within the previous five years. Twice divorced and the father of two children, one of whom had died almost three decades earlier, I was now writing in my spare time and earning a living as a grip in the movie industry. Still physically fit (my girlfriend had seen to it that I kept up with my yoga), I'd nevertheless grown acutely aware that I was about to age out of my chosen profession.

The problem of what to do with the rest of my life gaped open before me like the Grand Canyon glimpsed from the North Rim. Nearing retirement age without the means to retire, without even a college degree, and forced to ponder a new career like a twentysomething with his life still ahead of him, felt both pathetic and exhausting. It made me want to hibernate.

So, I climbed the steel-rung ladder to the loft bed in my small Upper West Side apartment, a perch with a view of the Hudson River. Lying back on the rumpled sheets and unfluffed pillows, I sighed with the resignation of a dying man. As I lay there, listening to the radiator hissing, the pressing problem of a career change slowly faded, and I think a part of me would willingly have died right there as an alternative to waking up with that problem still on my mind.

But instead of dying that afternoon, I had a dream—a mini-dream so brief it might more properly be called a vision: *I was walking along a path in the woods when suddenly my chest exploded, spewing out thousands of tiny seeds with fuzzy little tails that caught the wind and scattered everywhere.*

That's all there was to the dream vision. When I opened my eyes, I felt a sensation of utter serenity flooding my body. I had no idea what the vision might *mean*, but it felt blissful, and I welcomed the feeling like a man with a needle still dangling from his arm.

A clue to what this forest-path-seed vision might actually portend presented itself some weeks later, when I went outside to watch the sunset from a favorite spot in Riverside Park—an up-jutting lump of metamorphic bedrock that I'd dubbed Brain Rock because of its deep striations and cranial shape. I took along a notebook, as I always did in the park, and I plunked myself down on the westernmost slope of the brain—its prefrontal cortex, you might say. I was alone up there and could expect to be undisturbed in my sunset watching.

Settling my buttocks into a smooth declivity and zipping up my winter parka, I crossed my legs in half lotus, rested my notebook and pen on my lap, and looked out across the river to the west, where the sun lingered about three fingerbreadths above the New Jersey horizon. It was a mild February day. The sun was setting downriver from due west, and I could easily assess its descent. As I watched, I slipped unknowingly into a meditative state that involved attention but not thought. I was not *aware* of watching. My usual self-consciousness, with a notebook and pen at the ready, had for some reason morphed into that wonderful egoless state of mind that one can be aware of only in retrospect.

I remained lost for some time in this semiconscious realm, which bordered on but did not entirely collapse into sleep. I might have shut my eyes, because when my consciousness returned, the sun was already dipping into the horizon, cradled nicely between two apartment buildings across the river.

That's when I heard something right behind me, a slight shuffling sound, like a sneaker rubbing against rock. I spun around reflexively and saw twelve or thirteen people in their late teens, all of them in parkas and scarves, sitting in half lotus with notebooks and pens in their laps and looking at the sunset, as if in imitation of me.

Aghast at this mysterious but entirely waking vision—how had I not heard them approach?—I continued to stare at the group, but they paid me no mind at all. Not a single eye met mine, and they made no sign that my presence on the rock was interrupting their focus on the sunset. Not even a polite nod to the only adult among them. Nothing. They seemed not to exist on the same temporal plane as I, yet there they sat, for all the world like students in a classroom. But what had brought them together? Where was their teacher?

Feeling somewhat embarrassed to be in their line of sight, I stood up stiffly, gathered myself, and traversed down the right hemisphere of Brain Rock until I reached the little dirt path connecting it to the wider macadam walk, where I paused to look back at the young people still busy with their notebooks.

* * *

If linking these two visions—one a midday dream, one an actual event—into a narrative seems a little too neat, well, probably it is, but this is what the work of spirit—the work of change—looks like. Visions, and I choose the word advisedly, are pitons we can pound into the mountainside of life as we ascend it, so that when we descend into memory (and gratitude) we can make use of them along the way, as I am doing now. Visions often come unbidden, so they leave an indelible mark on the memory and have immense staying power. They possess a remarkable sturdiness, though sturdiness is perhaps all they have if we don't act on them. Like pitons on a rock face, they are useless if not strung together and put to some purpose. As the famous Lakota medicine man Black Elk observed in John G. Neihardt's *Black Elk Speaks*, visions are powerless unless they are "performed [. . .] on earth for the people to see."

In retrospect, I can say that *my* performance went into preproduction the next morning, when I walked thirty blocks uptown to the Office of the University Registrar at Columbia University. I'd attended Columbia's School of General Studies for four years, from 1960 to 1964, but I'd left in protest—without a degree—during my final semester.

All I wanted now, in April 2000, was my transcript from those days and permission to complete my degree so that I could get on with life in my old age. Compelled by financial circumstances and that good old inextinguishable need to survive—and for no higher reason—I was finally coming in from the cold.

The registrar's office located my records in the archives, and during my admissions interview the next day, the Dean of Students laughed and asked me, rhetorically, "Why are all you guys from the '60s coming back for a degree?" She was referring, I think, to the rebellious Columbia College students who had participated in the campus uprising of 1968, holding a dean hostage and occupying campus buildings, as a result of which many students either were expelled or dropped out.

I chuckled knowingly and shook my head, as if to say, "Yeah, those were the days."

But those were not *my* days. My reason for dropping out in protest was not political. In 1964, Vietnam was still a rumor and no threat to me. My reason was entirely personal, and it involved, in equal parts, impulsivity and stupidity. I'd been an atypical college student, having dropped out of my degree program at Lawrence College and having deferred my studies between 1958 and 1960 to help pioneer the sport of skydiving in the United States—an adrenaline-laced, ego-inflating experience that had involved a modicum of what we would now call "media exposure." I registered at Columbia in 1960, and by my senior year—when I was already three years married and had many hundreds of free falls to my credit—I was eager to have my way with my senior thesis before claiming my undergraduate degree in English and moving on to God knows what.

But, after repeated failed attempts to convince my senior seminar professor to accept my thesis subject, I informed the university that they could take their degree and shove it.

Forty years later, I was consumed with a new purpose and buoyed by the spirit of a familiar old space still resonant of seemingly simpler times: the broad Columbia campus with its iconic statue of Alma Mater on the steps of Low Library, directly across the quad from Butler Library, where the names of dead white European males (the Greeks and Romans) remained deeply etched into the lintel above the structure's fourteen Ionic columns.

My transcripts confirmed that I'd completed my major in the '60s but had dropped out owing fifteen credits (three per course). I took it without complaint when they insisted that I now complete twenty-one credits. (In my day, there'd been no diversity courses, and I would now need to fulfill a missing science requirement.)

I chose a class in Native American religions in order to read up on tribes other than my adoptive one, the Lakota Sioux, with whom I would soon be finishing up a four-year-long prayer cycle, in July. And I enrolled in a premed cognitive neuroscience course. The remaining fifteen credits I spread between the Department of Classics and Ancient Studies at Barnard College and workshops in fiction, nonfiction, and poetry in the Undergraduate Writing Program.

I didn't have the money to pay for these classes, so I jumped at the chance to obtain federal grants and student loans. Had I been more Christlike, I might have trashed all the Citibank pamphlets that were scattered around the quad clearly with the permission and encouragement of the administration. I might even have driven the moneylenders from the temple, once again sacrificing my degree. But I wasn't remotely Christlike; I just wanted to survive, and Columbia—whose wide campus walkways had become an oil-stained parking lot for corporate SUVs and long black limousines—had clearly ceased pretending it was an impregnable temple of learning.

I supplemented my loans and grants by working several days a week on movies—part-time work thrown to me by key grips who had once been members of my crew when I was a key. Two obscure Woody Allen films and Wes Anderson's *The Royal Tenenbaums* were three such projects.

I received my undergraduate degree in the spring of 2001. My first wife, who had helped to support my studies forty years earlier, graciously attended the ceremony, as did our daughter, Trellan.

R. W. (Johnny) Apple Jr., a longtime associate editor of *The New York Times* who had been a classmate of mine in 1960–61, was the graduation speaker. "I thought I saw some white hair walk across that stage," he told me later at a reception.

That summer of 2001, while standing on the tailgate of the grip truck at the end of a long day of filming, I received a call from a professor at the graduate writing program of Columbia University School of the Arts, telling me that I'd been accepted into their two-year MFA program. He said that he'd read my recent personal essay in *The Gettysburg Review*, and that while he couldn't imagine what more his program could teach me about writing than I already knew, they'd be honored to have me as a student. I reassured him that I still had plenty to learn, and that while I wasn't sure what I would *do* with an MFA degree, it felt right—and dizzyingly indulgent—to spend two more precious years in the bubble of studenthood.

* * *

My aforementioned visions and my new undergraduate degree notwithstanding, I still didn't suspect—it hadn't *hit* me yet—that I was on track to becoming a teacher. I was beginning to publish and earlier had tucked under my belt two month-long fellowships at the Virginia Center for the Creative Arts, which gave me nominal street cred in the writing world. None of those credentials meant anything in the *real* world of writing, which requires that you write at least a book. I knew that. But my youthful aspiration to be a big deal in that real world had long ago atrophied and died. I was more interested, now, in writing than in *being* a writer.

It took very little scaffolding to support my belief that I could hold my own in the company of writers and artists, that I wasn't just a laborer in the movie industry, that I had it in me after all. I could talk a good game, and I never missed an opportunity to present myself as a writer. In 1997, during my first visit to the Pine Ridge Reservation in South Dakota, I'd asked Wakinyan Sna Mani, a medicine man who shortly thereafter adopted me as his brother, "What do you have to do to become a medicine man?"

His answer: "Call yourself one."

Returning to New York City from the reservation that summer, I'd taken his advice to heart: I'd placed a quarter-page ad in *Poets & Writers* promoting myself as an "adviser to writers" and promising to help unearth "innate visions." In no time, and with no credentials or degrees, I was earning a small income from one-on-one sessions with aspiring writers. That I'd become an adviser to writers by calling myself one might account for the puzzlement expressed by the medicine man's wife when she later asked, "Why do you need a white man's degree?"

"Because I'm a white man," I said, as simply and as sadly as that.

* * *

Going back to school in one's sixties isn't all that unusual. The value of a continuing education consists in keeping one's mind alive: It prolongs inquisitiveness and curiosity, holds entropy and death at bay, and keeps one in touch with what's new. To learn just for the sake of learning is a process so marvelously free of the quid pro quo implicit in learning to prepare for a career that I wonder sometimes why colleges aren't swamped by sexagenarians.

But going back to school in one's sixties to get an advanced degree can illuminate disturbing realities about time. With one exception, no other student was anywhere near my age. Mostly in their twenties or early thirties, my fellow students seemed inordinately well bred. They proved highly accepting of my old-man presence, appreciative of my real-world experience, fully capable of critiquing my writing without being either obsequious or patronizing, and entirely open to and grateful for my feedback to them. If they had reservations about my presence among them, they never let on.

Occasionally, I would be invited to join writerly get-togethers—which I did, once or twice. My fellow students even took with good humor my tongue-in-cheek request to join the MFA program's group for writers of color, based on my self-identification as "pink." But I no longer drank alcohol or indulged in drugs, as I so avidly had at their age, and no one seemed to be talking very much about literature or writing, as I remembered doing at the West End Bar in the '60s. My investment in these gatherings proved meager and short-lived, and I'm sure my fellow students felt some relief when I announced that I was "heading home."

The woman I was heading home to, a published writer and yoga teacher, was thirty-eight years old. We were learning the hard way that, however much we assured each other that age didn't matter when it came to love and sex, the fact remained that age mattered very much on a day-to-day basis, and it would matter more urgently the older we got. Not for any mysterious or even moral reason but more simply and profoundly because one's age reflects where one inarguably *is* on the entropic scale that gives time its meaning.

Like the universe itself, we expand beyond our beginnings and move increasingly farther away from our original selves, evermore subject to hardening and accretion. To be old—or oldish, as I thought of myself at sixty-one—guarantees a broader perspective, if for no other reason than that most of our original body cells haven't survived the process of living. We aren't physically the same beings we were when young and filled with potential, any more than Earth is the same configuration it was when gaseous and swirling around the sun.

Only mind and memory can bridge the gap between people of different generations, and that bridge is often a construct of the imagination. The fact remains stubbornly the same: We are locked onto the escalator of time, each on our separate step. The perspective lent to the old is the product not of a growing proximity to some ultimate truth but of an ever-increasing *uncertainty*, confirming that there is no ultimate truth, only process. Perspective, then, is inseparable from process, which is to say inseparable from time-bound experience.

In a classroom or workshop setting, an elderly perspective can be expressed with humor and grace or with cynicism and resentment, depending upon one's authority at the workshop or seminar table.

While I loved being exposed to twenty- and thirtysome-things—to their concerns, perspectives, dreams, energy, and limitations—and while I managed to fool myself on occasion that I'd been reborn as one of them, in the end I found it difficult to suffer prolonged exposure to people who had not seen or done what I'd seen and done.

I was *not* one of them.

But neither was I a teacher, yet.

This state of limbo gave birth to a peculiar frustration, which sometimes leaked out as anger. In my second semester, I wrote a scathing essay about an obnoxious twentysomething I'd seen on a Riverside Drive bus, who had sprawled his selfish ass across three seats while listening to music with headset earphones and ignoring the seating needs of a busload of people three times his age. In the essay, I shamefully imagined—graphically and hyperbolically—pummeling the kid to teach him a lesson. I titled it "Neo Geek," barely concealing my suspicion that he was representative of an entire generation. Which, of course, he was not. Unsurprisingly, the essay was not well received in workshop, and my professor, who, like a good shrink, remained unperturbed by eruptions of the unconscious, suggested that I chill and move on to more productive subjects.

Uneasy with my commitment to an MFA degree, my girlfriend, who already had one, borrowed some money and flew off to Mongolia for a month-long trek across the tundra—a trek that precluded any phone contact with her. Upset at first, I came to relish the solitude, within which I could more comfortably ride out the limbo I was experiencing in school. Upon her return she presented me with a small piece of pottery in the shape of an *oboo*, which a Mongolian shaman had suggested she give to me. That and the news that she was moving out. Not without difficulty, we both embraced separate paths. She moved into her own quarters. We saw each other on and off, for a while.

Also, in my second semester, Spring 2002, I submitted for workshop the rough draft of what would become a sixty-page essay about my first encounter with Wakinyan, my Lakota brother. My straightforward, entirely self-deprecating narrative *was* well received by most of my fellow students. But, like a prophecy of the cancel culture to come, I was harshly reprimanded by one student in particular, who told me bluntly that I had no right to "steal" from another culture. It was my first encounter with the admonition against cultural appropriation, an admonition with which I am essentially sympathetic. But, in fact, I hadn't appropriated or stolen anything. I had neither sought a tribal identity nor accepted a tribal name. I'd simply described my encounter with—and the lessons I'd learned from—another culture at their invitation and with their permission and encouragement. I was infuriated that forbidding such a time-tested narrative about the transmission of human spirit and wisdom was even imaginable in a world whose cultural, religious, and even genetic history is, *for better or worse*, composed of nothing *but* theft, imitation, adaptation, and integration. Isn't Mercury the god of both thieves and writers?

* * *

In the nick of time, as I think of it now, and in the shadow of dire rumblings of a wrongheaded war, I enrolled in a class for would-be teachers, taught by the director of the MFA program. I'd always admired the director's calm demeanor, his generous availability, and his reputation as a teacher. But I found many of the assigned pedagogical materials dreary and naive, especially those that emphasized *rigor* and *assessment*. The idea of a "lesson plan," for instance, seemed ignorant of the dynamics of real-life learning, where risk and surprise (for teacher and student) seemed to me the keys to effective engagement. It went without saying, I thought, that the teacher would thoroughly know his or her subject matter. But if the teacher already "knew" how the class would proceed, what was left for the student to "experience" that couldn't better be "learned" by reading a book or going online in Starbucks? Why have a teacher at all?

The assigned readings actually upset me enough that I began earnestly to imagine subverting pedagogy altogether—should I ever get the chance. I fantasized a pedagogy that involved upending the notion of planning *anything,* especially "learning goals." Walking into a classroom empty-handed, so to speak, without a plan. How risky that would feel! How much more energetic to let the "lesson" emerge out of the energy already in the room!

When the director asked if I'd care to use the large conference table in his office to teach a noncredit workshop attended by eager Columbia College undergrads, I immediately said yes. "As long as I can teach it my way," I added.

"Of course," he said. "That's what we're looking for."

I remember a few days later lingering at the director's office door after arranging chairs around the conference table and eavesdropping as students began to gather. They seemed unusually excited. Assuming, I guess, that the old fellow lingering at the door was the director himself, one of the young men announced loudly to the others, "What a relief this is going to be, having a grad student for a teacher!"

"Yeah," said his buddy, "somebody *young* for a change!"

I braved my first workshop as a hardly young teacher—kneecapping the bugaboo of age by acting the role of a pathetically boring, ponderous, perhaps even tipsy, know-it-all old man, and then having the students describe my senile behavior in writing. The adjective "old" emerged after much politically correct hesitation, but finally naming the elephant in the room leveled the playing field. I came away from my first workshop wondering at the warm, spacious feeling in my chest. What *was* that? It differed so much from the purely intellectual satisfaction I was experiencing as a student among students in the graduate workshops. As the teacher, I felt unreservedly connected to the students—at the heart level. I could finally *touch* them, not physically, of course, but from a detached place that ironically allowed for greater intimacy.

* * *

A week after then-President George W. Bush unleashed Operation Iraqi Freedom on Baghdad, I started a second workshop for undergrads in the director's office. From the get-go, it was like a lovefest. I was hooked.

In May 2003, I completed my MFA requirements but put off receiving the degree in order to collect COBRA health insurance from the university, which would allow me to limp my way to Social Security eligibility at age sixty-five. I bid my fellow graduates goodbye, promising to "stay in touch," and I spent the summer in a tornado of uncertainty. From that whirlwind, no film work, teaching prospects, or even new relationships materialized. It dawned on me that I'd merely caught a ghostly glimpse of a hypothetical future as a teacher, the life I *might* have led, had I made wiser choices earlier.

I decided to leave the city and seek a place where—as I wrote in my notebook—I could "seed myself into the world before I die." Maybe I could teach on the reservation. Or rent a studio apartment in some about-to-blossom city like Lincoln, Nebraska. Or go to Mexico and apprentice to a sorcerer. I began to assess which of my many writing files and few possessions I could dump. My academically expanded world had shrunk back to its pre-degree Planck state, where infinite potential was forced to await a big bang.

There is a stage of failure that resembles relief: At least you are no longer in the throes of self-deception, you know the score, you are no longer burdened by hope. I'd quite quickly grown comfortable with that stage, and from hopelessness I was just beginning to fashion an oddly stoic stance with regard to my late-in-life prospects. I'd always landed on my feet, hadn't I? And when the time came that I no longer could, well, that would be called death, wouldn't it?

Then, on December 12, I received a letter from the chair of the Department of English at Gettysburg College, a small liberal arts institution located in south-central Pennsylvania. He was offering me, unsolicited, a two-workshop semester as an adjunct instructor of English, starting in January 2004. The provost would overlook my lack of degree in hand, asking only for a letter from Columbia confirming that I'd fulfilled the requirements. The college would pay travel expenses and find me a house for the semester.

My heart leapt at the offer, and I could feel my adrenaline surging. But having just become comfortable with my unworthiness and happy with my new insecurity, I considered turning down the offer. I suspected that the chair, a close friend of my erstwhile girlfriend, was unwisely being kind to an old man and thus overestimating my abilities, not to mention my just deserts. There were probably thousands of hungry young postgrads applying for teaching jobs like this.

I read the letter again, and then again, and it slowly dawned on me that this offer felt oddly meant to be. Not *fated* to be, by God or some force beyond my knowing, but somehow, and simply, already envisioned and thus already done, like the predictable reappearance of the moon as a crescent. I was being invited to *do* what was meant to *be,* to actively partake in the fruits of my trust in the unknown. It was like entering a supermarket, where the door opens *because* you walk through it.

Before I signed the contract, I looked up the word *adjunct* in *Merriam-Webster*: "something joined or added to another thing but not essentially a part of it."

That sounded just about perfect.

Teacher, Time to Go

2005

I was nineteen years old and a college dropout when I first picked up chalk and taught. I remember standing nervously in front of a packed classroom, worried that my twenty-five skydiving students, many of them in their thirties and forties, might notice a slight tremble in my hand as I drew a stick figure parachutist on the blackboard. When it finally dawned on me that their fear of dying was greater than my fear of teaching, I began to relax. There they sat, gazing helplessly in my direction, as if I held the keys to their future, which, in a way, I did.

At first, this gift of presumed authority felt undeserved, but I soon learned to treasure it and to relish my role in a process, which, because it was designed to encourage considerable risk, had the power to transform fear into joy and low self-esteem into confidence. I went on to teach the three-hour first-jump course on a daily basis for over a year. Eventually, I got bored with skydiving (John F. Kennedy was running for president that year) and moved to New York City to study literature at Columbia University. Perhaps because skydiving was a hard act to follow, forty-three years passed before I picked up the chalk again.

By the time I began teaching first-year English at Gettysburg College, in the spring semester of 2004, authority was no longer an issue for me. I came armed with enough life experience to handle the most recalcitrant student. I had begun to publish personal essays in literary reviews and was already teaching writing on a private basis. For me, the issue was not how I would quiet my own anxiety in front of a classroom but rather how I might instill enough anxiety in my students to simulate an atmosphere of risk. Having been around the track a few times, I felt certain I could rely on an arsenal of tactics when presented with unfamiliar challenges—even those facing a sixty-three-year-old novice adjunct teacher, saddled with two sections of Introduction to College Writing.

But on my first day of teaching, as I drove my rusting 1987 Honda Accord through a snowy student parking lot filled with shiny late model cars and SUVs, I began to feel deep misgivings about my prospects. I skidded to a stop in a faculty space and took a moment to stare out the windshield at one of Pennsylvania's oldest campuses. Chartered in 1832, Gettysburg College was a conservative institution. It exuded an aura of tradition and entitlement. The larger campus trees said it all: Some looked to have been rooted deep in the earth when the famous Civil War battle raged nearby. Abraham Lincoln had given his immortal address quite nearby.

As I sat in my car, with the heater turned on full blast, I struggled to envision my first class. All I knew about my students was that they had failed to pass the English placement test. My course was not only compulsory; it was probably reviled. Preparing for the worst, I emptied the contents of my backpack on the passenger seat and made one last inventory of my weapons. Two of them I pocketed; one I attached to my belt; the rest I returned to the backpack.

I eyed the campus once again and calculated that if I got out of the car right then and ambled slowly along the well shoveled diagonal walk that passed close by the college's historic Pennsylvania Hall, I would reach my classroom building with no time to spare. I intended to show up for class precisely one minute late.

* * *

Back when I taught the classroom portion of the first-jump course, I considered it my duty to present the theoretical aspects of skydiving in a way that would make students forget their nagging concern about not being able to summon sufficient courage when the time came to jump. (In those days, first-time parachutists were required to jump out of the plane alone; the chute was opened automatically with a static line.) I was obliged to lecture for an hour about inane things, like the aerodynamics of a human body in free fall and the porosity of various nylon canopies, while at the same time avoiding the real source of student fear: possible parachute failure. What resulted was a dynamic tension between the abstract information I was presenting and the almost palpable concern of the students. At certain times, I felt like a matador trying to distract and mesmerize a bull with a cape; at others, like a salesman conning a prospective customer into overlooking a defect in the product.

When I had finished presenting the classroom material—everything *except* emergency procedures—I would put down the chalk, erase the blackboard, and announce, "Well, that's it. Any questions?" Usually—when I had taught successfully—there would be none. Just eager faces signaling a readiness to be led to the next phase of instruction. That's when I would toss them a grenade: "Really, no questions? But what happens if your chute doesn't open?"

Invariably, everyone would laugh with surprise. Somehow, they had forgotten all about parachute malfunction! Now, suddenly, they found it plausible to forget about it while sitting in the wind-whipped door of a jump plane flying three thousand feet above the ground. Their fear had lost its sting.

I would then go on to address emergency procedures in a straightforward manner, just as I would soon be addressing strategies of composition *after* the fear of writing had been overcome. If the elephant in the classroom for a novice skydiver had been possible parachute failure, the elephant for my novice writing students would be the possible failure of their creative voice. It was not an exaggeration to assume that the two fears were roughly equivalent. The trick for the teacher, it seemed to me, was to produce the elephant for the students to see. And then to get out of the way and let them deal with it on their own.

* * *

At precisely 11:00 a.m., I paused on the third floor of Weidensall Hall, several yards away from room 304. I had scouted the classroom the previous afternoon and noted happily the lack of any high-tech teaching aids, such as computer consoles, projection screens, and video monitors. A long blackboard covered one wall of the room. Civil War lithographs hung on an adjacent wall, lit softly by two lace-curtained, east-facing windows.

Three rectangular tables had been pushed together to form a large workshop surface. I was pleased with the space.

I now took a deep breath, pulled my silly looking ski cap down over my forehead, and strode toward room 304. What I encountered in the classroom stopped me in my tracks. Huddled around the workshop table, cowering under a bright wash of morgue-like fluorescent light, sat seventeen sullen young people, all wearing parkas, scarves, and gloves, and clutching backpacks and soft drinks on their laps. They seemed ready to bolt at the slightest provocation. Every seat around the table was taken; not an inch of space remained. I hadn't counted on this.

I dropped my shoulders in a posture of defeat and removed my ski cap. I felt the tug of static electricity, certain that it had lifted my already unkempt gray hair into a mad-looking mess, as planned.

"Is this section 101-S?" I asked in a bewildered voice.

One noticeably tall student, seated with his back to me, glanced over his shoulder like a lizard and let loose an audible hiss of disgust.

I moved deeper into the room—not without trepidation, I must admit—and said something like, "Well now, let's see . . . where should *I* sit?" I made my way around the table like a beggar at a king's feast. No one moved. When I reached the blackboard end of the room (that *was* my territory, was it not?), I waited briefly to be offered a seat. With no seat forthcoming, I pointed at a bewildered-looking young woman who happened to be sitting in what should have been my spot. I jerked my thumb at her like a home plate umpire. She stood up and took a seat along the wall. After considerable jostling, I squeezed into the space she had vacated.

When I sat down, I noticed the classroom door was still open. "Close that, please," I said. A student at the far end of the table jumped to her feet, fumbled her bottle of Diet Pepsi, and scooted out the door, slamming it behind her. Sixteen freshmen remained—the number registered for the course—all of them gazing longingly at the closed door, perhaps contemplating a similar escape. No one, including me, had yet removed a single item of winter clothing.

"We're going to hit the ground running," I said. "Take out a sheet of paper and something to write with." I took two legal pads from my backpack and tossed them on the table for those who might have come unprepared.

The tall kid near the door rolled his eyes and slapped his open palms rudely on the table. The young man next to him shot me a perfect "last straw" expression. Another, obviously sporting a hangover, affected the glum look of a criminal about to be hanged. Clearly, these guys had expected me to zip through my syllabus—blab a little about the assignments, reveal my grading agenda, read them the usual riot act about lateness, absence, and incomplete work—then dismiss everyone early. The collective disappointment was as thick as smog.

"Write your name at the top of the page, please," I said.

I began to fumble nervously with my backpack's many zippers, opening and closing them rapidly, as if I were in a panic. Then, without looking anyone in the eye, I launched what I hoped would sound like a lecture: "To be a good writer," I intoned, "you must . . . above all else . . . be . . . *observant*." Stroking my chin, as if I had a goatee, I gazed around the table to ensure that everyone had registered the profundity of my dictate. A few students caved and dutifully pretended to take notes. Most just stared at their blank sheets of paper, as if the long road from kindergarten through college would never end.

"To be a good writer," I continued, groping blindly into my backpack, "you must . . . ah . . . you must . . . what you must do is be . . . the important thing to do is to be . . . or rather, to do the thing to be . . . or . . . what I mean is . . . "

Thirty-two eyeballs were now *locked* in my direction.

"Oh!" I said, "I almost forgot! I like to begin my classes by sharing wine with everyone." With that, I pulled out a bottle of red wine featuring a goat on the label. The student to my immediate left raised his eyebrows and eagerly pulled his chair closer to the table. Cradling the bottle in both hands, I presented the label for everyone to view.

"Did anyone bring a corkscrew?" I asked, looking pointedly at the young woman on my right.

"No," she said. "*I* didn't, anyway."

I snapped my fingers. "What am I thinking?" I said. "I have one right here!" I reached for a small leather sheath on my belt and extracted my pocketknife. I fiddled with the screwdrivers, the blades, the toothpick, and the awl. Finally, I pried out the corkscrew and began to scrape at the hard foil covering the cork. "The thing about writing," I continued, "is that . . . "

This time, I let my jaw go slack, as if I'd just suffered a minor stroke. I stared at the class and was met with expressions of polite horror. "Uh-oh," I groaned, "I forgot the cups." At this point, a student, who looked to me to be a football player, leaned sideways toward a pretty young woman who had been nuzzling up against his parka. Like a lawyer on a senate investigating committee, he covered his mouth with his hand and discreetly whispered something in her ear. She nodded and giggled in response, but she kept a wary eye on me at the same time, suspicious.

I put the still-unopened wine bottle on the table and began frantically searching for my cell phone, deep in the pockets of my parka. I came up with a quarter and two pennies, which I then fumbled nervously until the coins dropped on the floor.

The student on my right shoved back her chair, picked up the change, and set it on the table.

Finally locating my cell phone, I announced, "I *must* take this call." I stood up, turned my back to the class, and began whispering a one-sided conversation: "Hi, babe . . . I'm teaching a class right now. . . . Yes . . . yes. . . . No . . . no. . . . I can't, not now." After fifteen seconds of that, I put my phone away. Still facing the board, I asked, "Anyone know where the chalk is?"

When I turned back to the class, it was all I could do to keep from laughing. Sixteen heads were shaking side to side in a chorus of utter disbelief. Titters of laughter escaped a few firmly set lips. I found a scrap of chalk and scrawled a simple sentence on the blackboard, my handwriting drifting down insanely toward the end—"My name is"—and here I paused to affect a puzzled expression before I wrote my nickname on the board.

I turned from the board and sat down. "Okay," I said, "take ten minutes and write down everything that's happened in this room since I asked you to put your name on the page."

Off came the jackets, hats, and scarves! Up went the shirtsleeves! My young charges bent forward to the task of writing, with the fervent intensity of devotees bowed in prayer. They were *that* relieved to be rid of me—and shaken just enough to feel a sudden need to write.

I sat back and perused my syllabus. In some ways it felt strange to be teaching in a college setting. Under "Course Description," I had promised that by the end of the semester, students could expect to have learned "the strategies of organization and the specifics of execution" they would need "to achieve a confident writing voice." What I had not revealed was that, in my opinion, voice led to strategy, not the other way around. Voice contained its own strategy, which is what made every writer's approach unique. I wondered now if I would be able to recognize and honor so many individual voices when the pressures of the semester increased.

In any case, in addition to weekly reading responses, I would be requiring three drafts each of five types of essays—personal, comparison, persuasion, critical, and profile—as well as a final project, in which the students could pull out all the stops. My teaching agenda mimicked the way we used to teach skydiving: five static line jumps, then a free fall. My writing assignments came with built-in strategies of organization—the kind of stuff students could read about in the required text, if they hadn't already heard it a million times in high school. My job, as I saw it, was to listen for signs of life.

* * *

When the ten minutes were up, I could see around the table that, for all their initial eagerness, most of the students had clearly struggled to fill up the page or make good use of the time I had allotted. While perhaps relieved, at first, to get me off their backs, they obviously still had *teacher* weighing them down. You could almost smell the oppression coming off the page: *Is* this *what he wants me to write? Am I* allowed *to write this?*

I asked them to read their observations aloud. After each reading, I simply nodded to the reader then raised my eyebrows expectantly, as a signal to the next one. Disclaimers, either spoken or conveyed with body language, invariably preceded each effort. The readings were delivered in voices that issued from way back in the throat; some were nearly inaudible; others were as squawky as the first notes of a baby bird. The observations were cautious—some were simply lists—and many were made up of conflated information. A few students were more forthcoming than others in terms of sentence structure, but strict adherence to the letter of the assignment was typical. I didn't bother to listen for powers of observation, choice of tense, or evidence of style. I just listened.

Here is an example:

> D. took out wine and a corkscrew. His cell phone rang and he had a quick conversation. He dropped chalk on the ground and picked it up and wrote "My name is D." on the blackboard. He said the key to writing is being observant and then he forgot what he was going to say.

And another:

1. "The thing about writing is, you must be observant"
2. I forgot, wine
3. Corkscrew
4. Pocketknife
5. "The thing about writing is . . . I forgot what I was saying"
6. Laughter from the students
7. Cell phone buzzed—answered said he was busy hung up
8. Coin fell on the floor
9. Wrote on blackboard, My name is D., while the class laughed
10. Asked us to write down everything that happened since he told us to write our name on this paper

One student used his list to warm up his engine:

- offered wine
- coin fell
- cell phone was answered
- teacher wrote on the board

- The teacher asked what class this was (section S)
- The teacher proceeded to sit down, where he then offered us wine. He asked for a corkscrew, however nobody had one. The teacher's phone vibrated, and he proceeded to answer it. He wrote on the board that his name was D., and then he told the class to take out a sheet of paper and write everything that we observed.

"What's missing from all these descriptions?" I asked when we'd gone around the table.

Silence.

"If you sent them in an email to a friend, what do you think the response would be?"

The tall student by the door was the first to speak: "They wouldn't have a clue."

"Why?" I said.

He shrugged.

"Why?" I asked, again.

"I don't know," he said. "Basically, they'd just say what the fu . . ."

"What the what?"

" . . . fuck."

Everyone laughed.

"Yep," I said, "that's probably what they'd say. What else is missing from these descriptions?"

Silence fell upon the room again and reigned until it was almost unbearable, even for me. I did not want to have to answer the question myself with words like *emotion, voice,* or *opinion.* Before I was forced to do so, a student to my left finally spoke up.

"Frankly," he mumbled, "I thought somebody at this college probably made a big mistake hiring you."

"Why didn't you write that down?" I asked.

He just stared at me as if to say, *What do you think I am, nuts?*

"This is a workshop," I said. "There's nothing you're not allowed to write in this class. Nothing out of bounds, as long as it's on the page. *Nothing.* Let's take the next fifteen minutes and try again. Have fun with it."

* * *

I used the time to make notes for my two o'clock class and to ready next week's assignment for hand out. I toyed with the idea of reading aloud my strict rules about late submissions but then thought better of it. These students had peers who were dying in Iraq; they could read the rules on their own time. I did decide, however, that just before dismissing everyone, I would take a few minutes to address the issue of class participation throughout the semester. I figured I should probably wax eloquent about eagerness, empathy, and generosity—critical elements in any workshop process.

When the time came for the second reading, I asked my students to announce their names before they read, and I invited everyone to comment after each reading. Then I sat back and listened for their voices to emerge. Here are three typical results:

1. I knew coming into this class that this was a new professor coming to the college. Usually, someone knows something about the professor teaching the course. But no one knew anything about him (except whatever information was given in the email the college sent us, informing us about this new

professor, that is if they received it). Because it is freezing outside, when he walked in he was a little disheveled, as we all look when coming in from the cold. It crossed my mind that he may be a little nervous, it being a new atmosphere. Then I thought, no, he's used to this, he's been teaching for years (if I remember correctly from the email). When the series of odd events began, my mind was racing through possible explanations: "A bottle of wine?" H. whispered to me "he's a drunk," and I almost laughed. Then I thought, this guy's a wacko. When he started the conversation on the cell phone, I thought it might be an act. H. was convinced he was drunk; I was just confused. I knew there would be a point to this introduction, and personally I think it's brilliant.

2. D., then known to us only as our professor, told all of us that he liked to start out each class with a sharing of wine. This being told to our class of apprehensive college students by their new professor bewildered the faces in the room. I could almost see the other students' faces saying, "is this guy for real?" After being asked by the odd professor for a corkscrew, our now increasingly interested class listened as he realized he had his own corkscrew and watched him pull a pocketknife with a corkscrew out of his pocket. In mid-sentence he was interrupted by the apparent buzz of a cell phone call which he took. The charade of being quite the unorthodox teacher now sunk in to me and I started to look around and saw that I was a little slow in the realization that our professor was teaching us a lesson and wasn't just crazy.

3. As I sat in English class on the first day of the new semester, my teacher stumbled in the door and then took out a bottle of wine. At first, I thought this could be really good because if the teacher was a drunk his class was probably easy. Unless he was a mean drunk who hated young people because he was bitter, so old now. Then his cell phone didn't ring or vibrate but he somehow knew to answer it and talked on it for a while. Then a quarter, probably the change from buying the wine, rolled out of his pocket, and he wrote his name, D., on the board and gave up the act. He was no longer a cell-phone-answering, change-losing drunk. He was the teacher who asked me to write what I observed.

The readings produced a good deal of laughter. After we had gone all the way around, wonderful chaos ensued. Late-blooming reactions to my act—those that hadn't made it onto the page—got tossed back and forth across the workshop space, as if I were no longer in the room. An egalitarian spirit began to emerge, like steam from a wet bale of hay. As I watched, I was reminded of barreling down the runway with a planeload full of first-time parachutists, the roar of the engine drowning out anything further I might have planned to say.

Being [T]here

2013

You found it first on the other side of the mirror, and when you awoke from the dream, in your early thirties, you knew, as you've never known anything else in all your years, that what you'd found was *real*. The dream began with you sitting in a church pew, head bowed in prayer. Your eyes opened slowly, and you noticed that you were wearing brilliantly colored beaded moccasins. You stood abruptly, pushed open the wooden gate that separated the pew from the center aisle of the church, and fled. The dream then proposed a seemingly endless and entirely quotidian set of difficulties in The City and led eventually to an arduous climb through a pathless wood, where you passed an unfinished house—framed out but not yet sided—and where (after how many false sightings of the summit?) you squeezed with great difficulty between two tall boulders and suddenly emerged on the edge of a wondrous canyon. Below you flowed a wide, glistening river, and in the center of the river, partly submerged, was a sparkling granite armchair, stalwart and steady, waiting, throne-like, for you. You awoke to the rest of your life with a gasp, exhilarated by the iridescence of the water in the dream and tantalized by the mystery of the chair. You have looked for that river ever since.

* * *

She danced barefoot for you in the field near the airport, a choreography of pale limbs flashing in the tall prairie grass, as lithe as a breeze, and silk-bright in the noonday sun: visible for a moment, then gone, then visible again, her kinetic message of impermanence causing your eyes to tear up. You knew, even then, that her youthful exuberance, for all its power, could never diminish the years between you. And, of course, you'd already seen too much from the hill. *But what luck*, you thought, *and so worth the risk*: that fluid, wordless art she carried—her only luggage, really. Her inspired arrival that day snaked around your middle years: a magical flirtation lifting you briefly from the gray lake of time, like some dark heron laboring skyward at dusk. Surely your heart would remain safe in its chest, fastened as it was by the thick suck of living and the compulsory thrum of desire. She hung around for several years, weighed down eventually by inertia, before announcing her intention to rent a room in the home of a stranger—to find herself again, as we all must. You stood at the kitchen counter, your back to her, dicing scallions for the salad. *Weather is never just one thing*, you were thinking. *Wind is always working within the calm.* You had both stopped eating chocolate on the sofa by then anyway, and the Yankees weren't the team they used to be. Between innings, she would part her silk robe and straddle your naked lap, serving you a nipple on her upturned pinky.

* * *

Let go, John said. Let go of all you've been, and dwell here awhile on the muddy bank in drenched and shimmering clothes. Fuck the clock. Fuck the wallet. Fuck the sentence you rode in on. The needs of the congregation require that you be honest now. Close the deal with the fire on the far shore, its reflection reddening the little peaks of rippled water reaching out toward you this night. Revolution lifts its chin like a cat, sensing you first in the mist, then seeing that it is you in the flesh. Send significance that way. Feel buoyancy in the potential you will always (promise yourself) honor. Drink to it: Make possible everything, always. Pray: Make possible always everything to those who are new to this world. Reveal yourself, old man, to the river once again.

* * *

That time you stumbled, half in the bag, up to Robin's nest (she called it that), in SoHo, and felt your way across her pitch-dark loft, suddenly bumping into her lady friend from Minnesota. "Hello!" you said, kissing the friend, while Robin fumbled for the pull switch. You knew from the surprise in her friend's lips—and from her foolish tongue—that you could whisper in her ear the words *live with me now* and get away with it—that destiny was what you shaped for yourself by attaching desire to time and then loving the consequence. You lived with Robin's friend from that day until the time a few years later when she found herself ready to be serious, as we all must—her love for you (and yours for her) still as deep and sweet as a clear, clear well . . . but done, too, because you'd been there before with the children thing. She sent you a card depicting a unicorn leaning forward on a precipice and looking out at the void, along with her wish that you would find your truest self. You can treasure that image now in the rounding chug-a-chug-chug that remains.

* * *

What a lucky man you are. Practice small goodbyes. Goodbye, practice.

* * *

You know this much (because if it isn't this, it's nothing): Space (which is to say the betweenness of things) is where the substance lies. Or doesn't. Only from space can accumulation be achieved. Only in accumulation can the work of life be framed. The difficulty arises not from hardness or things that go bump in the night, not from the density of the walls, or from the ripe fruit just out of reach over the fence. The difficulty is right here, in the pain of having to die. The interval for love is composed of pure pain, or it won't be love at all. The vast distance between the sacrum and the heart can be measured in light-years. So many galaxies, so much plumbing and complexity, so much digestion and drowsiness, so much empty sleep. It's not the moon we must consider but the moon made invisible by the earth and sun.

* * *

What business is it of yours what anything means? What else has it ever meant?

* * *

Keats should have switched it up, should have written, *truth is beauty, beauty truth*. But he was young and overwhelmed with mind and meter. And so, of course, was the educated woman who slapped your dick when you suggested this. *You arrogant bastard. You would rewrite Keats?*

* * *

You're having a rough time with this, aren't you? It would have been seemlier, you realize now, to have kicked it at an early age, bought the farm in another market, so to speak. You've survived, old man, but you're a mess.

* * *

Today you were walking with a twenty-three-year-old friend in the park. She had wandered into your orbit, or you into hers, tugged somehow—both of you—in an innocent fashion. (You have learned not to argue with gravity; the chance of a comet colliding with Earth is . . . what?) So, you pointed out the sights— the usual shit, beginning with The Plaza Hotel and meandering north to the Alice in Wonderland statue and Literary Walk— and you deeply enjoyed the young woman's intermittent presence, her quiet curiosity punctuated by a frequent need to check for text messages on her cell—in other words, to find herself in time-full-ness, as we all must. Autumn sang in dry shades of red and orange, and you could remember hearing five-tone chimes in the wind when you were way, way younger, and it made you feel sudden and happy.

But how many times can you stand to see the now-shuttered carousel you rode on with your daughter in the '60s? Won't you ever grow sick of ghosts clinging like hibernating butterflies to the landmarks, tunnels, and pathways of your experience? The world has shifted, old man, a new lens has been clocked into place. The landmarks are accepting new memories, and your files have been moved.

Still, you persisted in tour-guide mode, trying hard to see all this afresh. You nodded toward a footbridge, a marvel of architecture that you had carried in your mind to Spain in 1966, when you were a few years older than this moccasin-footed girl at your side—using it for a scene with which you began a novel about love. No wonder it failed. The arc the footbridge describes (even now) wasn't clear to you then, yet it was all you needed to know about love and life: There's *this*, and it rises, then there's *that*. There *is* that. Remember? But given the chance, you'd begin again, wouldn't you? You'd remember all this and begin again. Throw up your hands, you old fool, and listen: Offer it up. Let go.

And that's what you did when you said to your dark-eyed young friend with glitter on her nails, as you steered her off the usual and proverbial path: "Let's cut over there and climb that huge rock to see what's on the other side," and as you said "the other side," you realized that you held it all—the whole ball of twine—in your hands at that moment, and it made you laugh with despair, if such a thing is possible. You led the way, and as you climbed the outcropping of rock, you began to see that the gentle-enough slope it described on this side would not be duplicated on the other side; very soon you were approaching the edge of a small cliff. You didn't slow down, but you were mindful of your footing, and just as you came to a stop on the edge, a beautiful child—golden, you'd have to say, like your daughter at that age—ran up and stood next to you on the edge. Bold and confident, she looked up at you, then down at the ground twenty feet below, then up at you again. *Not yet*, she seemed to say. *Not yet, old man.*

"How would *you* get down?" you asked the child, playfully.

"I'll show you!" she said.

And with that, she spun around and led you and your friend through a circuitous sequence of metamorphic crevices to flat and grassy ground. After which, your long-haired young friend with a silver ring in her nose went off to party with others of her kind—as we all must.

* * *

You don't want to know too much too early. Keep the mirror handy, the self intact. What's death but the crumbling silver backing on the opposite side of the glass? You feel bright tonight in the little glow of Christmas lights that illuminates the café you enjoy for its emptiness—for its perverse lack of clarity, its Halloween clientele, who tend to whisper instead of shout and who put their phones away and lean through the dimness toward each other. You feel bright in your red shirt, and conscious of your inner intensity after a day of miraculous confirmation that you are still connected to the web of green and living things. Feeling so deeply lit, you look up from your notebook to the window next to where you sit alone at a table for two, expecting to see your inner brightness reflected in the glass—your old-man visage tinged in red, perhaps—some hint of youth still there. But the outside light—that bright space of commerce and concrete and street—has overwhelmed the glass. You are invisible. It seems impossible, at first. No hint of you at all.

So, you squeeze into this—this impossibly thin, exquisitely persistent interval called solitude—wherein lurks the vast and timeless liberty of love. You may find it again on the other side of the mirror, but you won't know it back then.

Shade: A Letter from Gettysburg

2007

I tell myself that in times like these there has to be something for which one is willing to get shot, and for which, in all probability, one is actually going to get shot.

—Thomas Merton, *Conjectures of a Guilty Bystander*

"So I will disappear," said Thomas Merton, concluding his address to an international monastic conference in Bangkok on December 10, 1968. Merton, a Trappist monk and writer, planned to take an afternoon nap before a panel discussion that evening. He walked back to his guest cottage in the sweltering midday heat, took a shower, and, while standing in his bare feet on a tile floor, reached to turn on an improperly wired electric fan. The end came for him with a sustained jolt of direct current, at about two o'clock local time. He was fifty-three years old.

I thought of Merton the day before my sixty-fifth birthday, in 2005, while standing barefoot on a wobbly chair to change a light bulb over the kitchen sink in my rented house in Gettysburg, Pennsylvania. A rusted, poorly installed socket was making the task difficult. As I coaxed the old bulb loose, my mind drifted from Merton's tragic fate to a discussion I'd had during a family get-together sixteen years earlier.

That winter of 1989, Bill McKibben's book *The End of Nature* had been making waves by predicting the depletion of the ozone layer, the warming of the planet, and widespread species extinctions—shocking revelations at the time. My seventy-eight-year-old mother, after hearing my agitated reiteration of McKibben's statistics, shoved aside the vegetables she was preparing and tearfully asked, "Why is it that, of all the billions of people who've lived on the earth, *we* are the ones who must witness the time of the end?" I put my arm around her and made light of the subject, joking that we had at *least* six months before the end. But my eighty-year-old father, who had also read McKibben's book, did not conspire with me to be lighthearted for my mother's sake. "What makes me sad," he said, "is that we can't take with us into old age and death the assumption that nature, as we've always known it, will survive. *That*, it seems to me, is a first."

I changed the kitchen light bulb without incident and turned sixty-five the next day. Life goes on, both within me and around me, but I am left holding this intuition of The End.

* * *

I didn't learn about the tree-cutting program at Gettysburg National Military Park until I saw early evidence of its implementation. Just north of the hill known as Little Round Top, more than a hundred large trees—maples, oaks, tulip trees, mulberries, magnolias, cedars, hickories, and ashes—were felled and hauled away in a matter of weeks. The sudden and seemingly pointless cutting was deeply disturbing to me. When I walked the former woodlot just after the logging machinery had left, I had to choke back rage at the sight of the low-cut stumps, many of them two and three feet in diameter, and some as much as five feet across. Left standing for the pleasure of visitors to the national park were exactly fourteen eight-inch-diameter ash trees, their leaves shot through with disease, their bark scraped by logging machinery—scrawny, wobbly looking, giraffe-like stalks that seemed puzzled by their own survival.

Tourists can now rest assured that no trees will stop them from envisioning what the soldiers of Battery C, First New York Light Artillery, Fifth Corps, saw on July 2, 1863. Which, according to the information archived in the *Federal Register* of December 21, 1999, is precisely what the park service intended: "to rehabilitate the Gettysburg battlefield so that the features that were significant to the outcome of the battle . . . more nearly reflect their historic conditions."

When this logging project is complete, a forested area equivalent to 526 football fields will have been "restored" to match photographs taken in July 1863. At the time of this writing, 147 acres of woods have been cleared, and the remaining 429 acres are legally doomed. Any trees that have grown on the battlefield in the years since the Civil War will be removed; trees that were present in those days but have been cut or have died in the interim will be "replaced." The work has been swift, efficient, and neat. In a year no one will know those woods existed.

The lovely hilltop road leading to the Eternal Light Peace Memorial, dedicated by President Franklin D. Roosevelt on the seventy-fifth anniversary of the battle, has been stripped bare of the dozens of old oaks that once lined it. Restored to its original state, the once-wooded hilltop itself now resembles not an arboreal amphitheater positioned for a spectacular view to the west and south but a badly scalped bump of land hosting a stark granite platform. As a bonus, visitors can enjoy an unobstructed view, to the east and southeast, of the Giant supermarket, the Days Inn, the Hilton Garden Inn, the U-Haul franchise, the shopping mall, and the Gettysburg College sports facilities. The now-unfiltered din of traffic from surrounding highways makes it nearly impossible to conjure up the nineteenth century.

After five years of planning and protest, the forces in favor of historical restoration have prevailed over the voices of those who regard the stately woods as reassuring evidence that America has healed from its contentious history—not to mention those who simply cannot fathom the wholesale slaughter of hundred-year-old trees for *any* reason. The argument is over, and what I write here is not an attempt to persuade but an elegy for the kind of healing spirit that gave rise to this place.

Everyone understands that in the larger scheme of devastation caused by development and suburban sprawl, this particular alteration of the environment is relatively benign. The woods are not being replaced by shopping malls, after all. And at least the battlefield cannot be sold to developers. Opposing camps in this conflict have withdrawn and stood down for now, but the deep and irreconcilable divisions between them remain.

* * *

I teach composition and creative writing at Gettysburg College. Sometimes I illustrate the process of beginning an essay or story by drawing a thundercloud on the blackboard and sketching the start of a zigzag lightning strike: a series of unlinked dashes descending from the cloud at forty-five-degree angles to each other. Scientists call this a "stepped leader." You can't see a stepped leader, I tell my students. Those unlinked dashes represent intuition, the first tentative ideas for an essay, usually nebulous and vague, and as invisible to a reader as a stepped leader is to the naked eye. To produce visible lightning, the stepped leader must join with an upward reaching "ground leader." (I draw a little line from the ground to the lowest dash.) When the two leaders connect . . . *zap*! Lightning rushes *up* from the ground, not down from the cloud. Let grounded detail illuminate your intuition, I tell them.

Many cultures equate lightning with intuition. For the Lakota, for example, if you dream of lightning, you are likely what they call a *heyoka*—an intuitive who experiences brilliant flashes of inspiration but rarely understands their source. *Heyokas* are the irreverent contrarians, the sacred clowns who do everything backward during formal ceremonies. At a sun dance a *heyoka* might pretend to piss on the medicine man's altar, or sashay around like a woman, or splash his face with boiling water to cool off. *Heyokas* wear black-and-white costumes, and everything they do provokes laughter tinged with fear.

The Lakota believe that *heyokas* can cross the boundaries that exist between human beings and read people's minds. "Be careful not to look me in the eye," a *heyoka* once told me during one of my stays at the Pine Ridge Reservation in South Dakota. I asked him what he meant and then made the mistake of glancing at him while waiting for an answer. Only when I tried to tear my eyes away did I understand that he had somehow held me paralyzed with his gaze, as effectively as if I'd touched a bare electrical wire.

Shortly after that incident, two young Lakota, Mike and Tony, visited me at my apartment in New York City. I took them to the Statue of Liberty, and we got stuck in a long line waiting for the ferry. The captive crowd had attracted the usual array of street performers, one of whom—a man with dreadlocks—followed hapless pedestrians and mimicked the way they walked. He had an uncanny ability to duplicate the posture and pace of another individual and exaggerate the single element that seemed to define that person: the slouch, the urgency, the shyness, the arrogance. His imitations were hilarious, but they were also disturbing. I glanced at Mike and Tony to see their reactions; they both casually nodded their approval and said in unison, "Heyoka."

When I was a young man and insecure in my own skin, I used to compensate for my fear of lightning by getting all pumped up and challenging it to strike me as I pranced around soaking wet under a flashing sky. You wouldn't want to do that where Mike and Tony live. Out there, the many-fingered lightning sizzles across the Great Plains, striking indiscriminately at anything higher than the prairie grass. It's enough to make you run to your car and whimper like a dog.

In Gettysburg, lightning will strike a monument once in a while, but mostly it's the trees that take the hits. Once, while walking on a service road, I found a ten-foot-long splinter of bark and pulp that had been blasted from a nearby oak just minutes earlier. A surprising number of trees in the park bear the scars of lightning strikes. Some survive, but those that don't attract all sorts of insects and serve as feeding grounds for the population of redheaded woodpeckers in the battlefield woods.

* * *

If Thomas Merton screamed for help as he died, no one seems to have heard him. His Thai hosts found him lying on the tile floor, pinned beneath the fan, its blades still whirling in their cage. That was the same year Martin Luther King Jr. and Robert F. Kennedy were assassinated, and some speculated that Merton, too, had been murdered for his progressive beliefs.

I knew almost nothing about Merton at the time. His early autobiography, *The Seven Storey Mountain*, sat unopened on my bookshelf throughout the '60s. I don't know why I never got around to reading it; maybe it was because I wasn't Catholic, or because too much was happening in the public domain for me to be interested in the life story of a contemplative monk. President Kennedy's assassination had produced in me a strange addiction to the news of chaos and turmoil. It seemed as if every time you turned around, some well-known person was getting shot. Along with Martin Luther King Jr. and the Kennedy brothers, there were such disparate figures as Black militant leader Malcolm X, President Diệm of South Vietnam, pop artist Andy Warhol (who survived the assassination attempt), and revolutionary Che Guevara.

I was driving a taxicab in New York City on April 4, 1968, when a passenger told me that King had been gunned down on a balcony in Memphis. I remember feeling a wave of nausea. If there were people out there willing and able to kill our most visionary political and religious leaders, what did that say about the future of democracy? I drove up to Harlem and began giving people rides for free, my meter off. For a brief time that evening, everything seemed almost thrillingly clear: For all of us there was now a common enemy. Murderous racism had shown its face, and I could help beat the enemy by demonstrating my solidarity, as a white man, with my Black neighbors. Then an off-duty police detective jumped into the front seat of my cab and ordered me to drive him to the Bedford-Stuyvesant section of Brooklyn. By the time we arrived, a small riot was in bloom. After I let the detective out, a group of young people splintered off from the crowd and stormed my cab, pelting it with bottles. I ducked low behind the steering wheel and ran red lights as I sped away.

That same evening, exactly two months before he was gunned down himself, Senator Robert F. Kennedy, on a presidential campaign stop in Indianapolis, addressed a crowd of mostly Black inner-city residents. He told the crowd that he, too, had lost a brother to a white man's bullet. He quoted the Greek poet Aeschylus to universalize the suffering and pain, and he suggested that everyone go home and pray. Riots shook more than a hundred American cities that night, but not Indianapolis.

I had worked as an advance man for Bobby Kennedy during his 1964 US Senate race. President Kennedy had been assassinated in his motorcade in Dallas nine months earlier, but that did not deter Bobby from riding slowly in open convertibles along avenues and side streets all over New York State. I was sometimes obliged to ride with him, hanging on to his belt from behind while he leaned into the crowd to shake hands. At other times I would walk beside the car to protect people from being run over.

In Buffalo, when our campaign coincided for a day with that of President Lyndon B. Johnson, the head of the president's Secret Service detail asked me what kind of security we were traveling with for Bobby. He blanched when I told him that all we had was an on-leave New York City police detective armed with a .38-caliber pistol.

"I think I should tell you," he said, "that all the people we've rounded up seem to be after your candidate—not the president."

"*All* the people?" I said.

"Yeah," he answered, "they're coming out of the woodwork. We just caught some guy with a rifle lying in the high grass along the thruway."

It must have taken an iron will (the word *courage* doesn't entirely explain it; nor does the phrase *death wish*) for Bobby Kennedy to ride in an open motorcade and wade into crowds of admirers. He knew the risk. But he took seriously (and had copied into his notebook) the words Albert Camus recorded from a condemned Frenchman: "Knowing that you are going to die is nothing." As Evan Thomas recounted in his biography of Kennedy, in the early hours of June 5, 1968, about thirty seconds after a .22-caliber bullet lodged in his brain—and only a few seconds before he lost consciousness for good—Bobby lay on the kitchen floor at the Ambassador Hotel in Los Angeles, looking up at his wife, Ethel, who cradled his bleeding head in her hands.

"Is everybody else all right?" he asked.

As I write these words, news drifts in through my window from a neighbor's radio that President George W. Bush plans to visit a training center for border security guards in Texas today—another of his prepackaged appearances in front of government employees, calculated to strengthen his political base. When was the last time a political figure thought about anyone but himself and his party? And what is the consequence of this self-serving political charade? Perhaps it can be discerned in American democracy's great shadow, which we have now projected onto Iraq: civil war.

* * *

Ask people where they think Gettysburg is located, and they'll often say Virginia. (I thought this when I was young.) Perhaps they are conflating Robert E. Lee's defeat at Gettysburg with the fact that he signed the Treaty of Appomattox in his home state of Virginia. In any case, Gettysburg sits in a beautiful valley in south-central Pennsylvania, nine miles north of the Maryland border, which is also known as the Mason-Dixon Line, the division between North and South, "free" states and "slave" states, during the Civil War.

Gettysburg was hailed as good ground by generals on both sides. The place has power still. The same ten roads that led one hundred and seventy-two thousand Confederate and Union troops into battle still radiate from the borough today. Approach from any direction, and you will feel the agricultural richness and geological resonance of the valley. In the summer, rolling thunderstorms patrol the sky.

When I was a boy, I lived on the edge of the Ward Pound Ridge Reservation, a four-thousand-acre preserve in New York's northern Westchester County. I spent a lot of idle time in the woods and fields of that preserve, just as I now spend idle time on the expansive Gettysburg battlefield. Like the battlefield, the reservation consisted of an enchanting mix of woods and fields, set apart and quiet, yet so alive with wildlife that you could sometimes imagine humankind started there.

I used to walk the three-mile dirt road that bisected the reservation to a small nature museum run by a naturalist named Mr. Wheeler. I think he must have suffered from Parkinson's disease. Stoop-shouldered and old before his time, he moved slowly and sometimes seemed to be in pain, but he never failed to smile broadly when he saw me, or to beckon me into his musty world with a wave of his palsied hand. He spoke with a raspy, breathless voice as he shuffled along the stone floor, narrating the contents of each display: jars crammed with pickled snakes; stuffed raptors hanging on brass wires; a dust-covered, yellow-eyed bobcat frozen in mid-prowl on the windowsill; bugs and butterflies pinned to sun-bleached cardboard; arrowheads locked in glass cabinets; and minerals galore. Some of these displays allowed you to identify an object by matching it with its name. Two tenpenny nails—one for the object, one for the name—were wired to a battery and would set off a buzzer if you matched them right.

About three decades later, in the early '80s, I lived in a rural area not far from where I'd grown up. Mr. Wheeler had died many years before, but I fancied that if I could restore my memory of him—touch him with a tenpenny nail, as it were—I might learn something about myself as a child. I tried writing a story about the way he would ritually end our visits by scooping a cupful of sunflower seeds and making an offering to the sky. Little black-capped chickadees would swoop down from the roof and cling to the edge of the cup, two or three at once, feeding from it even as the old man's hand shook with an embarrassing violence.

But I simply couldn't write the story—nothing worked. I threw away page after unsuccessful page until finally, at about ten o'clock one winter night, I gave up entirely and went outside to shoot baskets in front of the garage. To clear my mind, shooting baskets worked almost as well as meditation. Finally, I tossed the basketball into an empty planter, glanced overhead at the stars, and headed back toward the house.

No sooner had I begun walking than I heard a rapid fluttering right above my head. The sound sent a chill up my spine. A chickadee appeared in front of my face and landed on the stone walkway at my feet. Partly hopping, partly flying, the bird preceded me to the house and then perched on a Christmas wreath attached to the front door, which I opened gently. The chickadee flew inside and sat for a few minutes atop an open bathroom door, where I snapped its picture with an Instamatic. It spent the rest of the night resting on a beam while I watched it for hours from the sofa. At first light, I opened the front door, and it flew away with a single peep.

A bird expert has assured me you will never see a chickadee fly at night. That I have a poorly lit snapshot of the bird does not erase the paper-thin boundary between the material world and that of the spirit; it simply confirms that the causal perspective with which we negotiate the real world vanishes when we cross that boundary. Tourists by the thousands cross it every day in Gettysburg. You can see it in their faces as they silently imagine the battle—and perhaps intuit its resonance in the here and now. And therein lies the power of the whole enterprise to which Gettysburg National Military Park was dedicated: memory.

The past cannot be restored, but if allowed it will manifest in the present as spirit. To manipulate the process by which spirit is evoked—by removing any evidence that time has passed, or by tampering with a place where so many souls have died—might just short-circuit it. I guess, after they're done clearing the trees, we'll find out.

* * *

"We are numbered in billions," Merton writes in *Raids on the Unspeakable*, " . . . worked to the point of insensibility, dazed by information, drugged by entertainment, surfeited with everything, nauseated with the human race and with ourselves, nauseated with life."

The nausea of which Merton writes is what we used to call *despair* or *angst*, and what experts today refer to by an array of psychiatric names: anxiety, clinical depression, bipolar disorder, post-traumatic stress disorder, and attention deficit disorder—not to mention erectile dysfunction. You can take an assortment of pills for the nausea of modern despair: the pain of a lost love, the fear of failure, the dread of poor sexual performance. Many of my students take such medications. These pills are pushed on network television in slick, long-winded commercials interspersed with brief news segments calculated to *cause* anxiety—reports of suicide bombers, child molesters, suspected threats to national security, nascent pandemics, kidnappings, genocide. This mind-numbing, socially engineered cocktail has left many young people insensible to prophetic nuance. It is as if they have arrived at adulthood with their alarm systems disabled.

In the classes I teach, I must take care to avoid making any negative statements that might label me as antagonistic to popular culture. Having been taught to assess attitude rather than substance, young people have developed an eagle eye for affect. For them, affect *is* substance. I get around this problem by cheerily assigning stories about suffering and death. And I never lecture.

When I assign E. B. White's essay "Once More to the Lake" to my composition class, I lure students in by noting that White also wrote *Charlotte's Web* and *Stuart Little*. (They have all seen the movies.) "Once More to the Lake" is about death and trepidation, but its bleak mood is rescued from despair by the notion of heritage and continuity. At the time he wrote the essay, in 1941, White had outlived his father, who used to bring the entire family to this particular Maine lake during the summer. White transcends the premonition of his own mortality by imagining that his young son will one day return to the lake, continuing the tradition. It is all quite patrician and predictable, really. White's voice exudes generations of entitlement. But almost everyone loves the essay and has no problem responding to it, even students who might never have seen a pristine lake. All are struck by White's subtle evocation of death and admire how the author uses death's shadow to give texture to a bland summer day. They seem aroused, even mesmerized, by his description of a gathering thunderstorm, and by the release of a perennial spirit when the children swim in the rain after the lightning has passed.

* * *

At the beginning of the fall semester, more than seven hundred freshmen Gettysburg College students assemble to walk south down Carlisle and Baltimore Streets to Evergreen Cemetery, near where historians believe Abraham Lincoln delivered his famous address on November 19, 1863. Traffic is held up for miles in several directions as the students march to the cemetery lawn, where they will listen to a reading of the Gettysburg Address.

Two years ago, I went to the cemetery early, hoping to locate the grave of the poet Marianne Moore before the arrival of the students. I wound up wandering the nearby battlefield until I came to the area directly across the road from Evergreen, a place called East Cemetery Hill: ground that, on the second day of battle, was taken and then lost by Confederate soldiers. I parked my butt on an old stone wall and relaxed in the shade of a spreading ash, one of five large trees that grew into and around the wall. I could have sat a little farther down the hill, beneath a huge tulip tree whose twenty-foot circumference was girdled with a faded orange tape that read DO NOT CUT. But my perfectly adequate ash tree, whose twelve-foot circumference had garnered it no such reprieve, provided me a better view of the entrance to Evergreen Cemetery. I heard a slight breeze rustle the leaves, felt the stillness of the afternoon, and relished the shade that, because it was growing late, seemed to be building everywhere.

And that's when I began to hear it, the approach of hundreds of students. You can hear a similar sound in late autumn, farther out on the battlefield, when enormous flocks of migrating Canada geese descend on a patch of open marshland. As the students grew near, I thought that even the songbirds must have been impressed by the high-pitched cacophony of so many uninitiated young people.

What could all those kids have been talking about individually to raise the collective clamor to such a level? I don't know. I'm not sure that I want to know. There they were, approaching a cemetery to listen to a recital of the Gettysburg Address, that great, sad oration, but if I shut my eyes, I could imagine a massive cocktail party in progress. The tens of thousands of soldiers who marched along this same road, canteens and swords clanging, must have sounded low-key by comparison. Here they came, this blissfully naive and blessedly upbeat gaggle of tightly packed teenagers—agitated, eager, self-conscious—about to descend on the sacred burial ground of the ancestors. The slow procession was preceded by a single police car, motorcade-style.

* * *

During one of my winter walks through the battlefield, I saw a man with hands clasped behind his back, blond hair streaming from beneath a broad-brimmed cavalry hat, his black riding boots set apart in a stance that affected the authority of a commanding officer. In the light of the setting sun, he began solemnly pacing a fence line that had been, on July 3, 1863, one of the obstacles to Pickett's Charge, when thousands of

Confederate soldiers had swept in futile fashion across the nearly mile-long field to the west. The man seemed to be assessing the lay of the land or perhaps imagining himself surveying a line of Union troops before the bombardment on day three of the battle. I couldn't resist walking up to him and telling him he looked much like George A. Custer, and I wondered if he could tell me whether the famous cavalryman had fought in the battle of Gettysburg.

"Wh-wh-wh-why, yes, he d-d-d-d-did," answered the man. He told me with some difficulty that Custer had fought a small skirmish a ways to the east of where we stood. I saw now that the man's blond hair had the rough consistency of a horse's mane and must have been colored with cheap dye. I asked if anyone else ever remarked on his resemblance to Custer. Yes, they did, he answered. "And you m-m-m-may be interested to know that Cu-Cu-Cu-Custer stuttered, too." He told me he lived in New York State and came here every weekend, though he didn't like going to the place where Custer actually fought, because it was "too spooky out there." His eyes grew damp as he spoke about the number of men who had died on that spot. By the time we finished talking, his stutter had disappeared.

After my encounter with George Custer, the chain saws and steel-treaded tree clippers advanced from several directions on an area known as Devil's Den. The loggers worked quickly to fell the trees, but the huge trunk segments remained stacked along the road for months. I walked there every evening during the winter and early spring, and the sight of the carnage made my throat grow dry and my mind concoct absurd fantasies of violence and revenge. I thought of sabotaging logging equipment: putting sugar in the gas tanks, flattening tires, spiking trees. I even allowed myself to imagine committing cold-blooded murder: sniping at loggers from up on Little Round

Top, ambushing the vehicles with a loaded shotgun, blowing up culverts, torching gas tanks. I told myself it wouldn't matter if I died in the attack.

Those trees had been there to teach patience and posture, a counterpoint to the desperation of war. My worst fantasies rushed to fill the void created by their loss—harmlessly, of course, because I'm old. But the idea was out of the bag.

There is a scene in Michael Shaara's Civil War novel, *The Killer Angels*, in which Union Colonel Joshua Chamberlain recounts to a friend an argument he had with a minister. This man of the cloth was also a serious advocate of slavery and claimed that Black men were *not* men but more like horses. "I was really thinking of killing him," Sharaa's version of Chamberlain says, "wiping him off the earth, and it was then I realized for the first time that if it was necessary to kill them [proponents of slavery], then I would kill them."

For months I walked despairingly past the piles of wood chips, the remains of old trees that had provided shade for generations of visitors—shade for the overweight, shade for the old and infirm, shade for the infants, watercolorists, veterans, and lovers, all of whom must now cower from the heat in idling, air-conditioned buses, or huge SUVs, or oversized pickup trucks, lest they become puddles of bubbling flesh among the sun-cooked boulders of Devil's Den—or, on a cloudy day, the target of lightning strikes that were once easily absorbed by large trees.

True, those trees were not there when Confederate sharpshooters hid behind the rocks and picked off Union officers on Little Round Top, just across the way to the east. And, true, visitors to the battlefield enjoy a more accurate view of the way things were. But the breadth and height of those trees, and the way they sometimes blocked what was once a clear view, were the only real evidence that what happened then is not still happening—or about to happen—now.

There are two sides to any argument, I teach my students. But the fulcrum of an argument, like the base of a seesaw, must be the collective, the transcendent, good. Without that fulcrum, the ideal of reasoned and balanced argument collapses. Debate becomes a playground for bullies. My patience with argument has snapped.

* * *

I love a good graveyard. My parents' ashes are buried in Mount Auburn Cemetery, in Cambridge, Massachusetts, which was dedicated on September 24, 1831. Mount Auburn was the first large American cemetery conceived according to the Athenian model, which recognized death as integrally linked with life and celebrated nature—specifically trees and birds—as a reminder of the life-death continuum. The Gettysburg National Cemetery became the second such graveyard. But in Gettysburg, the cemetery resides in the middle of what was once a battlefield, and the battlefield—because so many fought and died there, and because there are so many monuments attesting to that fact—has the feel of a cemetery. Indeed, cemetery and battlefield would be indistinguishable if not for a wrought iron fence.

Birds ignore the fence, of course, and treat the two properties as a single preserve. It is sometimes fun to imagine them as the winged spirits of the dead: blue herons traversing the domed evening sky; turkey vultures soaring over Little Round Top; mockingbirds singing up a storm while perched atop the heads of sculpted riflemen; finches, cardinals, jays, swallows, orioles, and woodpeckers all darting everywhere, protected by the surrounding woods. Here's how Joshua Chamberlain put it in his dedication of the Maine monuments at Gettysburg, on the evening of October 3, 1889: "In great deeds something abides. On great fields something stays. Forms change and pass; bodies disappear; but spirits linger, to consecrate ground for the vision-place of souls."

Even if lingering spirits aren't your idea of fun, I'll guarantee that if you visit in the spring, you will be impressed by the clouds of grackles and starlings that appear as if from some invisible seam in the sky on the western horizon, advancing by the thousands to swarm above, around, and behind Big Round Top, cackling amid the leafless branches, feathers iridescent in the light of the setting sun.

For me, Thomas Merton speaks from that twilight stratum where day ends and night begins. He was able to balance both states of mind—light and dark, sun and shade—finding in the biblical notion of end-time a promise of fulfillment, and in fulfillment the promise of a new beginning. He was careful to distinguish between biblical eschatology and secular anxiety, which he defined in *Raids on the Unspeakable* as "the pathological *fear of the violent end,*" calling it a "thinly disguised *hope for the violent end* [emphasis his]." He used the biblical "Time of the End" as a metaphor to encourage people—Americans, in particular—to turn away from the material abyss, where one is no longer governed by the heart but propelled instead by the forces of blind fear and narrow greed.

From Bangkok, courtesy of President Johnson, Merton's body was flown back to the States in a US Air Force plane, along with the coffins of the American soldiers killed in Vietnam that week.

* * *

I must have read and heard the Gettysburg Address a hundred times. I still can't listen to it without wanting to weep. As the writer Garry Wills has pointed out, the speech violates all the rules of rhetoric. But Lincoln did not need to prepare the ground for his audience; he was standing on it. The hard specifics of war, which are missing from the address, were buried in the earth all around him. Death's stench filled in the blanks. The speech is pure lightning.

I am closer in age by almost half a century than my students to the three-day slaughter that prompted that speech. Both my grandfathers were born in the decade of the Civil War. My great-grandfather's cavalry sword sits in the corner as I write. I even once had the privilege of drinking bourbon with an old man who was born to slaves in Georgia. I can feel the Civil War in my bones.

And now I live nearby it.

* * *

Just before the summer solstice last year, while walking on the battlefield, I came across a redheaded woodpecker lying in the middle of United States Avenue. A thinned-out woodlot lines the south side of the avenue, and a vast field stretches to the north. The bird must have been whacked by a vehicle as it flew across the road between woods and field. I assumed it was dead. It lay motionless on the pavement, one black-and-white wing splayed, its bright crimson head turned sharply to the side. Its left eye looked dazed and bloodshot, like the eye of a drunk after a bar fight.

When I squatted to pick up the woodpecker, thinking of moving it to a grassy burial place on the shoulder of the road, it suddenly struggled to flap its open wing. I gathered the creature into my hand, holding both wings tight against its body. Happy to see that its neck wasn't broken, I walked to a stone wall, where I sat on a rock and tried to give the bird some solace. It lay still in my grasp, its beak parted, one clear eye staring at me. I touched its stiff, long tongue, but it didn't bite or peck my finger. I stroked its smooth head, which looked like a red hood pulled down over its neck and throat. Some minutes passed, during which I managed to clean its wings of the loose fluff produced by the trauma, and the bird grew more alert. Its heartbeat seemed normal enough. After checking that no cars were approaching, I slowly opened my hand to let it fly away. But it just sat there contentedly, as if nesting. Even when I made a gentle tossing motion, urging it toward flight, it didn't budge. The bird reminded me of my English composition students the previous spring when I'd told them, midway through the final class—after pizza and a few stories—that I was done with them, and they were free to leave early. They'd just sat there, refusing to break the circle of our group.

The sun was close to setting. I carried the bird across the road and into the woodlot, where I spoke to it about the need to get home before dark. I had to pry its sharp, four-clawed feet from my index finger. Only then did it fly to a nearby oak, where it clung crazily to the rough bark, its body falling back from the tree trunk like that of an exhausted window washer leaning away from a ledge. Disappointed, I tramped through low brush and reached out to offer my help again, but just as I touched it, the bird flew toward another oak deeper in the woods, swooping abruptly before it landed—correctly this time—high up on the trunk.

The Drowning

2001

The first time I saw a dead child, I was a child myself. I stood then, as I do now in my imagination, on the south bank of the Cross River, one of two feeder streams that supply the three-mile-long New York State reservoir bordering the river's little namesake town where I grew up. From this riverbank I can see the rural intersection of New York State Routes 35 and 121 several hundred yards to the north, and I can just make out, through the trees, the small general store—the intersection's only place of commerce.

Catty-corner across from the store, under the shade of a large maple tree, sits the old stone fountain, with its semicircular seating area, where my childhood buddies and I used to gather on hot summer afternoons to gulp down cold soda pops and improvise mischief. The fountain functioned only sporadically in 1948, the year I'm recalling here. But before World War II, its continuously flowing spout was said to have provided cool spring water to passersby—and to thirsty horses that drank from a small trough, hollowed out of granite, which caught the spillover from the spout meant for humans.

Carved into a stone plaque just above that spout, you'll find the moss-covered inscription:

> Spirits of Water, Earth and Sky,
> All gather here,
> Where once dwelt one who like this spring
> Was sparkling, sweet and clear.

"Who once dwelt here?" we boys asked each other, laughing riotously. "Who! Who! An owl?"

It is from that fountain that Johnny Edgerton, Sydney Huck-vale, Lewis Holly, and I set out one Sunday afternoon, in July 1948, in search of snakes, turtles, and arrowheads. Johnny and Sydney, both ten years old, led the way down the road from the fountain and across the small cement bridge, where the Cross River feeds into the reservoir. Lewis and I, both eight, tagged along. We all carried lever action Daisy BB Guns slung over our shoulders.

We didn't stop here at the riverbank, because a family of four had parked a station wagon nearby and was picnicking and fishing at our favorite spot. Instead, we turned east up the then-unpaved entrance to the Ward Pound Ridge Reservation, a four-thousand-acre tract of county-park land where Lenape people once lived and hunted. We followed the dirt road, which paralleled the river, for about five hundred yards. After passing a little swamp, we came to a grassy sweep where white-tailed deer slept at night. We left the road and cut north into a stand of white pines. Beyond the pines, we scrambled over a stone wall, lingered for a while at our secret campsite, then slid down a treacherously steep embankment to the river itself. From there we began to make our way back west along the river toward this spot, my chosen perspective for this account.

Should it go without saying that childhood was radically different then—that the kind of psychic innocence to which we were privy cannot possibly exist anymore? What kind of information was in the air, after all? And how was it even disseminated? Not with microwaves or television (quite yet). Certainly not via the Internet and cellular devices. And World War II was over now, so the wider world remained just that—wide and remote: from our perspective, all-American. Information seemed to come to us on the wind. Imagination and invention took up the slack.

I won't pretend that I recall the specifics of our conversation as we walked back along the river's edge, poking at rotten logs and turning over rocks. But I'm pretty certain that the presence of the family picnicking in our spot did not go unremarked. We would have assumed that they came from White Plains, or New York City fifty miles to the south, and it was their urban origin that made them strangers to us. The mere presence of "city slickers," as we called them, (and this included any fishermen or boaters whose faces we didn't recognize as local), with their unapologetic invasion of what we considered to be *our* territory—*our* river, *our* reservoir, *our* reservation—brought out profound and ridiculously childish expressions of xenophobia. Who knows where such behavior comes from in children? I suspect the world war had much to do with it; we were defending Cross River from invasion the way our nation had defended itself from Hitler. We regularly went about unchaining chained-up rowboats, letting air out of car tires, and lobbing huge rocks into otherwise tranquil fishing waters to the astonishment of the targets of our inexplicable angst. We styled ourselves on the Underwater Demolition Teams we learned about from movies, the teams later dubbed Navy SEALs.

I still retain trace proprietary feelings regarding this pristine place, which seems odd, since I'm now a sixty-one-year-old city slicker myself—and since my parents have both died. The house where my younger brother and sister and I grew up—the one next to the Baptist church just a few hundred yards south of this spot—now belongs to another family.

On the face of it, I needn't imagine standing here at all, and perhaps wouldn't had I not, back in 1972, buried my son's ashes in an old, old cemetery in the reservation. Born with Down syndrome, Chelsey, my second child, died of a then-inoperable heart condition at the age of eighteen months. His brief life was difficult and terribly wearing on him, but his unabashed gaiety was a blessing for my wife and daughter and me. So, it is now my son's grave that anchors me to this place. For which I can be grateful: It is time, at age sixty-one, to look back like this at my first face-to-face encounter with death.

* * *

Johnny Edgerton was our ringleader, a daring, impulsive kid who several years earlier had earned his leadership cred by riding his brakeless, balloon-tired bicycle down what we called the Hill Road and crashing it straight into a stone wall at the bottom of the hill. When he was discharged from the hospital, after suffering a severe concussion, we began following him unquestioningly.

When our little band of boys came to the place where the Cross River broke out of the woods and widened before narrowing again to meet the reservoir, Johnny signaled with a flattened hand that we should halt and stay down low. Sydney Huckvale, next in command, repeated the gesture. Then, on Johnny's signal, we fanned out, so as not to be caught, all four of us at once, by a single burst of enemy machine-gun fire. We darted this way and that, across slippery rocks and into the cover of some reeds and cattails. Johnny dropped to his knees. So did we. He reached into his shirt pocket and pulled out a limp Camel cigarette. He let me light it with a matchstick, and then he and Sydney smoked it to the nub, while Lewis and I breathed in the delicious secondary smoke.

Sydney buried the butt and the dead match, so as to leave no trace, then patted the earth the way we'd seen untrackable Indians do in movies. We crawled side by side on our bellies, keeping a nervous lookout for copperheads. Finally, we came to the edge of the reeds and saw the picnicking family on the near riverbank about twenty-five yards to the west.

Did we discuss a plan of "attack"? I don't remember. But we crawled through some low grass, until we found a good place to spy and assess the situation. A tall man, presumably the father, stood on the shore, fishing with a short rod. He wore wire-rim sunglasses, a white sleeveless undershirt, and military fatigues neatly bloused halfway up his paratrooper boots. Behind him, a large bosomy woman—his wife, I assumed—reclined on a folding wood-and-canvas lawn chair. A floppy straw hat obscured her face, but her bright red dress, bunched as it was around her hips, exposed a pair of voluminous legs. Pink slippers dangled from her toes. Nearby, a girl who looked to be about my age, her yellow-beribboned braids framing her face, sat sorting wildflowers in the shade of a young maple. A lanky boy, maybe twelve years old and clearly the girl's brother, stood on the edge of a stone abutment at the south end of the concrete bridge. He used a casting pole longer than his father's.

To complete the scene, a local man wearing a cowboy hat fished from the center of the bridge, which was the best spot if you hoped to catch bass.

I doubt that we would have dared to fire our BB guns into the water, with the family so close by—we had no easy escape route. But we might have tried imitating the call of a white hawk, which Lewis had learned how to do, or made ferocious growling noises, hoping to scare the city slickers.

In any case, I'll never know what kind of commando tactics we might have employed, because the lanky boy was now swimming in the deep water below the stone abutment. We all looked at each other in outrage: The boy was violating one of the cardinal regulations posted on trees all around the reservoir—all reservoirs—NO SWIMMING. Just because we broke the rule occasionally didn't mean *anyone* could. (Actually, I couldn't swim yet, but I often cooled off by wading into shallow water.)

"Hey!" yelled Johnny. "No swimming here!"

As the boy began to flail and splash, we all took up the chorus. "Hey! No swimming!"

The boy sputtered and waved wildly at us, yelling words we couldn't quite understand.

Suddenly, the man who'd been fishing from the bridge pulled himself over its concrete wall and leapt fully clothed into the water fifteen feet below. His cowboy hat flew off and landed beside him. Ignoring it, he swam toward the flailing boy.

The four of us looked at each other.

"Jeez," said Johnny.

When we looked back toward the boy, he was gone. An ominous ripple spread out across the water.

I can't for the life of me remember what transpired during the next minute or so. Either I ran toward the event with my companions or I drifted toward it slowly on my own, as a cinematic portrayal might have me do. In no time, it seems now, I was standing amid the chaotic family scene. The rotund mother was running up and down the shore, wailing and flapping her arms like a Canada goose protecting her young. Her husband, who had stepped into the water initially, was now sitting on the shore fumbling with the wet laces of his paratrooper boots. Clearly, like me, he couldn't swim, but his attempt to remove his boots before entering the water struck me as alarming and strange.

When the bridge man reached the spot where the boy had disappeared, he dove repeatedly beneath the surface but kept coming up for air empty-handed. A car skidded loudly to a stop near the bridge. The driver, after deciphering the scene, leapt a wire guardrail, ran down the embankment, and plunged fully clothed into the water. The little girl was now chasing up and down the shore after her mother, tugging at her braids and screeching.

For once, Johnny was speechless. Sydney and Lewis, too. We all stood there, awestruck. Several minutes must have passed before the two men in the water hauled the boy out and dropped him on the muddy embankment. The bridge man kicked aside an ice chest and dragged the boy's inert body face down onto the family's picnic blanket. Dripping wet himself, he knelt and turned the boy's head to one side. The driver of the car placed the boy's hands beneath his head and arranged the arms, elbows out. Then, the bridge man began artificial respiration, which I'd seen older kids practicing in the school gymnasium. Kneeling at the victim's head, you placed both hands flat on the victim's back, over the lungs, and pressed down with all your weight. Then, you lifted the bent elbows upward (opening the lungs), and you repeated the process, over and over again. I remember telling myself that when my time came to practice in the gym, I'd better pay attention and get it right. Once the bridge man's rhythm had been established, the driver of the car went to call for help.

The mother, her bosom heaving, circled the blanket.

"Is my boy gonna die? Is my boy dead?"

The bridge man told her to hush and go stand in the shade. The mother and her little girl moved obediently under the small maple. Standing apart, they covered their eyes and sobbed. The bridge man's efforts grew increasingly intense and desperate.

I didn't like looking at the boy's expressionless face, which was turned in my direction. But I couldn't look away. His eyes were closed, his expression undisturbed. Brackish water trickled onto the blanket from between his motionless lips. He seemed so sad. I remember expecting him to open his eyes any second now, wanting them to open so I could see his relief. They *had* to open. Soon, his mouth wasn't dribbling anymore, which I took to be a good sign. I wanted to say something that would make him wake up, but I had no words. I remember forcefully shifting my gaze away, not wanting to miss the boy's revival but needing to look over my shoulder toward the father, who was standing motionless in white socks, holding one dripping boot in each hand.

The trouble with curiosity, it seems to me now, is that it requires you to accept what you see. Not that you must accept what you've seen as either right or wrong, meaningful or meaningless, inevitable or random, but rather that you must accept what you've seen as inexorably connected with your *choice* to look. Curiosity has emotional consequences. You can't *unsee* what you've seen, and what you've seen involves you irreparably. Often forever.

Whether I turned to look at the father because I already sensed that the bridge man's efforts would be in vain or because I simply did not want to see what the boy was going to look like when it was determined he was dead doesn't matter. What matters to me now is that, even then, I was curious to know this event from the father's point of view. He never did step forward, just stood there on the slippery riverbank, paralyzed, watching the bridge man work on the inert body of his son. Even when the long, bullet-shaped ambulance arrived, the father stood on the periphery, stunned and wordless.

I imagine, now, inhabiting his point of view—being him, so to speak—while the ambulance driver takes over for the bridge man, using a contraption called an inhalator. *It isn't over yet*, he must be thinking—there's always hope—but the way the bridge man sits back on his heels and bows his head signals a certain undeniable finality.

The mother suddenly throws her hands in the air and charges at the water like a wild buffalo. The bridge man, still on his knees, lunges out, tackles her, and pins her down.

A county patrolman arrives, followed by onlookers who have parked their cars along the guardrail. There are questions to be answered and logistics to be determined about who will go in what vehicle to the hospital. Two young men cover the boy with a green surplus US Army blanket.

I had expected my own son's body to be covered with at least one sheet, when my wife and I asked to see him at NewYork-Presbyterian Hospital, in Manhattan. It was four o'clock on a cold and dark November morning. We'd left our six-year-old daughter at our apartment, in my mother's care. The nurse led us down a hospital corridor, tried several locked doors, until finally an unlocked one opened, revealing a cramped fluorescent-lit utility closet. There was Chelsey, eyes wide-open, his now-stiffened body lying stark naked and face up on a cold steel-top tray table that had been carelessly stored there until someone had the time to properly deal with it. The sight paralyzed me, paralyzed both of us, I think. Even the anger I felt in the moment failed to surface under the sheer tonnage of the sight. There were, and still are, no words to describe the cold horror of the scene. Yet my curiosity held me motionless until I could absorb the reality, as if I might be able to pocket it before closing the closet door.

On the riverbank, a crowd gathers at the back of the green ambulance. The boy's blanketed body, having been transferred onto a canvas stretcher, is placed on a stationary bench inside the vehicle. Mother and daughter, dazed and exhausted, are helped into the vehicle beside the boy. The back door closes. The ambulance pulls off the grass and swings onto Route 121, heading north. It drives toward the intersection with its waterless stone fountain, red light twirling, siren off.

The boy's father walks to the family station wagon and tosses his boots in the back. He sits down on the edge of the driver's seat and removes his muddy socks.

My own father is calling me home from the front porch of our house. He uses the distinctive whistle of a bobwhite—a shrill two-syllable birdcall ending on a high note, which he achieves by hooking two spread fingers into his mouth, tucking in his lips, and blowing out full blast.

The shrill sound jolts me into a parallel reality, in which Johnny and Lewis and Sydney and I, sobered by what we've witnessed, begin wordlessly heading our separate ways home. I wonder if my father has been aware of the commotion so near our house, and if he's been in any way alarmed or worried about me. I'll be able to tell by the expression on his face when he sees that I am safe.

From a Long Life,
a Moment

2002

My first conscious attempt to secure the future came on a sunny July morning in 1950, when I was ten years old. The camp I attended that summer overlooked crystalline Silver Lake, in Barnard, Vermont. Every day, exactly one hour after breakfast, all of us campers would pile out of our log cabin dormitories and run barefoot down a grassy hillside to the roped-off swimming area, where our counselors awaited us. Little patches of white clover, teeming with brown honeybees, turned the descent into a kind of free-for-all slalom run—requiring quick shifts, this way and that, to avoid being stung.

Once in a while someone did get stung, and on that particular day, it was me. I yelped and hopped around on one foot while the other kids raced toward the lake. I sat down on my towel to examine the tiny stinger mark on my big toe. I winced and whimpered and squeezed out a few tears. After the pain subsided, I studied how the bees were working the clover all around me, each bee clinging to a separate blossom, not at all perturbed by my presence. Slowly, I became aware that, except for the bees, I was alone on the hillside; the voices of the other boys were distant now, their shrieks mingling with the shrill blast of a counselor's whistle.

As my feeling of aloneness blossomed, so did my sense of self, until suddenly it occurred to me that I actually *existed*—sitting on a hillside on the planet Earth. Something I can only describe as urgency took a hold of me, and I made a silent but solemn promise: *I am going to remember this moment for as long as I live.* I must have known something about the fragile nature of human memory because immediately I amended the promise: *I am going to remember this moment like an elephant—forever.* I picked up my towel and made my way carefully down the hill to the lake. *Bees and elephants*, I chanted quietly, *elephants and bees. Forever and ever.*

I did not yet picture myself as anyone in particular—certainly not the painfully shy and deeply ambitious boy I now know myself to have been—which is to say that there was nothing melodramatic about my promise. On the contrary, it was one of the simplest, purest, and most private moments of my life. I could not possibly have imagined how thick and treacherous the future would turn out to be, or how many memories, far more consequential than a beesting, would not survive the pitfalls of time. But I did understand that to remember such a thing "forever" would be a challenge, and that to intentionally populate the distant future with a memory of self-awakening might prove undoable. Casting that awakening into an unknowable time felt a little like throwing a lifeline into a dark sea, a line that I can now say I have happened upon from time to time and have dutifully tossed into the future again, as I do now, in the middle of my seventh decade on the planet.

One Draft at a Time:
The Rewards of Process

2007

Kathy Dougherty arrived at my fourth-floor college office exactly on time and panting like a sprinter. A painful grimace replaced her typically open and sweet expression.

"Those damn stairs!" she gasped. "How do you do it?"

"They get easier with practice," I said, "especially when you lug a ton of books up here four times a day."

Kathy, nearly forty-five years my junior and burdened only by a five-page essay, shot me a look of disdain.

I laughed.

"Take a load off," I told her, indicating a stiff-backed armchair in the corner of the room. I sat down in a matching chair, from which I would be able to monitor the arrival of another student during the drop-in office hour.

Kathy remained standing in the doorway. "I'm having a terrible time writing this nonfiction personal essay thing," she said.

"Have a seat," I said, pointing at the chair again.

Hesitantly, she stepped into the small room and planted her feet about a yard from my chair. Clutching the essay in her fist, she looked like an actor preparing to audition for a part.

"Sit," I said—sternly this time, as if speaking to a dog.

But she seemed not to hear me and launched instead into an agitated description of her struggle to write sensitive personal material. I sank down in my chair, like a hapless moviegoer stuck in the front row of a theater. To be honest, I'd been dreading Kathy's visit. During lunch, I'd read a copy of her first draft—a chaotic, untitled rant, which described Kathy's feelings about her stormy family life, her difficulty scraping together funds for tuition, and the rage she felt for her mother, on whom she blamed her family's breakup and subsequent troubles.

I deserved the chaotic rant, of course, having prompted my multigenre creative writing class to write freely about their most painful experience. They had three weeks before they would switch genres and try their hands at short fiction. Now I would have to coax Kathy, draft by draft, into producing a transcendent personal essay.

"So, what do you want me to include in the paper, exactly?" asked Kathy, shifting her weight and cocking her left hip. "I can't possibly get the whole story in. There's just way too much stuff." She turned her right foot out and began tapping her sandal on the carpet.

"What do *you* want to include?" I asked, refusing to be distracted by the anxious rhythm of her tapping shoe.

"I mean, like, how long does it have to be?"

"I don't know, Kathy. You tell me. How long does it have to be?"

She rolled her eyes and exhaled loudly, as if she'd heard this kind of response before, which she had—from me—in a first-year composition class two years earlier. *It's up to you,* I'd told her then.

"It's up to you," I reminded her now.

"But the paper *sucks*," she said. "It just *sucks*. It's like blah-blah and it just keeps . . . " She paused in her assessment, apparently distracted by the image of a reclining nude on a postcard taped to the wall above my computer. " . . . I don't know what I'm doing."

"I think you do," I told her.

"No, I don't!" She stamped her foot and covered her ears with her hands. "I've tried writing about all this before and it never turns out right." She dropped her arms and sighed.

"Your first paragraph's a mess, Kathy, I'll give you that. You begin with your bank balance, jump to your already estranged parents, list your college loans, bitch about a blown semester in Australia, and allude to summer jobs you worked during your high school years. Dump it, the whole paragraph. Highlight it, paste it somewhere, and scavenge from it. First paragraphs almost never wind up being first anyway."

"Then how should I start?"

"Read me your second paragraph."

Kathy stared at her essay, then began to read: "My parents met at Farmington High School, in Farmington, Connecticut."

"Stop," I said.

"What?"

"Give me that."

She passed me the paper. "Listen," I said, and I read the sentence aloud for her, not once but twice. "See how quiet and simple it is?"

Kathy tipped her head and allowed that she saw my point.

"That's how you start. The story makes you angry, doesn't it?"

"Pissed. Totally pissed. I can't even begin to tell you how much I hate my bitch of a mother."

"You want to kill her, right?"

"Yep. Tear her eyes out."

"Fine. But don't betray your anger at the outset. Play *against* it. Ground the reader, like you do in that sentence. Patiently write what happened after your parents met, and how the breakup came about—with the boyfriend—and how you learned about it. Calmly bring yourself and your siblings into the picture. Make the *reader* want to kill your mother."

I passed Kathy's paper back to her. She stood there a moment longer, pondering her second paragraph then flipping through the other pages. I cracked my neck and rested my eyes on the magical smile of a dolphin beaming at me from a wall calendar near the door. Apparently satisfied with my feedback, Kathy folded her essay in half and stuffed it into her back pocket.

"That's it?" she asked.

* * *

Kathy was lucky. Some female students her age suffer from the illusion that their mothers are their best friends—an illusion fostered, perhaps, by the culture's obsession with youth and the way that obsession blurs the boundary between adolescence and adulthood. It often takes three drafts of la-di-da banter before these students unearth the smoldering anger the illusion has invariably caused, and by then it's too late in the semester to make sense of it. Kathy, although she claimed to hate her mother, at least saw the woman as a distinct individual, which is to say that she had no problem making her the villain of a personal essay—a real villain with real motives causing real havoc.

A villain does not a narrative make, but the energy a villain can constellate—in this case, rage—serves the three-draft process well. A first draft need do nothing more than illuminate the lay of the land, giving the student a glimpse of the territory to be covered in a second draft, which will be the context and frame of the narrative. If in the third draft a student has achieved a sustained narrative, supported by individual scenes and ending on a nuanced note, I'm happy.

In Kathy's untitled second draft, she added a startling scene where her father gathers the children in the living room and tells them tearfully that their mother is having sex with his best friend. The story of Kathy's painful home life also emerges more fully, grounded in scenes between her siblings and her mother, accounts of ruined family holidays, and excerpts from emotionally devasting phone calls and emails.

In the final draft, titled "Tuition," the father fades a bit too conveniently into the woodwork of the struggle, but Kathy harnesses the original chaos into a surprisingly cohesive portrait of maternal neglect. Toward the end, her patient narrative voice gives way to her expressed determination "to break away from the ties that still connect me to my mother." She resolves "to live a life free of the hurt she has caused."

The word *tuition* derives from the Latin *tuitio*, "protection," and *tueri*, "to look at" or "to look after." Though Kathy may have been unaware of such etymology, her title—which obviously refers to the cost of her education—also hints at the deeper nature of her struggle and her victory. It springs directly from the context of her essay. Her mother has failed to provide a true guardianship, so Kathy breaks free and becomes her own guardian— sworn to look after herself.

* * *

To help students negotiate the transition from nonfiction to fiction, I urge them to shift their focus from personal pain to personal desire: What is it that you want more than anything else in all the world? I have them write the answer on a scrap of paper, and I ask them to keep the answer to themselves. Once they've pocketed the scrap, or tucked it away in their notebooks, I tell them that the protagonist of their short story wants the very same thing, except something is standing in the way. "Now begin the story," I say.

It is a provocative exercise and usually triggers a whirlwind of creative chaos, visible in the expressions of every student: puzzlement, panic, and intense, self-conscious imagining. During what remains of the workshop session, students read aloud their responses to my prompt, and I toss back suggestions about point of view and tense. Often when students have written in the first person, I will ask them to read again, this time using "he" or "she." Or if they have chosen to write in the present tense, I will sometimes ask them to read it again, using the past. Invariably, by the end of the class, a pall has descended upon the room, and I find myself subjected to fifteen cold and unforgiving stares. That's when the workshop becomes a cohesive group—when we share the devastating and better-left-unsaid truth that the difference between creative success and creative failure is determined not by inspiration but by choice.

During the silence, I try, however briefly, to meet every eye in the room. On this particular occasion, when my gaze settled on Kathy Dougherty, I was met with a subtle but complicit smile: *Got it*, she seemed to say. Five days later, she submitted the first draft of a short story titled "Respect."

If asked to bet, I would have wagered that her story was a predictable rehash of the mother-daughter conflict, a slick way for Kathy to keep the experience at arm's length by fictionalizing it. But there was no reference to a mother anywhere to be found. The protagonist of the story is a strapped-for-cash college student named Laura. The person standing in the way of what she wants is her father. When he stubbornly insists that she attend college no farther than two hundred miles from home, Laura rebels and flies from Massachusetts to Arizona, where she lands a job as a pole dancer in a strip club, thereby supporting herself and earning tuition at the college of *her* choice. Though the genre and the narrative have changed, the core issue in Kathy's life is being reimagined and dealt with anew. She begins the story in the middle of things and on a slightly klutzy note, with an unidentified speaker groping and heckling Laura during her act. The story ends five pages later when the passive-aggressive father shows up at the club to reclaim his daughter:

> The look in his eyes was heartbreaking, and in that moment she no longer felt numb. The hurt and shame hit her like a brick wall.
> "Are you ready to . . . " he began.
> " . . . go home?" she finished.
> He turned his eyes away to give her the respect she deserved as she gathered her things.

Here, it's the father who earns the respect that Laura ostensibly set out to achieve for herself. He satisfies his *own* demand for respect under the pretext of rescuing his daughter's self-respect. When Kathy workshopped the first draft, I saw the opportunity to address, in a generic way, the dramatic principle of life articulated by Mick Jagger: that you can't always get what you want, but that sometimes you can get what you need. "Maybe Laura doesn't go home with her father," I suggested. Then I yakked for a while about suspending judgment, risking discovery, and creating sympathy—all the stuff that I'd absorbed from my own writing teachers. "Inhabit the killer," I told the class, "inhabit the whore." Kathy sat across the workshop table from me, scribbling furiously.

In her second draft, Kathy uses the same awkward opening, but we now learn that Laura was the captain of her field hockey team in high school; she agrees to a semester at her father's alma mater, Boston College, before insisting on her college of choice, Arizona State. When the father calls her an "ungrateful, selfish, awful daughter," Laura leaves home and flies out west, where she soon runs into "an older gentleman" at a bar—a man her father would have called "guido trailer trash." She takes the job as a pole dancer, and this time we actually see her mount the stage and face the ridicule of nasty customers: "Hey, honey, my grandmother moves better than you," one of them says. Laura teaches herself "to be numb" to the abuse and to focus on the prize: tuition. With the groundwork for her character fully established, and Laura's onstage experience revealed, Kathy has her protagonist turn away from her father when he asks at the end if she is ready to reunite with the family and be a respectable woman again. "She held her head high, even though in his eyes she had become a common whore."

The first sentence of Kathy's nine-page final draft, which arrived with the bold-font title "Palm Trees, Red Thongs, and the Power of a Dream," reads: "All Laura had ever wanted to do was travel." Gone is the klutzy opening. The patience with which she then grounds the reader pays off in a touching new scene where Laura greets the owner of the club on her first day of work. He gives her "a big hug and a fatherly peck on the forehead," leads her to the dressing room, where he gives her a robe and a skimpy costume, then leaves her alone. "She put on the bra and thong in front of the mirror and could not stop staring at herself. Her athletic body melded perfectly with the costume, and for the first time in her life she felt sexy." Laura suffers the same abuse from customers that she suffered in the second draft, but this time her patient pursuit of self-respect is utterly convincing and transcendent:

> Driven by the money, she had become good at what she did. With each night and every dance, she had become increasingly confident. About a month after her first night at the club she was moved up front. The bigger stage, brighter lights, and larger and higher-paying crowd made her excited for the big night. When her heel hit the main stage, on the first beat of Jessica Simpson's "These Boots Are Made for Walkin'," she felt a rush of power. Sliding up and down the pole, keeping it between her legs, and wrapping her body tightly around it, she worked the crowd. Lawyers, doctors, construction workers, and honest hardworking men watched as she shook her breasts and swayed her hips across the stage. Every eye in the room was on her.

In this final draft, Laura tells her father in a choking voice, "You just don't get it." Then: "She turned around and walked away, the tears he had provoked streaming down her face. [. . .] She was paying for her dream, one pole at a time."

By acknowledging the pain her character feels, rather than having her character cop to the pain her father displays, Kathy has opened the door to the resolution of the story—a resolution that might very well reverberate beyond the boundaries of fiction. And she arrived there one draft at a time.

April in Autumn:
A Meditation on First

2012

It goes without saying (and thus must be said) that there is no path for First: no footprints under the leaves, no intelligible topography, no message carved in the bark. Just omens composed of approach, appearing as shape and shadow. First takes the lead and moves in single file because light is the only solution to darkness—which is death, which is Last.

First must be famously cruel.

It's been decades since she dug her nails into your back and pleaded with you (finally, like an offering) to kill her. You knew what a metaphor was, so you pinned her prickly knees back to her ears and clutched the roots of her braids as you might some wild mare's mane, and you rode her dangerous energy until the buzzer sounded. You'd already engaged in months and months of nonstop sex—been late for work a dozen times, left the dishes sprinkled with cleanser since February.

* * *

There is nothing ever left to do but die. But the business of First is to find, not finish. So, when the time came, you piled her stuff by the door and changed the locks. She was quite beautiful—and is still—and you had felt in the curve of her breast not the weight of tissue and fat but the heft that desire imposes on result: You sensed, even then, the consequence of want.

But maybe it's less what First wants than what First feels compelled to be. Sometimes you feel like the personification of Wonder; like a living window sailing through space in awe of the happening Now. It would be wrong to say that you presume to live only in the Now, since everything, including space, has another side and must therefore be complex and shaped of minutes. Even the famously instantaneous quark undergoes a deep inelastic scattering—which is doubt, which is death. You've read that no successful quantum theory of gravity exists, but you suspect they've overlooked failure. The strong interaction of exotic things is simply the mutual attraction of red and yellow, which is orange, which is desire.

* * *

You know (because you've risked it here on the edge) that reach results in touch, and that expectation leads only to despair. Look at the mansions! November reads aloud the penultimate chapter of wind, sweeps bright-yellow gingko leaves into neat brick cul-de-sacs behind Prairie Lights Books in Iowa City: All the houses will blow down, be they brick or straw. What counts today—right now—is the crystalline stab of sunlight through the leafless branches—and of course what you discern in the shadowed alley. You once saw a naked apparition fleeing loneliness in an alley darkened by fire escapes—then you met her, fully clothed. Unspeakable things happen in a mostly invisible universe. We swim in what we are to become. We are already in what we will swim, which is not only life (and not yet death).

* * *

How risky it is to be born, to wriggle free of the ropy cord, to walk away from the dense encumbrance of knowing and move through this (life) without making sense of it all. You catch yourself at times having occupied a space unspoiled by intent. It may soon become a habit you won't be able to kick. She warned you, centuries ago it seems: This messiness, it's communicable.

* * *

What? In solitude you fear the company of the other, which is death? Ah, so it's Last that's nagging you now? Finish instead of find? The alphabet is running dry, the Zee-ness is upon you, eh? Go on, scribble the fucking *Z* right here on the page. (Do it, you.) Good. Now draw a direct line between the point at which your pen first touched the paper and the point where your pen stopped. What does it look like now, that shape? Any sand left in the downward-facing triangle? Focus on the pinch point, that impossibly little squeeze between do and done, through which all letters tumble between First and Last. When Last has come, it'll be time for First again, because nothing-left is where possibility thrives—where you must find me to find I to find we, which is love.

Avoid the bind in the cable, the build in the wave, the trap in the throat, the snare in the bottomless pit of relief. Inhabit First like that fatal light blasting through the slats in the window blinds. Just love randomly. Take that stranger, for instance (your students would call her "random"), the one sitting at a nearby café table in the bookstore, rim-lit with bounced sunlight, which has just moved from the framed famous-writer letter on the wall to the open book on her table. Fish in that light. Be a fisher of women. Catch her eye as you stare at her from First. Watch her head tilt slightly in thought, and notice how her lithe fingers stroke the pale skin above her dark eyebrow. Her legs are clothed in smooth black cotton and crossed—left over right. Her posture reflects a subtle awareness of audience. Undress her gently (with soft scissors) while she highlights the work some Iowa workshop professor has assigned her. You could teach her that nothing she underlines, nothing she finds relevant on the page, will outlast this light she sits in, feels warm in, leans even farther into, and soon—at precisely this moment, yes—she tilts her head fully and smiles at you.

She may not remember it, but this is the infinite ripple of First. Like this, it begins, snatched up and kidnapped by light. Memoir overflows the bookshelves here; it has nearly over-whelmed the literary sea, but she, sitting there, is everything Now to me (you see?). Watch how you are I, and I are you-and-she. The messiness of dissolve (the willing dissolution of resolve) is contagious—it is love—and it spreads the way a slightest kind glance will blossom in a crowded New York City subway car and become, all on its own, a ton of consciousness hurtling through the dark tunnel. First shares without hanging around for credit. First prays without you knowing it, pays be-hind your back. In its wake you awake to what it was. No per-manent home for light. Just light and what it exposes into being.

The eye, they think, (and if they don't, they should) began as a shadow on a cell (and the eye opened eventually, over eons). Pores open, after all, and the wet pussy and the stiff penis and the overstuffed anus open, and the ears, mouth, nose, and throat open, and you find yourself wet and bloody and full of alphabet, feeling for the breast, for the rounding promise of curve, for the first sign of Things To Come. As you reach out, you imagine that it will not end for you (ever) as it has for others, whom you dimly remember have died and left you here to be born again alone. It will not stop for you because the last letter in the squeeze is the squeeze itself, and the squeeze will last and last, until you ever must upend omega and allow room for some new and remarkable onliness, some alpha composed of particle and light, with eyes made of shadow, who will one day look up from wherever he sits (or she) in the vertical horizontality we think of as space—which by then will most likely no longer be the Prairie Lights bookstore and coffee shop and (who knows?) may not even be a prairie—and God knows what aspect that eventual light will contain of you and your nowness, then. Trust the urgency of wait. Wonder what it would feel like to run your forefinger gently up and down the ridge of her beautiful straight nose while she puzzles (and maybe feels) what has been written in her text.

She massages her right wrist with long white fingertips. Why on earth is she studying, and what for, for God's sake, what for? You yourself have been doing it for decades, underlining texts and scribbling *Yes!* in the margins and highlighting important phrases, all the while puzzling at the brilliance of other minds than yours—the hysterical wildness of someone else's articulated truth—and now you're just a melting mess of autumn light: an old man plucking the last of the cabbage and the few cold brussels sprouts left. First absorbing the last of it, First unleashed from collared mind and unwilling to look back—what for, for God's sake, what for? What's back there but the residue of thrust and a fading contrail of spent fuel? The privilege of Now lies in watching it play out ahead. Watch as first becomes Last, watch yourself last and last as Last gives way to First. You go first, Alphonse. Tell us what you see beyond the squeeze. Ah, she cocked her head at the sound of that! See? She begins to listen, her hand cupping her ear in a totally unconscious fashion. She's found not-enough on the page, perhaps, or just too damn little in her prefrontal cortex—that damp arena of planning and knowing that she must march in all day. She hears in what she studies . . . something. Her legs uncross and fall lazily apart, the right foot now resting on a little ledge, her posture becoming more erect. The flesh of her inner thigh would describe a loose clothesline; her calf a parenthesis. You'd almost be interested in what she's reading and writing because the furrows on her forehead are gone, and her eyes, though looking down, have opened more widely. Whatever-it-is seems to be occurring in concert with your own tranquility of Be, within the light which is passing over the last of the famous-writer letters on the wall and moving onto a patch of pale ochre. It will soon (and sadly) disappear altogether. The warmth will leave the scene, the sharper shadows merge with generality, and by the time you arise from this chair (your chair, sir), sequence will have turned into common sense, and sense into a subdued, no-longer-relevant residue of rub, like the delicious disappointment of sex, when you're still alive but impossibly done.

* * *

Done. She's distracted now, no longer puzzled (and wasn't it puzzlement that shaped her and you, gave birth to the impulse, made you move into First?). Her slender right arm dangles softly alongside the back leg of her chair. She has found in this moment her footing in time. And whatever has happened between you and her in the ongoing Firstness, the freshness of imagination and invention, is crumbling in anticipation of Done—the soon-to-be-diminishing day—while you and everyone else in the room whirl wildly toward noon (by the clock in Iowa). And how can something so goddamn pure and primary as this nearly forever Nowness just disintegrate and vanish into Then?

She massages her wrist again then grasps it, as if feeling for a pulse, and in the process exposes her wedding ring. You want to reassure her: It doesn't matter that you are married. It's important to have a roof over your head. What counts is this narrowing light that funnels us like fine sand into the squeeze of here and now, and the unpluggable suck that forces us to expand in response. Let's be lucky and live big in this squeeze, this noisy silence of chatter and music—no matter what. If she checks her watch again, tell her you know what time it is. To teach you must know what time it is, while keeping the time in question. Unfold the question of time into a narrowing of space, and there you will find the tug and shape of invisible things.

* * *

The reflecting pool beside a pyramid was meant (I propose) to disorder the pyramid's shape. Water ripples. The blood within us ripples, too, but with difficulty. Blood is simply a complication of water. Do you get this? Do you really understand what my *I* is telling you? Everything within is a complication of without. Your fire has heat but can't possibly be pure; your water is too thickly ridden with red; your air suffers from process; and your earth is simply shit.

Cows know. Stop listening to the gabfest on channels and wavelengths in the licensed world; stop checking the fucking GPS and listening to the woman who knows it all. Watch, instead, the mystery unfolding in a cow's breath at dawn. Inhale the still-green world cast in gold and silver light and notice (exhale!) how the cow abides the cold earth and takes what is dealt.

* * *

Ah! Her thighs have shifted your way and her knees fall slowly apart. You receive without flinching this steadier gaze, imagining in her parted lips a wet invitation, a breathy opening in the vast and icy stretch of No. She sits only two small tables away and you can sense the damp heat from within, without help from her thin smile. You savor the agony of thirst, remembering when you really could be never done and could kill. The evidence of defeat lies everywhere—the sense of purpose you've both shared, to make sense of what you were either studying or observing, now lies exhausted between you like an old throw rug on the floor. The sun has slid farther along its mere foul ball of an arc, and you must be content to reach more deeply, and with the patience of a redwood, into the awesome marrow of Be.

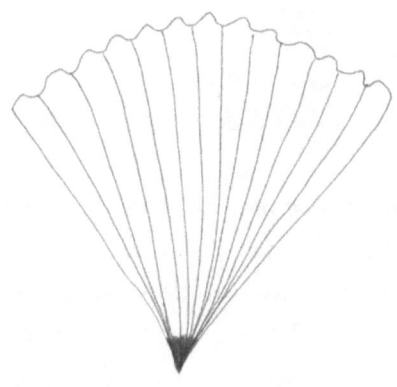

Letting Go

2024

As with a professional athlete, there hovers over the college professor an informal admonition to know when to quit: to recognize that dreaded, indeterminate moment when cutting-edge wisdom, gained from years of attention to a subject as well as repetitive performances in the classroom, begins to lose its vitality—first for the teacher and then for the student.

For the college professor who has taken the arduous, credentialed route to a secure teaching position by earning an undergraduate degree, a master's, and a PhD, then enduring a precarious multiyear trial period called tenure track, success often results in being tied forevermore to the same institution, the same academic department, the same academic office, the same colleagues, and the same narrow subject matter, all in service to research and/or to teaching an unending stream of youth. That stream, like Heracleitus's river of time, seems forever fresh, the flow of students forever young, but as the semesters pass, the teacher grows older and older, until one day, he or she wakes up old.

I was lucky. I *began* old. At age sixty-three, after attending a two-year MFA program at Columbia University School of the Arts, I was invited to teach undergraduate writing, as an adjunct, at a small liberal arts college in Pennsylvania. I had *not* been obliged to spend decades in academia, so the potential for growing stale promised to be mitigated by the limited number of active years left to me. Surely, the dreaded moment of reckoning would not be my concern.

I'd come about my academic appointment naturally and without ceremony. Suddenly, without any prompting from me, people were calling me "Professor." Some even called me "Doctor." At the outset, my formal title was "adjunct instructor," but it soon got bumped to "adjunct assistant professor," then "adjunct associate professor." One year, I taught full-time as a visiting assistant professor, and I was paid a tenured professor's salary, tripling my adjunct income. (A dangerous precedent that the administration did not care to repeat, for fear of locking me legally into full-time status.)

To supplement my meager adjunct salary, the college graciously offered me a part-time administrative position as coordinator of the Peer Learning Associates Program, which effectively (though not formally) made me a full-time employee of the college.

For the first eight years, I worked without health benefits. But I received Social Security and Medicare, and the institution contributed 10 percent of my earnings into a TIAA retirement account. My adjunct salary (one of the more generous in the nation) went up every year, and I was treated as an equal (more or less) by all my associates. I was soon offered a first-year seminar of my own design (most adjuncts weren't); I was assigned student advisees (most adjuncts weren't); I supervised a number of senior-level independent studies (most adjuncts didn't); I took on unpaid committee work for the First-Year Program (no other adjuncts did).

Over the course of seventeen-and-a-half years, I gave talks and/or readings at various venues across campus, mentored English majors and writing minors, and made myself available 24-7 to any student who needed me. I published a prizewinning memoir-in-essays. I availed myself of professional grants and traveled at the college's expense to writing conferences all over the country, where I also gave panel talks. I faithfully attended author dinners and readings and was allowed a voice (though not a vote) at English department meetings. I worked closely with the Center for Career Engagement and the Center for Public Service, and I hosted and cohosted a number of provocative, high-profile public speakers. For my own edification, I attended Friday afternoon sessions called e-Race, where students of color gathered in a circle to share their grievances. For my amusement, I attended many of the college-wide faculty meetings, secretly thanking my lucky stars that I wasn't tenured. I underwent yearly assessments by senior faculty. When asked, I allowed other faculty, and their spouses, to take my creative writing workshops, as long as they did so as active participants, even though assessing their writing increased my workload.

I actually wanted *more* work, but adjuncts suffer the proverbial glass ceiling, regardless of their qualifications or demonstrated enthusiasm. For instance, despite my having spent thirty years working on movie sets actually *making* movies based on written scripts, I failed to earn a course devoted solely to screenwriting—a genre I was already teaching in a four-genre course. Eventually, I gave up my attempts to be awarded innovative writing classes of my own design, similar to the summer workshops I was already teaching at other venues.

Luckily, and unlike many younger adjuncts and tenured folk, I had no still-dependent children, so I felt free to ignore the pitiful salary and to simply act *as if* I were a full-time tenured teacher, embracing whatever work came to me, free of any quid pro quo. I thought of teaching as a gift, and of the feeling it produced in me as payment enough. I happily took on even the most recalcitrant students sent to me by the dean of academic advising. I answered student emails at all hours of the day or night. I sometimes received four-in-the-morning calls from students in tears about a death in the family or some existential anxiety.

With a lifetime of worldly experience behind me and no more ambitions to fulfill, family to raise, or tenure requirements to meet, I jumped at the chance to teach in my own peculiar style, which I'll describe here as internally rigorous but entirely unpredictable, unplanned, and nonpedagogical. I borrowed heavily from the Tibetan style of teaching called "crazy wisdom," sometimes also referred to as "nothing special." This involved taking spontaneous risks and sometimes pushing boundaries based on what was happening in the moment in the classroom. Despite a few raised eyebrows, I was allowed free rein to pursue this style, even by faculty to whom my popularity with students must have felt a little off-putting. ("Who *is* this guy?" I overheard one ask, while I was sitting in a bathroom stall.)

For many years, I had two offices: one administrative, one academic, both in the same building. I was rarely forced to share my academic space, which I'd personalized with a lot of student art, including a large framed charcoal nude.

To many of my students I was known simply as Dusty, which I took as a sign of respect. Emails and texts that began with "Hey Dust" warmed my heart as much as those beginning "Dear Professor," a moniker some students found more comfortable.

An English department administrative assistant told me once that reading my student evaluations was like observing a lovefest. So much did I enjoy teaching at the college level that I'd come to anticipate dying in the saddle, so to speak, even fantasizing humorously that one day I'd just fold my arms on the seminar table, lower my grizzled old head onto them, and "leave." It would serve as my final creative writing prompt.

* * *

But I wasn't going to get off that easily. None of us were. During the 2020 spring break, just before I turned eighty, as COVID-19 was spreading unchecked globally, word went out that the campus was closing, effective immediately. Spring break would be extended one week, and all classes would henceforth be taught remotely, until further notice.

Students, professors, and administrative staff scrambled to learn the technical aspects and vagaries of remote teaching. Soon there was talk of dire financial consequences for the institution. Layoffs and cutbacks were announced. Adjuncts were casually, almost carelessly, informed that we would be the first to go; tenured professors would be assigned our intro courses, if push came to shove.

In practice, during the online experience I managed to retain some of the intimacy of the workshop and seminar tables, but nothing I did reproduced the good vibes of the in-person venue. How could it? Zoom provided a handy facsimile of togetherness but removed completely the sensory experience of teaching—for students and teachers alike. While I could view each member of my sixteen-person classes on a single virtual "page," gone was the gritty complexity of the workshop setting, an elbow-rubbing experience that involved engaging all five senses. Roughly 90 percent of human communication is nonverbal. Gestures play a huge (and apparently primary) part in the way we "speak" and in the way we are "heard." Gone were the telling and helpful subtleties—the sidelong glances, puzzled frowns, whispered asides, and spontaneous blushes; gone was the smell of snacks and coffee, even the odor of recently smoked pot; gone the sounds of gum snapping and pens clicking; gone the subtle body vibes between students. Student images were stacked shoulder to shoulder on the computer screen, but the students themselves were sometimes sitting literally continents apart. The workshop table as *context* completely disappeared. With only one mic open at a time, I could no longer hear collective laughter or be responsive to sudden tears, which had been a big element of workshop interaction; and there was no "room tone," as we called it in the movie business—no consistent ambience. Students were confined like prisoners in separate cells—at home in their childhood bedrooms, some with pets, each with different lighting, each in a different posture and in various modes of dress or undress. Sixteen different environments depicted in sixteen tiny frames, absent smell, taste, and touch.

Some brave teachers chose to switch to "hybrid" teaching, which required cameras in the classroom in order to record the experience and transmit it to those students who were immunocompromised, isolated in quarantine, or otherwise indisposed—an insane process that obliged professors to address remote and in-person students simultaneously, while trapped under fluorescent lights, imprisoned behind a plastic barrier, and wearing a mask.

* * *

Compounding the problems brought about by the pandemic was an odd but perhaps predictable erosion of trust in the time-tested notion that education is an ongoing, open-ended *process*, rather than a strictly definable, boxed and beribboned *product*. Trust in learning, above learning outcomes; trust in serendipitously encountered knowledge—through exposure to many subjects—above knowledge earned purely by strict attention to specialized career-oriented goals.

In my experience of it, this erosion of trust began long before the pandemic, somewhere in the mid-2010s. It appeared first as a strangely legalistic, top-down, assessment-based administrative rigidity, and it attached like a cancer to the nascent DEI and #MeToo movements. With the help of the new smartphone and social media, it metastasized, bottom-up, throughout the campus, indeed throughout campuses everywhere. No longer were students eager to learn. Suddenly, they were social warriors. With access to everything, they already *knew* everything. It was no longer necessary to walk in the shoes of previous generations, to study—through history, art, music, and literature—how we got where we are. They'd *already* got where they were in a magical, persistently available present, with instant access to everything, which ironically gave them access to nothing, because the learning pathway had been robbed of *process,* part of which involved absorption over time. They had not been compelled to re-experience—through literature and the arts—the lives of their ancestors. They were offered those lives on a programmatic platter. Often, when I told personal stories from my sometimes-eventful life, students would fact-check me while I was speaking. *How amazing,* they would say, *that what you describe can be confirmed on my iPhone!*

Control of the classroom—what was taught and the manner in which it was taught—increasingly passed into the hands of data-driven administrators. With sometimes naive faculty blessings, control of first-year seminars was now being shared by administrative personnel who were invited into the classroom, where they would essentially co-teach alongside the teacher, bringing into the educational process their often rigid and programmatic ideas—their expectations of product. Often, these same administrators would email my students independently, reminding them of their obligations as students, and thereby undermining my more freewheeling style of allowing organic blossoming. A little of this behavior went a long way toward souring student enthusiasm. Many wished that I hadn't gone along with the misguided program, which, while perhaps well intentioned, had shattered the traditional and wise distinction between faculty freedom and administrative regulation.

For instance, on the first day of a first-year seminar, I mentioned to the assembled sixteen students that later in the semester we would put on a performance in the school theater, and that we would need to begin thinking about what that performance might be. To my delight they jumped at the chance and suggested that we should do something about Beyoncé and JAY-Z. The two performers were top of mind because they had both just reached billionaire status. I had no interest in such a choice, but I played along and asked who would play Beyoncé.

A handsome young fellow to my right raised his hand and said proudly, "I'll be Beyoncé."

There was a lot of laughter.

"Okay," I said, "and who will play JAY-Z?"

A young blonde woman from Ohio, sitting at the far end of the table, raised her hand tentatively. "I'll be JAY-Z."

Again, laughter. Laughter is good on the first day of class. Laughter is how strangers learn to hold hands.

"Of course, I'll have to wear blackface makeup," the student added, blushing brightly.

"Uh-huh," I said, waiting for student reaction to her suggestion. None was forthcoming, so I said, "Well, what would this performance be about?" I happened to glance at the administrator assigned to my class, who was flashing me angry and demanding looks.

Ignoring her, I started to query students further, going around the seminar table counterclockwise, ignoring for the moment the racial elephant in the room. We entertained various ideas for a performance, even while the administrator shifted anxiously in her seat.

When we'd come around to the final student, I nodded to him.

"Whatever we decide to do," he said, "I think we should be careful not to hurt anyone's feelings unnecessarily."

Bingo, I thought.

"How do you mean?" I asked, allowing space for the elephant to clarify.

"Well, a lot of people find blackface makeup offensive," he suggested.

Murmurs of assent arose around the table.

"Indeed," I said. "So, what would you suggest?"

"Maybe I don't need any makeup?" suggested the girl who would play JAY-Z.

That was process in a nutshell. And it came from *within,* instead of being imposed from without by some authoritative, shaming voice.

We moved on. The first class ended happily and with laughter. But when the students had left, the administrator lingered. She berated me in front of another faculty member, now in the room, for not stepping in and quashing the idea of blackface the minute it surfaced. I felt utterly betrayed by this intrusion and at the same time helpless to convey my style of teaching to anyone who would presume to intrude on it so rudely.

I use this incident to example what academia was like at ground level, how ethical and moral issues had become detached from the learning experience, even before the pandemic, and how process (the essence of teaching and learning) can be short-circuited by the product-based demands of administrative mindsets.

To demonstrate how product-based thinking can filter into *student* mindsets, allow me one more example:

A graduating business major in one of the last classes of my spring-semester creative writing workshop proudly read aloud a long poem he'd written describing his first free fall the previous summer at a nearby skydiving facility. The poem took as long to read as his free fall had lasted—sixty seconds. It developed pleasantly until the point where the narrator (with his instructor harnessed to him but never mentioned in the poem) suddenly ponders the possibility that his parachute might malfunction (an oh-my-God-what-would-that-be-like moment), and then the poem ends with his uneventful, happy-to-be-alive landing. His mother sought me out at his graduation to thank me for inspiring her son suddenly to embrace reading and writing poetry, even to question his chosen major. But immediately following his reading in our workshop, a very bright student and one of the best writers in the class, a student I admired greatly for her maturity, looked sternly across the table at the novice poet, pointed her finger at him with extreme emphasis, and told him that he could never again read aloud a poem like that without a trigger warning.

"And why is that, may I ask?" I asked her.

"Because it made me think of suicide," she answered.

Several of her fellow students sitting alongside her nodded sagely in agreement. I glanced at the poet, who looked as if he'd been literally stabbed by her shaming admonishment.

I managed to make it clear that such an admonition would never apply to my class, but I was otherwise rendered speechless that one of my favorite students had seen fit to import, as if by edict, the timid administrative caution against even hinting at the word *suicide* in the presence of supposedly sensitive students. This would have rendered Hamlet's "to be, or not to be" soliloquy an unteachable gem of English literature and, perhaps more importantly, would have underestimated the courage and resilience of young minds.

* * *

I taught in remote mode for another year. In Fall 2020, I struggled to get my footing in my Voice of the Rebel seminar, a class that in the past had championed any and all forms of free speech. I now found myself preemptively forbidding essays that proposed to argue clear political falsehoods or QAnon propaganda. Instead of listening and being open, a quality that students really respond to in a teacher, I preempted what I anticipated would be lies and disallowed certain cited sources of information. My patience grew onionskin thin. Hints that the abovementioned "dreaded moment" of retirement was near swarmed my dreams. I'd lost my trust in certain students, which had *never* happened before. I'd always been able to exercise endless patience with problem students, having been a problem student myself. I'd disciplined myself to shed any and all expectations, thus short-circuiting disappointment and displeasure. But my instinct to teach freely, in the moment, without fear of consequence, now felt stressed and stilted, hence compromised. Some of what I tried fell flat. At the close of my fall-semester classes, student evaluations assessed me kindly, but I knew I'd let them—and myself—down.

Also at the end of the fall semester, I resigned my position as peer learning coordinator, after being told by a newly hired dean (whom I had warmly welcomed and at whose request I'd helped adjust to her new position) that under no circumstances was I to talk to or meet with student advisees outside billable hours and without informing her first. (She was gone within the academic year, but any hope for a teaching and advising protocol based on unspoken mutual trust had been extinguished.)

Quitting my administrative job meant that I now had one foot out the door.

The Capitol riot of January 6, 2021—heaped upon the exhaustion caused by the pandemic, not to mention the epidemic of fear caused by racial tensions—cast such a miserable pall over the opening of the spring semester that the whole purpose of a college education suddenly seemed suspect. Many students began opting for gap semesters or gap years, and some sought transfers, threatening the college's already dwindling retention rate. Classes with low enrollment and/or nonmonetizable subject matter (i.e., the liberal arts) became endangered species in comparison with STEM subjects. The timeworn idea that one studied at a liberal arts college not to earn big bucks after graduation but to learn about the civilization into which one had been born collapsed under the weight of rising tuition costs and the financial pressures of student loans.

On top of all this, and as part of a nearly two-year-long "strategic planning" agenda, the college, under new leadership, seized the opportunity to offer buyout packages to employees as young as fifty. Partly because of pandemic exhaustion, but also fearing a more autocratic regime, teachers and other employees were, as more than one administrator told me in confidence, "leaving in droves."

The new strategic plan, many, many months in the making and jargon heavy to the point of hilarity, felt oddly cloying as it responded to the shifting landscape of higher education. Announcements of new administrative hires seemed to outpace those of academic hires. Suddenly, deans were sprouting up everywhere. The college, ostensibly a liberal arts institution, was giving way to a top-heavy administration with an increasingly larger say in the development of a new academic curriculum, much of it bald-facedly aimed at increasing student retention. Acronyms that had sprung up in service to the perfectly laudable aspirations of diversity, equity, and inclusion (DEI) now joined the already acronym-riddled emails coming from the new president and the soon-to-be-outgoing provost. (A partial list: BARC, SPC, BOLD, CRC, PLC, SRC, SEI, EPACC, FERC, IACUC, IBC, IRB, APPC, ASC, GSPC, FFC, FGC, FPC, SERC, COLA—not to mention all the curricular subcommittees, whose acronyms had yet TBA.)

Updates from the administration, while extolling the sacrifices and loyalty of "our community," were rendered weirdly impersonal and unmistakably tinged with cautious legalese, promising, as they did, to help us all "navigate" the treacherous future, as if such a thing were actually possible. Worse, they seemed to be espousing rote recitations of obedience to new codes of behavior. Caught up in the justifiable public outrage following the murder of George Floyd, an administrative eagerness to be in step with the times and on the right side of federal grants led to a collective amnesia about the lessons of another George, named Orwell. Suddenly, administrative edicts sounded like parodies of Newspeak. They issued not from any real compassion but from a cold and calculating left-brain insistence that ethics and morality were composed of a moldable (and monetary) substance.

Having lived through the McCarthy era (during which my aunt Anne Revere's Academy-Award-winning movie career was effectively canceled by the Hollywood blacklist) and having witnessed on TV, as a child, the unforgivable behavior of the House Un-American Activities Committee, I reacted viscerally to what *The New York Times* writer John McWhorter rightly condemned as "woke racism" in his book by that title. I voiced my objections out loud to anyone who would listen; texted and emailed my opposition to what I felt were knee-jerk, fear-based, McCarthy-ish department policies—unnecessary edicts of social justice solidarity that expressed blanket condemnation of *any* form of expression that *anyone* might find offensive or objectionable. For some reason, we now had to avow in writing that we were not, as a department, racist, sexist, homophobic, misogynist, or any other kind of -ist; in other words, we had to sign an institutional loyalty oath. But wasn't the real point of consciousness-raising that as human beings and as a department, we *were*—historically and perhaps still—all these things? To what Big Brother or Big Sister were we now being asked to genuflect?

I was heartened to receive a few reply emails from colleagues agreeing with my objections and praising my "courage" in speaking up, but none of these were reply-all replies. In other words, no one *openly* agreed with me. And many of those who replied privately to me soon became signatories to what was essentially a loyalty oath issued by the English department, to be posted on faculty-office doors.

I understood *intellectually* that all this behavior exampled academia's much-parodied practice of making mountains out of molehills. But what I was beginning to *feel* within the academic community was something quite different. I felt a strange dread. Not for my personal safety or job security, just good old inexpressible, existential dread. I've since come to suspect it is a dread shared by anyone who has taken a stance during a long life. The river of rime is always sweeping us along. We're born into the world of our parents, a world to which we cling until we can process and shape it as our own, even as it washes into the hands of our grown children and grandchildren. In the end, we are forced to cede control entirely, and in old age we tend to project our own mortality onto the future. What we hear coming from downstream—since we will never actually get to *see* it—will probably always be a massive waterfall.

* * *

Needless to say, I didn't support the department's loyalty oath. Nor did I agree to take a mandated survey, ginned up by some company in California and aimed at assessing a professor's "cultural literacy."

When a request was sent out to first-year seminar professors, by the newly anointed "senior associate provost" (whatever that absurd title meant), asking professors to use class time to supervise a survey designed to assess student retention—with the caveat that we *not let the students know the aim of the survey*—I lost it. Replying to him and copying my reply to those he'd copied, I said that I found his request deceitful, that he was welcome to send the survey to students directly, and that I wanted nothing to do with the administration's bald-faced hype and would not spend class time (nor betray my students by) playing his game.

The senior associate provost replied that he was sorry I wasn't a "team player." (Within a year, he took a job at another college and has since been inaugurated as that new "team's" president.)

* * *

I'd taught for almost eighteen years without a break (no paid—or even unpaid—sabbaticals for adjuncts). I hadn't taught on campus for over a year, though I had met with students and advisees for one-on-one conferences in local open-air settings.

In April 2021, I wrote the few people to whom it mattered that I would be leaving in May and not returning in the fall. Adjuncts don't formally "retire," I learned, which I suppose makes sense if they aren't seen as an integral part of the institution. They don't even get to fade away; they just cease to be and, effectively, cease even to have been. The adjunct's connection to the college (including email archives and progress reports of former students, as well as library, gym, and parking privileges) is typically severed.

I was told by the department's administrative assistant that to "retire," I needed only to clean out my one remaining office after exam week (graduation would be conducted online only), turn in my office and mail room keys, and that would be it.

Then one day in late April 2021, I received a priority-mail package on my home doorstep, containing four small retirement gifts and a nice card from the English department Chair, requesting that I attend a farewell Zoom session of the final department meeting of the academic year. Among the gifts were a hardbound edition of Blake Bailey's just-released biography of the novelist Philip Roth, published by W. W. Norton & Company, and a copy of *The New York Times Book Review* of April 1, 2021, featuring Cynthia Ozick's review of Bailey's biography, in which she praised it as "a narrative masterwork both of wholeness and particularity, of crises wedded to character, of character erupting into insight, insight into desire, and desire into destiny."

The first twenty minutes of the year-end English department meeting were devoted to sharing how everyone had managed to "survive" the semester. The remaining forty minutes began with the chair's complimentary appraisal of my contributions to the department, emphasizing the way I had stood up for freedom of expression and the exercise of narrative voice. She explained that she had ordered the Blake Bailey biography of Philip Roth two days *before* it was canceled by its publisher W. W. Norton & Company, because of public allegations of sexual misbehavior on the part of Bailey. She noted my interest in Roth's lifetime work, and she now surmised that maybe the canceled biography was even more appropriate for me, since I'd been such an advocate for free speech and for the importance of exploring desire as a means of attaining narrative voice.

I told her, not entirely jokingly, that my proudest achievement at the college had been to *avoid* being canceled, despite the many risks I'd taken. I had openly hugged students—in my offices, in hallways, on campus pathways, in student centers, and at graduations; I'd insisted (against unwritten policy) on closed-door office-hour conferences, to allow for, *yes*, more intimacy and privacy; as a writing teacher, I had encouraged students to narrate their most painful life experiences and to investigate them deeply in essay form (a distinct no-no in trauma-sensitive academia); likewise, I had encouraged students to fully harness and consciously employ libido when their writing called for it; I had put *no* restraints on *written* language or subject matter, however edgy or seemingly inappropriate. In the interest of narrative clarity, I'd disallowed the pronouns *they/them*, if used to obscure gender rather than simply indicate the plural—the original purpose those pronouns served. (Creating a *new* substitute pronoun to disguise gender was fine by me). I'd treated students as adults by withholding personal judgment and behavioral guidelines. (How else can one fully *experience* another person or their work?) I had emphasized voice over craft in writing, since the latter properly follows upon the former. And rather than forbidding mention of the word *suicide*, as we were instructed (even warned) to do by human resources, I'd invited students to consider an open discussion of suicide as essential to understanding what it means to be human in this world. In this way, I had created what for all but two resistant students (out of roughly eleven hundred) proved to be a "safe space," according to their teaching evaluations. Not a *risk-free* space, as modern parents and administrators might wish, but a space that gave risk and anxiety a lot of breathing room to grow into creativity and love. Not kindergarten nap time but college wake-up time.

In my department's goodbye Zoom session, I *did* condemn the cancellation of Blake Bailey's biography, on principle, having no means to determine the truth or falsehood of the accusations against the author. Another publisher took the book right away, but the stain left by Norton's cancellation proved indelible—for Bailey, I'm sure, and posthumously for Roth, who'd spent his career—bravely, honestly, and often profoundly—investigating male libido *from the male point of view*, his prerogative, surely.

Several colleagues gave heartwarming assessments of my time in the English department. It was all very cordial, and I felt grateful for the compliments, though it was a little like attending my own memorial service.

I thanked everyone, saying I was both moved and humbled. A couple of weeks later I was informed that I could keep my college email—a special dispensation, for which I remain immensely grateful.

And that was it. I'm free. Sort of. What I'm left with now, absent the dread, is a profound nostalgia for the human world as it manifested itself in academia as recently as ten years ago. A world where intuition freely fed into process and process could at least hold its own against the data-driven, product-obsessed mentality that is now hiding in plain sight behind a cloak of old-fashioned reason. I hear a roaring Niagara around the bend downstream.

At Once

2023

let's live suddenly without thinking

under honest trees,
          a stream

does.

—e. e. cummings

It's mid-July 2014, and I'm attending a seventieth birthday party for my girlfriend Betsy's younger sister. It's a sunny afternoon and fifty-odd guests are packed into an airy Massachusetts summerhouse a few minutes' drive from the ocean. I suspect that Betsy, whom I've been seeing for less than a month, has abandoned me in order to assess from across the room how I hold up amidst this heady academic crowd. So far, I've happily engaged in conversation about the most recent status of the SETI Institute's search for exoplanets; the pedagogical merits of math circles; and the precession of the equinox as posited by the Greek astronomer Ptolemy. But not once has anyone asked my name or how I happen to be in the room, which makes me think they must already know. I feel like the groom whom no one has met until the wedding reception.

I place my sweaty glass of water on a cork coaster and plunk down at the end of a long, comfy sofa. I scan the large room and spot tall, elegant Betsy, more properly introduced as Elizabeth Dane, holding forth in a group that includes five or six distinctly interested older men. Suddenly, an attractive woman about half my age sits down eagerly on the other end of the sofa and slides toward me with an expression of great anticipation. I don't want to be inquired into at this moment, but she slides closer still. "What I want to know," she says, excitedly, "is how did you get so lucky?" And with that, she points to Betsy, who at that very moment is glancing smilingly over her shoulder in our direction.

Elizabeth and I were born three weeks apart in Boston's Massachusetts General Hospital, in the Year of the Metal Dragon, 1940. Our paths converged more closely fifteen years later at the Putney School in Vermont, a coeducational private school with a mere two hundred students. Despite the intimate class sizes, neither of us can recall exchanging a single word during our three concurrent years there. Not even at our graduation in 1958, where, after enduring a long speech by Eleanor Roosevelt, we received the high school diplomas that now hang next to each other in our upstairs hall. These personalized documents, illustrated in watercolor by a fellow student, depict long-limbed Betsy hanging upside down from a bending birch branch, her hair swinging freely; and me sitting with my back against a very different, less yielding tree, reading a book with the name CAMUS inked on its cover. She seems the very picture of a carefree, studious girl, and I a bad boy, already anticipating a future filled with existential rebellion.

All of which is to say that we didn't really meet until our class's forty-fifth reunion, a weekend event in June 2003. I was nearing the end of a month-long swing through New England, visiting friends I hadn't seen in years. I'd also recently ended an intense five-year relationship with a woman twenty-three years my junior. So, it was in a blissfully free why-not mood that I joined the registration line in the new arts building. I pinned a name tag to my green linen shirt, pocketed the weekend schedule, and began perusing class memorabilia spread out on kraft-papered tables and pinned to portable partition walls. I funneled through the display like a leaf caught in a stream, until suddenly I found myself stopped in front of a tall, graceful woman with walnut hair and green eyes. Her dress was a mustardy color, as I recall. She wore an expression of slight puzzlement and had an expectant youthful air that conveyed an interior sense of humor about this whole reunion thing.

Hello, Betsy, I thought, surprised that her name had come to mind so easily. She held out her hand as though to keep me at a distance. I hadn't been about to hug her, but her instinct to prevent me from doing so seemed immensely sage, since the antennae in my fingertips had already detected (if not yet decoded) the potential for intimacy. Not that it mattered. Such promising moments aren't exactly uncommon in life. And she wore a silver wedding ring. I don't remember what we said in that moment, or during the next day's alumni events that led up to the dance on Saturday night. But it was the dance that did it.

As a high school student, the prospect of choosing a partner and committing to a slow dance would have sent me outside for an illegal smoke with my buddies. But time can sharpen the libido's appetite in surprising ways, even as it winnows the options. I remember folding Betsy's right hand into my left and drawing our elbows close between us. For a while, we didn't even bother to move our feet to the music; we just swayed in place. The compelling quality of her touch—our mutual touch—the smell of her hair, the tenor of her voice in my ear, the ease with which we'd come together—completely surprised me. I began to wonder if maybe, at age sixty-three, I'd finally found . . . But the notion was absurd: She was married.

Nevertheless, we left the dance together (having danced with no one else) and stepped into the soft night air. We walked along a moon-dappled dirt road that led downhill to the alumni house. When I spied a huge bullfrog sitting boldly in the middle of the road, caught dramatically in a patch of bright moonlight, I stooped to pick it up. It obliged me by sitting patiently on my palm as I introduced it mock-formally to Betsy, whom it seemed to like. I took that as a good sign, and said so. The frog's apparent trust in us relieved me of whatever caution I might have otherwise brought to this moment, and I put my arm round Betsy's waist, drawing her close to my hip. We stared into the creature's unblinking gaze for several minutes, before I bent down again and offered it release, which it took another few minutes to accept.

We continued walking along the dirt road, talking about our marriages (two each, Betsy's second entering its fourth decade). I learned about her career as a professor at Hunter College in New York City, about how she and her husband and their two adopted children had moved to Helena, Montana, and how subsequently, when the kids were grown, they had moved again to Tucson, Arizona. I described how my career as a key grip in the film business had come to its natural conclusion and how

I'd just that month completed my two-year pursuit of an MFA at Columbia University School of the Arts. "I have no idea what I'll do now," I told her.

We parted at the entrance to the alumni house and slept in separate preassigned rooms. After breakfast on Sunday morning, Betsy traveled back to New York City with a fellow alumna. She was scheduled to fly out of LaGuardia the next day. I drove back to the city alone, then called her from my apartment, convincing her to meet me the next day, before her flight. We met at my apartment and walked the winding paths of Central Park for several hours, ending up at a small French bistro just off Madison Avenue, where we lingered over tea and fizzy water and lemon tortes for four hours. The late-spring weather seemed to fuel an undeniable mutual attraction and perhaps inspired our amazement that our paths had never crossed in the city. We'd been undergraduates on campuses a mere block apart in the early '60s, she at Barnard, I at Columbia. We discovered that we'd once lived in back-to-back buildings on the Upper West Side; we'd even raised children on that side of town and had perhaps even unknowingly stood on the same street corner waiting for the light to change, or on the bread line at Zabar's.

Betsy flew back to Tucson that evening. The following day, she emailed me saying how much fun she'd had and expressing her desire to visit again soon. She often flew to the city, she said. I replied recklessly that I'd enjoyed her company so much I'd follow her to Timbuktu, if necessary. Inevitably, my name came up one too many times in Betsy's conversations with her husband, which led to some drama between them, which resulted in her decision to break off any future contact with me. And that was the end of that.

Until a decade later, in 2013, when I read in the fall issue of the *Putney Post* an entry under "Alumni Notes," written by one

Elizabeth Dane, in which she mentioned the death six months earlier of her husband from brain cancer. She described her newfound readiness to move on from the life they'd shared—to look for new paths. She concluded the entry with this sentence: "It is amazing to me how the human spirit can be consumed by immense sadness and at the same time can countenance the boundless thrill of being alive." I replied with my condolences and expressed my interest in hearing her thoughts about "new paths," should she ever want to share them. Several seasons passed. No response. I had bellowed the embers of what I'd remembered as a mutual desire only to discover that those embers must have grown cold. Hardly a surprise, I told myself. So much had changed in our lives.

I'd been teaching in the English department at Gettysburg College for ten years. At the urging of a few matchmaking colleagues, I'd hooked up with a bright and savvy woman twenty years my junior, a writer and editor, and a newcomer to the college. During our time living together, we'd carved out a little niche in the world of literary nonfiction, and I'd published a prizewinning (though hardly moneymaking) memoir-in-essays. When our live-in relationship lost its luster, we agreed to part ways. I became the monk I now figured I was destined to be. I could walk to the college, devote all my time to students, and still hit New York City to see my daughter whenever I chose. At age seventy-three, I was done with love relationships.

After the May graduation of Gettysburg's class of 2014, I drove to New York to mull things over: see friends, take down the storm windows, watch sunsets from a bench down by the Hudson River. One afternoon, I clicked on an email message addressed to the Putney class of '58. It was Betsy, asking if anyone was thinking of going to our fifty-sixth reunion, and if so, would they be able to provide her with a bed in the city and a ride to Vermont? I had zero interest in going to a fifty-sixth re-union, but I was definitely interested in sharing my bed. Which is how, precisely eleven years to the minute after our first cautious encounter in the new arts building at Putney, I opened my apartment door to encounter Betsy already leaning across the threshold, like a runner toward the tape, as if even the time it would take to open the door fully would prove unbearable.

That night, all night, we lay on my king-size loft bed, with its view of the river, our seventy-four-year-old bodies smoothed magically young again by the forgiving light of yet another full Strawberry Moon.

* * *

It's now spring 2021, the season in which we will both turn eighty-one. We live in the spacious house Betsy purchased when she moved to Gettysburg to be with me. It sits a few miles from the college campus where I still teach. We revel in our lives together. We enjoy our gardens and neighbors—many of whom are former teaching colleagues—and like most of them, we call ourselves husband and wife, though we've never had a formal ceremony, never sworn to have and to hold forever forward, "for better, for worse, for richer, for poorer."

When we came together, the quantifiable struggles hinted at by the words *better* and *worse*, *richer* and *poorer*—the predictable angers, resentments, jealousies, infidelities, competitiveness, and professional demands typical of marital relationships—had already been played out. Grievances of any kind now seemed petty and inconsequential when compared with the luck and joy we felt at having found each other in such a circuitous yet oddly intentional way.

Before the pandemic hit, we traveled in Europe, spent partial summers out west, and entertained current and former students. During it, we Zoomed with friends, read books, shared podcasts, and talked endlessly.

We support our respective passions and private pursuits (writing for me and music for Betsy), and until recently we have enjoyed good health. We seem to have obviated the need to engage most of the rocky shoals warned about in the marriage vow, having negotiated them in earlier years. We honor our very different and divergent histories—our essential solitudes—which is where real steadiness in marriage can be found.

Now, having received a particular medical prognosis, we are forced to consider the inevitable approach of a new kind of solitude: for one of us it will consist of going on alone; for the other it will consist of going alone. Death *will* us part. It's part of the "I do." But death cannot erase, for either of us, the living certainty that we grabbed the moment to come together when that moment presented itself. Knowing that we had little time, we wasted none. To think of oneself as courageous, to know for certain that one has been demonstrably courageous in love, is the real "I do." We can now say to each other, *We did it.* We did not shrink in the face of all the obvious and often comic absurdities of late love: the ghosts of former loves; the incremental loss of hearing and even memory; the incessant entropy of human flesh and bone—any one of which realities might have served as a persuasive excuse not to act, a convincing argument that it was too late for love.

It is always too late for love. But the risk left untaken, the love not dared, the ring not snatched at once would have made of all our ongoing joy a hollow "what if."

SELECTED
TALKS

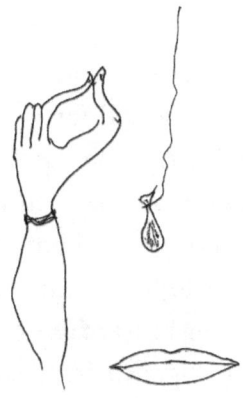

The Role of Uncertainty
in Craft

Association of Writing & Writing Programs Conference,
Washington, DC, February 2011

On June 12, 1970, a Pittsburgh Pirates pitcher named Dock Ellis threw a no-hitter in a game against the San Diego Padres. Fourteen years later, in 1984, Ellis revealed that he'd pitched the entire game under the influence of LSD. "Sometimes I saw the catcher, sometimes I didn't," he reported. "I started having the crazy idea in the fourth inning that Richard Nixon was the home plate umpire, and once I thought I was pitching to Jimi Hendrix, who to me was holding a guitar and swinging it over the plate."

For decades, Dock Ellis's feat ranked high in my mind—right up there with the guy who tied forty-five helium balloons to his lawn chair—as one of a handful of stunts that perennially inspired me to wonder what it would be like to just let go of all sanity and pass freely back and forth through what Joseph Campbell referred to in *The Hero with a Thousand Faces* as the *shimenawa*. The *shimenawa*, a rope used to demarcate sacred space in Japan, is, in Campbell's account of the hero's journey, the hymen-like barrier that separates the indescribable realm of chaos—that pure peril at the heart of raw experience—from the quotidian demands of intelligible narrative.

What would it feel like to be so present in the game and yet so absent; to be so aware of the cheering fans, yet immune to the demands of audience; so completely wacko, yet somehow grounded and in command of craft—and all that in a record-book kind of way?

Well . . . last fall, in my seventh year as a creative writing teacher (I came to this profession late), I got a taste of what Dock Ellis must have felt like when throwing sometimes a golf ball, sometimes a basketball, at a catcher who wasn't reliably there. I think of it now as a kind of controlled demolition of self.

* * *

I begin all my creative writing classes by eliciting from my students their most profound experience of pain. It seems a good place to begin. By accessing pain in a public way, the students' sense of security is put at risk, albeit within the cozy environment of the workshop. I usually feel quite confident and certain, teaching the personal essay in this fashion. But on the first day of class last fall, the dike separating me, the teacher, from the sea of pain I had just evoked in my students, collapsed, and I was suddenly awash in pain myself. It was very strange and quite riveting. As I looked around, I saw that my students had somehow morphed into teachers. I had become the only student in the room. All the pain at the workshop table was now mine—and my fault as well. All the ignorance became mine, too, and I saw myself as totally inadequate to the task of teaching. Suddenly, I knew nothing at all about creative writing. When printed student essays began to flood in during the following week, I could barely utter a word in response to them. My meager observations felt weak, and my ritual attention to narrative strategies sounded, to me, both rote and absurd.

One student's account of his struggle with depression after the suicide of his close friend seemed far better than anything I could have written. His writing was so raw and beautiful I could barely stand it. A young woman to my right wrote about the way her father beat her senseless and how it had made her into the brave creature she now was; she did this without once using a passive construction or a weak verb. It took all my strength to conjure up some small advice for her second draft. The belligerent jock at the other end of the table became a warrior, wielding unintentional tense shifts to prove to me that past and future did not exist. A health sciences major used a tedious story of injuring her ankle during a track meet in order to mock what I now saw as my own narrative sluggishness—a kind of parody in which her injured ankle magically became my Achilles' heel. A philosophy major exposed my ignorance of Spinoza, and in no time we were dueling in some quantum world where light—especially mine—was no longer the quickest thing in the universe. I felt as inadequate as Freud must have felt when he fainted in the presence of Carl Jung. I experienced myself as a cosmic failure whose talented students were urging him to turn in his academic robes and go leap off the roof. They began using non sequiturs and comma splices in order to jar me from the head of the table. Fragments and phrases soon became the only forms I could hear or trust. Take us at face value, they all seemed to say. Stop correcting us. Stop it with the models. Stop telling us to be safe and write what we know—and to show, not tell. Put your money where your mouth is, and show/tell us something new. Lead us into the place of not-knowing and uncertainty that you seem to be inhabiting right now.

So, I did. I let go. I just pitched. It wasn't quite as desperate as it probably sounds, but then again maybe it was, because I'd been reduced to circling in blue ink the occasional word or phrase I liked. I nodded to students a lot and that seemed to help, and sometimes I even raised my brow in approval. I let others speak more than might have been prudent had the chair of the English department stepped into the room.

Through it all, I knew nothing, in the normal sense. It was really quite alarming.

Which is to say, in retrospect, energetic.

* * *

As it turned out, my not-knowing opened the door to what my students needed to know—that not-knowing became their permission to discover, so to speak, and because of our mutual bewilderment and shared alarm, we let go of the whole idea of authority and classroom: We let go of grades, we let go of schedule, we let go of time. People stayed late. There was a lot of laughter. What bloomed in the rubble felt meaningful. We began to recognize shared motifs of fire and wind and for some reason the path of falling leaves; we realized—and all at the same moment—the importance of ripple on water. Unintentional tense shifts—when left uncorrected and even flirted with—produced surprising emotional range, and our flagrant embrace of not-knowing resulted in a kind of crack-the-whip momentum, a collective and dangerous spin that everyone managed to hang on to—even through the subsequent genres of fiction, screenplay, and poetry—everyone except for one student who insisted he already knew how to write, and even he crawled back onto the gymnasium floor at the end.

As did I—in my own work—in the evenings.

I began to think that maybe my personal-essay mindset had a built-in impediment, a humorless instinct for self-preservation, a literal flatness and was-ness, a fear of surprise. Maybe I hadn't been exploiting the gap between the question a factual detail unwittingly poses and the answer it implies—that gap where, as Chögyam Trungpa suggests in *Crazy Wisdom*, "intelligent uncertainty" resides.

In that gap, sparks occur.

What would happen, for instance, if I paused in my nonfiction description of, say, my father, who was an artist, lying dead under a sheet? What if I dropped some figurative acid and watched myself doing something I didn't really do: What if I lifted the sheet covering his body? What if I discovered, as I'm doing right now, a little pansy struggling in the sun where his brave heart used to pound, struggling with drought in the dry dirt far from home, like the pansy in the pot on my porch last summer? Who is my father then? Since it is my father we're talking about in this way, I can attest in a totally nonfiction—and thus truthful—way that too much traveling as an only child prevented him from venturing very far from home as an adult. Which is fine. But I arrived at the truth not by remembering and thus accessing something I already knew to be a fact, but in a more authentic way: by trespassing into the world of imagination, into a place where what I found under the sheet in 1995 was the pansy struggling on my porch in 2010.

How could that be nonfiction?

Well, Dock Ellis wasn't planning to pitch the day he dropped acid; apparently he had lost track of time and discovered his mistake right after he dropped it. But Ellis showed up. It was what it was at the time. The world was what it was at that moment.

I never—as nonfiction would seem to require of me—actually lifted the sheet my father died in, nor would I have necessarily discovered a pansy growing there had I done so, but now that I have, I did in fact do so, and I don't owe it to anyone to say how, when, or why, or to explain that I'm imagining it all—not until years later, maybe—or now, or never.

What grew from my artist father's heart was a resilience that survived a drought—with all its connotations for him and his family. The pansy describes perfectly his persistent faith in art, even in the face of his biggest fear—which we all share—the fear of *art* itself.

Art more than death, I'd have to say.

Don't be afraid to dissolve and demolish the walls of this genre. Go outside in the bright morning and shovel snow. Come back snow-blind. Walls don't define the space in which we write. Open space defines where we will eventually decide to erect a wall or two.

There is in each of us a crazy zone where anything you throw from the pitcher's mound will work—where you simply cannot miss. It lies in the gap between question and answer—between a fact and its resonance—and in that gap resonance becomes fact. Go there. Stay there for nine innings. It is a deep, revealing, and rewarding place.

Crossing the Boundary
Between Fact and Art

Conversations and Connections Panel Talk,
Washington, DC, April 2009

As Paul Maliszewski's book *Fakers* suggests, there is no shortage of people willing to cross the boundary between fact and fiction for the sake of telling a good story: The human imagination is capable of embellishing even the dullest of lives. But, as writers, we have rules: If you are writing nonfiction, you must use facts to convey the truth; if you are writing fiction, you are allowed to employ imagination to convey whatever, *as if* it were truth. Fiction can resemble nonfiction in its detail and information, and nonfiction can resemble fiction in its narrative style. But when asked, "Did this really happen?" the memoirist must be able to answer yes, whereas the novelist need not.

This distinction between the genres, which is really a contract between writer and reader, serves the marketplace well, and it puts boundaries around our notions of "truth." Break the contract and you'll likely wind up being shamed by Oprah, sued by readers, and blacklisted by editors.

Pretty simple, right? So, what's the problem?

The problem, as I see it, is this: What's missing from the rule book is any consideration of *process*. In particular, that point in the writing process where the fiction and nonfiction mindsets begin to intermingle and merge freely, without interference from some internal or external Big Brother. If we are very honest with ourselves, we will acknowledge that all forms of writing are a mix of memory, research, and construct. In the case of memoir, memory is the vehicle by which the material arrives; construct is the means by which it is delivered to the page.

Imagine a memory arriving in a UPS delivery truck at your front door, which is sort of what happens, isn't it? Since memory isn't substantive, picture it as, say, pink air. The truck driver lowers the tailgate, rolls up the door, and takes out a box of pink air labeled: "The first time I saw my parents fight." You take the box into your house and sit down with it in front of your computer. With one hand hovering over the keyboard and the other holding a mat knife, you prepare to transfer the contents of the box to the written page. You slice open the box's seal, flip up the lid, inhale as much of the contents as you can, and start typing. Let's hope you've inhaled deeply, because you get exactly one shot at uncorrupted memory. When your breath runs out, the content of the box is gone, and you are left with your memory on the page. Is it still your memory? No. It is a construct of your memory. The construct will probably be full of disconnected data, unsupported detail, and inexplicable gaps in the action. So, you'll have to fix it; you'll shape it, so as to make sense of it for yourself and for your reader. You will, in fact—there is no avoiding this—revise the construct, holding as tightly as you can to the "truth" of the original memory, but with each revision you will inevitably move farther from the remembered truth in order to concentrate on the reconstructed truth. That's just how it works. Writing a memory disturbs the memory because it materializes it. And it's the *material* we work with, not the pink air, and it's the material that the reader gets. The memory remains, of course, but its vitality has been sapped, which explains perhaps why we feel a therapeutic effect after writing down painful memories about events in our past.

Fiction writers are fond of saying that their characters take on a life of their own—that they often seem quite real. The memoirist has the opposite experience: The memory that once seemed so shiningly real—a situation, an event, or a dialogue— is actually dulled in the process of writing it, so much so that when one is asked to spontaneously recount a scene from one's life that one has already written about, the memory is somewhat difficult to access. The scene, or the memory of it, having been reconstructed and perhaps even published, has lost its vitality as a memory. It's kind of sad, really. As someone wrote, "If you cherish your memories, don't become a writer."

What is this process, really, this materialization, this reshaping of memory into memoir or personal essay? Hopefully, as we discuss boundaries and rules, we can call the process art. If it isn't art, why bother?

Since I'm not intimately familiar with the process of other writers, let me talk about my own experience with this. One day in the fall of 2003, I was sitting in an MFA nonfiction workshop at Columbia University. My fellow students were mostly in their late twenties, and they were getting on my nerves with their oh-so-sure-of-themselves personas.

It was making me grumpy, so I scribbled a sentence in my notebook that read "You're twenty-seven years old and you don't have a clue yet, do you?" When I got home that evening, I transcribed the sentence in my computer, thinking to begin a rant about my classmates and the whole MFA program at Columbia, but as soon as I did, I realized that it wasn't going to be a rant about them but rather about me—about clueless me at age twenty-seven.

I kept the second person and the present tense and proceeded to write about myself in 1967—a would-be writer who is sitting sideways in an open window, five floors up, on West Eighty-Fifth Street, in New York City, drinking beer from a frosted mug, and looking down at a Black man in a red bandanna. Bandanna Man is totally stoned on heroin, trying to step over a crack in the sidewalk. He's making a big production of it, and this allows me to digress and describe other things that occur or have occurred on that block—all the street life, including a murder I once witnessed from my window, and the shenanigans of a flamboyant pimp named Renaldo. By the end of the piece, which is only three pages long, the reader understands that what the cocky, arrogant twenty-seven-year-old sitting in the window doesn't get is that he's going to wind up just like Bandanna Man, overwhelmed by the dissipated life, and that Bandanna Man's inability to step over the crack in the sidewalk mirrors the young writer's—*my*—failure to knuckle down and write.

It's a harsh piece, self-critical and in-your-face because of the second person. The details of the street are exactly as I remember them—Bandanna Man *was* a real character on that street, where a murder did take place, as described, and I *did* witness it; Renaldo the pimp *was* a fixture on the block; a phosphorous-tipped match stuck in the crack of the sidewalk *was* what Bandanna Man was having trouble stepping over (to him it probably appeared as big as a log); the clacking of dominoes and the static from transistor radios *were* the dominant sounds on that street in the '60s, et cetera, et cetera.

When I read this brief piece, called "When You Finish Your Beer," at a writing conference at Kenyon College, it received a rousing response. Many students came up to me afterward and thanked me for what they called a "warning" about the dangers of the drinking life for writers. The next evening, I had dinner with some of the faculty, and the novelist Brad Kessler told me that he'd really enjoyed my reading, admired the way the piece was written, thought the use of the second person was just perfect.

"Thanks," I said, "I'm glad you liked it."

We clinked glasses to that, and Brad leaned closer to me and confided, "But I know it's fiction."

"What?" I said, not a little surprised by his assertion.

"That's okay, I liked it," he said. "But I know it's fiction. And good stuff, too."

Coming from Brad, a terrific novelist, this probably should have seemed a compliment, but I found it disconcerting, and I surprised myself when, rather than protesting that it was non-fiction, I responded simply, "You think so, eh?"

Brad nodded and smiled at me conspiratorially. "I'm sure of it," he said.

I took another bite of salmon and simply smiled back.

But he had me thinking. Was what I had written fiction? In order to achieve the extreme compression of material, I'd taken one liberty with perspective: I'd made Renaldo's ground-floor apartment fully visible from my perch on the windowsill, when in fact his apartment was on the same side of the street as mine. And I'd used a pair of binoculars (which I, like many apartment dwellers, did keep handy by the window) to determine that an unstruck match caught in the sidewalk crack was the source of Bandanna Man's difficulty, when, in fact, back in 1967, I'd actually left my window perch and gone down to the street to see what was bugging the guy. (Hang me for that, if you want, but I feel strongly that adjustments of this kind, if they serve the greater good of the piece and don't distort the truth, are entirely legitimate.)

But the point is, I didn't protest Brad's assertion. I've wondered about that since. Why did I allow his allegation to go unchallenged? Perhaps because, for me, the piece itself, like every other piece of personal nonfiction I've written, no longer felt like nonfiction or memoir but like something entirely other—something that resembled art. It no longer mattered to me that the material was true—it was, but the truth had lost its original urgency, as had the need to be critical of that twenty-seven-year-old self. What mattered was that the memory had been transformed, from the pink air that memory is into a meaningful, transcendent text. The text, unlike the memory, now existed in the world. Separate from me, no longer attached to the memory that gave it birth.

Or perhaps I didn't protest because, somehow, I understood then what I understand more clearly now by writing this: That just as the fiction writer struggles to achieve the illusion of reality, thus rewarding the reader's willing suspension of disbelief, the memoirist struggles to achieve an implicit or shaped reality, which is to say a kind of fiction. And, such being the case, if one can compliment the novelist by saying, "It seems so true," then the equivalent accolade for the memoirist might be "It reads like fiction."

Personally, I'll settle for that, any day.

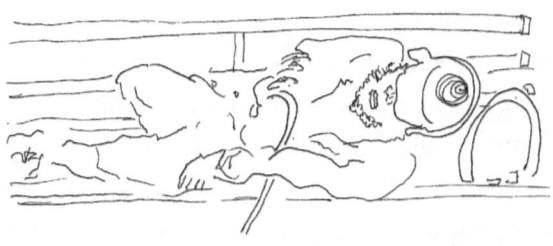

Can Compassion Be Taught?

NonfictionNOW Conference,
Iowa City, Iowa, November 2010

In the summer of 1997, a Lakota Sioux medicine man from the Pine Ridge Reservation formally adopted me as his brother. In the subsequent three years, I made a number of trips from New York City to South Dakota to participate in various rituals and to work, in a loose way, as my new brother's apprentice. I returned home from the first of these trips, in 1998, all pumped up to write about the historical roots of reservation life, with an eye to shedding light on the dire conditions there.

I began my research in the main branch of the New York Public Library—downstairs, where the microfiche was stored. I spent six hours without a break that first day, browsing through decades' worth of newspaper articles about the Lakota—dreary and familiar accounts of broken treaties, alcoholism, entrenched poverty, and suicidal despair. It was exhausting reading. Overwhelmed by reportage, I grew strangely resistant to the material. By three o'clock, my blood sugar was depleted and my brain frazzled. Statistics and information that should have *fueled* my compassion had actually dulled it. What good, I wondered, could possibly come from my rehashing all this information?

Feeling slightly ashamed of my insufficient drive, I gathered my papers and prepared to leave the library. But as I did, I heard my ever-resilient ego—that good old lifesaving "I"—asserting itself amidst the ashes of my ambition: *Forget the Lakota,* it whispered consolingly. *What about* me? *Where do* I *fit into all this?* Then, suddenly, a totally gratuitous question arose in my mind: What was happening with the Lakota Sioux on the day I was born? I reached for the 1940 periodical index the way a drowning man might reach for a rope and turned quickly to the date of my birth.

Bingo, there it was: a *New York Times* article, datelined Bedford, Pennsylvania, April 13, that read "Sioux Chief Dies in Auto Crash." My heart stirred at this. I had a Lakota story, and the story could be connected to *me.* I could deal with that.

I printed out the little article, bought an egg salad sandwich on rye with a pickle from a vendor on Forty-Second Street, and a few days later found myself rooting around in a dimly lit, nineteenth-century dungeon that served as a storage basement beneath the historic courthouse in Bedford, Pennsylvania. In a dank corner cell, I literally stumbled on a tipped-over file cabinet with a drawer that contained a coroner's inquest report for one Chief White Wolf, age seventy-two, who had been traveling to Washington, DC, to testify before Congress regarding the upcoming fiftieth anniversary of the Wounded Knee Massacre. He had suffered severe head injuries in the crash and died on the eve of my birth—taking his last breath right about the time my mother's water broke.

No one in Bedford had ever heard of a Chief White Wolf, not even the young family that now operated a buffalo farm and a Native American crafts concession located right at the crash site. Clearly, this was my story to tell, but all I had to work with was the coroner's report and a rather perilous conceit: that the seemingly random concurrence of White Wolf's death and my birth might in some way be seen to transcend mere coincidence and thus illustrate the interconnectedness of all life—a concept, incidentally, that is central to Lakota rituals, as it is to Buddhism, quantum theory, and, for that matter, essay writing.

Interestingly, the word *conceit* denotes both an excessive sense of self-worth and an organizing principle. The two meanings are not mutually exclusive. Though I hadn't given my White Wolf conceit much thought at the time, I was reminded of its ego-driven origins last autumn, while teaching a writing-intensive first-year seminar during which we discussed the writings of iconic American rebels.

The students had no problem with Thomas Paine's ideas, since the American Revolution had led to the life of ease they now enjoyed; nor did they protest the writings of Frederick Douglass and Martin Luther King Jr.—everyone agreed that slavery and racism were abhorrent. But they drew the line starting somewhere around Malcolm X. They complained that Malcolm's demeanor was edgy, snide, and threatening. Trained by media pundits to judge behavior rather than discern motive and intent—and thus reluctant to put themselves in Malcolm's shoes—they dismissed his street-smart strategies as "inappropriate" and "confrontational."

This also held true for Mark Rudd, former member of the militant Marxist group known as Weather Underground. In his memoir, Rudd openly confesses his naive idealism as a college student facing the draft in 1968, as well as his deep fear of leadership and his perhaps compensatory sexual promiscuity. In response—and without having met him in person—my students complained that Mark was a naive and brainwashed idealist, that he should have embraced his leadership role if he was so charismatic, and that he was a sexual braggart. In other words, they could not distinguish the rueful voice of the now-sixty-three-year-old memoirist from the persona of the youthful radical that Rudd—as a memoirist—was obliged to inhabit.

Male and female students alike panned Inga Muscio, the author of *Cunt: A Declaration of Independence*, her provocative ideas and voice proving completely intolerable, though she was only thirty-two when she published it in 1998—hardly a dinosaur from another age.

While this empathic distancing is endemic in American society today—our Internet "activism" notwithstanding—it is also true that empathic distance is a perfectly natural teenage phenomenon. Young people throughout history have struggled to imagine the lives of their elders—how could they not? They have so little *experience*.

The word *experience* comes from the Latin word *ex*, or "from," and the base verb *per*, which is also the root of the word *periculum*, meaning "risk" or "peril." To bridge generations requires us to risk engaging the *experience* of our elders—and when we finally become elders, to risk engaging the *experience* of young people. Unfortunately for all of us in this Information Age, information alone does not reproduce experience. On the contrary, it clouds the profound relevance of experience—its *feeling*-centric nature—and diminishes its well-known power to teach. However provocative it may be, information is inherently risk-free. To learn about the sexual revolution of the '60s is not to have lived through the upheaval and chaos that decade brought to relationships. To enjoy the fruits of feminism today is not to have been an early militant against violence to women. To disapprove of American wars now is not to have confronted a draft board and faced imprisonment in 1968.

Memoir offers a way across these temporal divides, of course, but it requires the reader to risk engagement and to withhold judgment—to withhold one's own "I" while another "I" speaks. Clearly, my students were resisting this, which I found distressing and ominous, until, as I was looking at them one day after midterms, I was reminded of myself and my information burnout in the New York Public Library. Here I was, trying to elicit compassion from my students without first giving them the tools to unlock that compassion. I had failed to ground them in *feeling*. A medicine man would probably have recommended a sweat lodge ceremony, the purpose of which is to remind participants what it means to be human.

* * *

The French philosopher Simone Weil once observed that because mere chance can strip us of everything we own, all we really possess in this world is the power to say "I," which means that the only free act given to us is the *destruction* of the "I." Implicit in this notion is the understanding that you must first credit the *existence* of the ego before you can move beyond it.

I would need to cut my students the slack I had cut myself.

"Okay," I told my seminar, on a dreary November morning, "for our research visit to the college library, I want you to bring your date of birth: month, day, year, and time."

"Why?" demanded M., a student who had nicknamed himself God and on whom I could rely to kick off a lively conversation.

"Because your final essay is going to be about someone who died as you were being born," I told the class.

A few moments of stunned silence were followed by a barrage of questions: What does that have to do with rebels in America? What does that have to do with *anything*? What if we can't find anybody to write about? What if the person we find is just a random person—a nobody? How can you write about someone you don't know? Does this mean talking to the family? To all these questions I answered, as I always do, "I don't know. You tell me."

A Chilean-born student, a wrestler who had trouble staying awake most days, came up to me after class a week later and said, "Professor, I'm the kind of guy who needs structure. I need you to give me some guidelines about this assignment."

"Just go there," I suggested. "You'll figure it out." He looked at me with an expression that suggested he was debating whether to sucker punch me or kick my legs out and pin me to the classroom floor.

At first, the resistance from everyone was fierce. Even the student who had just joined the soon-to-be-defunct local chapter of Students for a Democratic Society, and who had been emailing back and forth with Mark Rudd, couldn't see the point of my assignment. To a person, they opposed the idea on the grounds that it was a waste of time. "This is just puerile," one girl suggested. Another asked me, "Have *you* ever tried this?" When I said yes, she asked how it had turned out. "I published the essay," I answered.

The students' objections dwindled after their first experience with microfiche. Something about being able to browse backward through time, watching newspaper pages fly by until an appropriate obituary appeared, gave them the illusion of travel, different certainly than the instant appearance on the screen of some googled request. After a few weeks, I didn't hear one complaint. I began to worry that they had conspired to blow off the assignment (half hoping they would, just as a sign of life), but I decided to leave them alone.

* * *

In the last weeks of the semester, we read and responded to increasingly edgy strategies of political and environmental resistance, including blowing up dams, spiking trees on land leased by lumber companies, and dissolving government agencies altogether. Some students were inspired to develop a strategy to force the college administration into being more transparent about the college's endowment fund. The effort (which was successful) gave them some insight into the pitfalls of organization and leadership; the lazier students added an element of unhelpful negativity. But the project brought them no closer to forgiving Malcolm X for allowing the persona of an ex-con into his early speeches, or Mark Rudd for being angry enough to shape (and wear) a ring made from the scrap metal of a US fighter plane downed by North Vietnam, or Inga Muscio for her graphic description of her own abortion and her militant stance on confronting rapists.

On the final day of class, before I collected the papers for grading, several of the students read their essays out loud. As it turned out, the young Chilean wrestler had been born the day the author Graham Greene died. His surprisingly energetic and complex essay interwove the pride he felt in his Chilean origins with the poetry of Greene's Chilean friend, Pablo Neruda. Toward the end of the essay, the student described at length the physical pain he suffered when he had the image of the Chilean coat of arms tattooed on his back; he interrupted his reading to take off his shirt and show us the red-white-and-blue crest, with a stag on one side and an eagle on the other, inked across his broad shoulders.

One young woman wrote extensively about the artist and humanist Nancy Dryfoos, born in 1918, with whom, as it turned out, she shared a heritage and a passion for art. The student's approach and style were as clear as crystal, and her effort lacked even a tiny hint of academic jargon. She inhabited Dryfoos for four pages then merged seamlessly into a disquisition on her own artistic nature. Toward the end, she brought her meditation back to Dryfoos:

> A perfectly preened woman, Nancy Dryfoos stared back at me from my computer screen. The most striking thing about this snapshot, a window into a life gone by, was not her stunning appearance or elite company, but her smile . . . the smile of one completely at ease with herself, possessing both pride and confidence.

A bearded student, T., whose contrarian brilliance reminded me of Christopher Hitchens's, described his journey from deep cynicism about this assignment to his surprise that a bond did indeed exist between him and his "random" person, George Mortorff, born in 1915. "Life, on the individual level," he wrote, "has a significance that can't be seen through a casual glance." As if to emphasize his epiphany, the random person's daughter called T.'s cell phone during our last class, asking if she could meet with him one more time just to reminisce some more about her father. That sealed it for T. I thought he was going to cry right there at the table.

All the information we had shared during the semester was nothing compared to the compassion and surprise at the heart of these essays. Almost without exception, the implicit "I" provided by the prompt gave the writer permission to explicitly inhabit the experience of the "other."

At our best, we all begin writing from a place of solitude—from the self. To expect young writers to self-start without first allowing them to embrace the "I" is folly; the results, all too often, will lack narrative vividness and authority and, ultimately, compassion.

Consider one of these final essays, written by a student, J., who had earned the nickname Buddha by sitting silently (and barefoot) to my left all semester. J. picked for his subject a guy named Jack Bobo, who had died in Gettysburg, Pennsylvania, the day J. was born.

During his research, J. learned that when Jack was born in Hardy County, West Virginia, in 1902, the river that ran through the field behind the family house had flooded its banks—something the river almost never did, thus creating a family legend. After an astonishing seven-page description of Jack's meandering and happy life, for which J. used the controlling metaphor of the river, here is how he ended his essay—and how I will answer the perhaps rhetorical question posed by the title of this talk:

> On the day Jack Bobo died, his brother Presley could not make it to Gettysburg to pay his respects. He still lived on the family plot in Hardy County, West Virginia, and on that day, he was called by his neighbors to the field. Presley looked out into the field and could not believe his eyes. The stream was flooding its banks again. As the stream overran its banks, *my* eyes opened for the first time, and what came next can only be described as a flood of life.

Smithereens

In Praise of the Essay Symposium,
New York, NY, October 2011

Some years ago, I escorted a girlfriend of mine to Greenwich Village to get her horoscope read by an astrologer named Cassandra. The private session lasted about an hour, and after it I chatted with Cassandra outside her office. Small talk done, she asked me, "So, Dusty, when were *you* born?"

"April thirteenth," I told her.

"Ah, yes," she sighed, "the Day of the Iconoclast."

I was still working in the movie business, which meant, among other things, that I was surviving on as little self-awareness as possible, and I had to think for a moment to remember what an iconoclast was.

"A breaker of molds," said Cassandra helpfully.

"Right," I said. "I knew that! From the Greek."

I had in fact known what an iconoclast was, but I'd never connected the word to anything as basic as my birthday—a date I share with such contrarians and mold busters as Thomas Jefferson, Christopher Hitchens, Samuel Beckett, Butch Cassidy, and Alfred Butts, the inventor of Scrabble. I understand better now that the word *iconoclastic* pretty much sums up my contrary life—and my contrary teaching.

This semester, about a month ago, I assigned E. B. White's essay "Once More to the Lake" for the first time to a writing-intensive seminar in which we just take off in whatever direction feels right, using rebellious voices in American history as prompts. The aim is to rescue students from the adolescent mire by duplicating in the classroom the kind of chaotic energy that produced those iconic rebellious voices in the first place—voices from the American Revolution, the Civil War, the '60s, and so on.

I love White's essay. It appeared in 1941, the work of a poster-boy WASP, who, like me, spent his early summers at a lake in New England, and who in this essay returns to that lake with his young son. It is pure indulgence—the culmination of several decades of musing about the lake—undertaken by a lucky man, who by then had become the quintessential voice of *The New Yorker* magazine.

My students had no clue why I'd assigned the essay—sandwiched as it was without warning or logical chronology between the writings of Thomas Paine and Frederick Douglass. I figured that springing it on them like this might jar them loose from obedience to the syllabus, challenge us all to think on our feet, and maybe give me something to talk about here today. I had no agenda, but I had asked the students to highlight phrases and words that interested them, and now we sat around the seminar table, staring at our xeroxed copies of the story, mutual bewilderment enveloping us like fog—two hours of class still to go.

"Well," I said, finally, "what do you think?"

In unison, all sixteen students bowed their heads, as if in mourning for some long-ago era when they could just go out and play. They looked like reprimanded hound dogs in a kennel. Something about this kind of knee-jerk timidity—perhaps the way it reminded me of my own at that age—really pissed me off.

Impulsively, I ripped my copy of the essay in half—two double-sided pages, right down the middle. All the bowed heads flew up in surprise. I snarled and ripped the essay again and again, then mangled the mess of paper in my hands and threw the crumpled result furiously on the table. A few shards of paper had fallen into my lap, so I passed one of them to a young man seated next to me. He stared at the pathetic scrap the way a beggar might stare at a dirty penny dropped in his cup.

"What do you see there?" I prompted. "Read us a fragment."

The student frowned at me suspiciously then read out loud: "There had been no years."

The room grew ominously quiet, as if we'd all heard a mouse in the walls. The silence, uncomfortable at first, soon turned unbearable—wonderfully pregnant.

Peter, a tall student seated across from me, shifted restlessly in his seat and announced, "I hate this essay."

"Really," I said. "Why?"

"I had to read it in high school, and I hated it then and I hate it now."

"Why do you hate it?" I asked.

"Because he's an old man who should just go get a life."

The hush in the room grew even deeper. It was lost on no one that I was an old man.

"What did your high school teacher say when you told him you hated it?" I asked.

"I didn't tell him," said Peter. "We weren't allowed to."

Murmurs of agreement rippled around the room, as in an old movie when the townspeople rouse themselves to fight off the villains. Almost everyone agreed: Honest self-expression had not been encouraged in high school.

"I went to a lake just like that," piped up a guy with his hat on backward. "A three-day weekend with my family. I couldn't wait till it was over."

"Why?" I asked him.

"Our cell phones didn't work."

"Did that scare you?"

"It sucked," he said. "I didn't know what was happening in the world. At night it was creepy—just insects. The GPS was out, too."

"I have a built-in compass," offered another student, proudly. "I always know where north is, don't ask me why."

Suddenly, the hounds were loose, off and running.

In White's essay, his son, Joel, insists on renting a boat with an outboard motor, preferring its clatter to the purring inboard motor of his father's time. The sound of outboards has clearly begun to overwhelm the provocative silence of the lake in the evening. The paving of paradise has begun. Solitude—that ageless value—is at risk. Or so it seems to sophisticated readers like us, who talk a good game when it comes to solitude.

But solitude is scary—scary to White, who has already confessed that he prefers the noisy sea to the lake; scary to White's son; and even scarier to my students. And soon, that's what we were talking about in the seminar—not the essay with its carefully crafted observations but the fear those observations had provoked in us. The fear, like the dread aroused by old-time fairy tales, had an energy all its own. It leapt from the high-lighted fragments of text and eloped with our personal experiences of dread.

I was reminded of the previous year's seminar, when I'd asked the class, "What are you guys afraid of, really?" I'd hoped for an answer that would illuminate their fear of activism and taking to the streets. What I got was much better. "I know what I'm afraid of," said one girl. "Death. What the fuck is that!"

And now Death was in the room again this year. Personal encounters with scary nature, claustrophobic family vacations, rumors of drownings and abductions, fate and its place in life. It was as if E. B. White had turned on the autopilot and was listening to us with earphones.

A girl from Indiana found it alarming that she needed to check email so much; a shy boy with a shock of red hair falling over one eye, agreed: "We're all hooked on being connected. Where is that coming from?"

We began talking in a wide-ranging way about what it means to be connected—and connected to what? What it means to be afraid of the night. The implicit value of nighttime to our appreciation of the day and how perhaps the flip side of technology is that it steals the night from our lives. Referring to the closing scene of White's essay, in which children reenter the water after a thunderstorm moves on, one student marveled at how lightning is "so scary awesome, the way it moves from the ground up." This allowed me to pontificate about the value of the grounded detail in White's essay. But I needn't have bothered. They'd already "got it" on a feeling level and would, as it turned out, model it in subsequent written responses without any urging from me.

Had these students followed my lead and ripped up their essays, we might have left the classroom early, a single-file line of joyous monks, no longer needing "to try" (as in the French *essayer*) along with the essayist, or to be "tried by" the tedium of academic inquiry.

But they didn't shred their essays, because they are young, and I had done so only because I'm old. Their highlighted fragments, transmitted to me verbally during the course of our two-hour discussion, made of the essay what my fellow iconoclast Alfred Butts made of the alphabet when he created Scrabble. Not a linear construction, as we learn it in school, but a jumble, a surprise, and a participation. Here, with apologies to E. B. White, is our pieced-together mosaic of "Once More to the Lake," beginning with White's spiritual evocation of Nature:

> The stillness of the cathedral. This was the big scene, still the big scene. The return of light, hope, and spirits. The American family at play. Peace, goodness, and jollity. How you could have it eating out of your hand if you got close to it spiritually. You remember one thing and that suddenly reminds you of another. Girls, donuts dipped in sugar, minnows in a bottle. Summertime, oh summertime. Then the kettle drum, then the snare. Shadow[s] doubling the attendance. Icy garment. The chill of Death.

I am deeply suspicious of the verb *to teach*, especially when it takes the form of one person presuming to impose received wisdom on another. What do any of us know, after all? It's all unfolding, all the time. And it's always new. Science itself—that great empirical know-it-all—is quaking in its boots as it looks into the quantum box it has opened.

I don't want to teach the essay; I want to ask it, and I want my students to ask it without any front-loading from me. The value of old constructs is not a given for the young. White's father's experience of the lake is nothing but a mirage to White himself, until he encounters it "once more" in essayistic fashion—by colliding his memory into the brick-wall reality of death.

The old needs constantly to be torn from its pedestal and shattered in order to be recognized. Its value to us as teachers of process lies not in its construction (which is a done deal, after all) nor in its deconstruction (on that road lies the utter ruin of all meaning) but rather in its reconstruction (where a young reader can make of the shards a fresh mosaic). White knew this instinctively: Death is the last word in his essay, and it springs at us like a cobra. From such an urbane voice as White's, it feels like an assassination, or a suicide—or at the very least, a shattering. He shreds his own essay, right in front of us. It's an outrageous act. A betrayal. A leveling and tarring over of the sacred ground he's just spent eight pages evoking.

But that's it, isn't it, the universal truth at the heart of White's essay: that paradise ain't really paradise 'til you know what it feels like when it's gone.

Failure

Association of Writing & Writing Programs Conference,
Boston, MA, 2013

In the fall of 2001, after completing the bachelor's degree I had walked away from, in protest, in the '60s, I enrolled in Columbia University's MFA writing program. Almost everyone on the campus looked alarmingly young, of course, but as I was leaving Butler Library one day, a woman about my age rushed up to me and asked breathily, "Dusty, is that you?"

She told me her name and said, "You probably don't remember me from our senior year, back in '64, but we used to hang out at the West End Bar, drinking beer and talking books and politics."

"Ah, right!" I said, faking it. "Did we do anything else?"

"No," she said, laughing, "but you made a big impression on me. You seemed so sure of yourself. When I asked what you wanted to do with your life, you answered, 'I'll either be a great American novelist or president of the United States. I haven't decided which.'"

I don't remember saying such an arrogant thing (which probably means I did), but I suspect that mattering meant more to me in my twenties than meaning itself, and the less I seemed to matter, as the years went on, the more urgent my need to matter became.

I didn't think I was needy in this way until one evening in the late '80s, when I found myself standing in the Upper West Side apartment of a successful novelist named Tim Murari. Tim's wife and my wife were friends in the movie business. I was trying desperately to get out of that business by writing a commercial novel, so I tagged along hoping to glean some wisdom from a pro. Tim sat stoically in his study, listening to my description of the writer's block that had me mired in the early chapters of my planned five-hundred-page tome. When I finished, Tim stifled a yawn and stood up dismissively.

"Oh well," he said, "it doesn't matter."

It was at that moment, I think, that my hunger to matter morphed into a kind of existential anguish. Armed with Rainer Maria Rilke's admonition to be determined in my necessity to write, I went back to work with a vengeance.

But three years and four hundred pages later, when my completed novel had failed to find a publisher, even with a top agent, I felt completely betrayed by the habit of ambition that had sustained me for years. The myth I'd created early on, fueled by my parents, teachers, and friends, that because I could write I was therefore a writer, that because I could craft a sentence I must have something to say, that because I had something to say, the world was waiting with bated breath to hear it—the whole construct simply vanished, leaving me, in my fifties, balanced precariously on the lip of an enormous void. In that void there was nothing to see.

I suspect that everyone in this room has gazed out into that darkness, perhaps more than once, and in both big and small ways. As a creative writing teacher, I observe on a daily basis the signs of vertigo, nausea, shame, and panic etched into the crestfallen expressions of students who fail to get the critical response they expect from a workshop, or from me. The Kleenex box in my college office runs out of tissues once a week. Failure is a big deal emotionally—but why?

What does the void—and the sudden absence of hope the void creates—reveal to us? The short answer is that failure resembles death, with its absence of hope. And death, we are reminded, backgrounds everything we do. We could leave it at that and walk away. But there's something strangely energizing about the absence of hope. And clues to this energy might lie in etymology.

The word *failure* derives from the Latin *fallere*, meaning "to deceive, to escape from." The word is far too pernicious at its root to serve simply as an antonym for the word *success*. If our use of the word is to mean anything—and if our experience of it is to teach us anything—failure must be seen as rooted in deception. And since writing is a solitary process, we're talking here about *self*-deception.

By definition, self-deception is an unconscious act. We don't *intend* to self-deceive. And, indeed, the whole purpose of writing is to become increasingly self-aware. More than a few of us on our deathbeds will likely discover that self-awareness is all our writing has brought us. Perhaps we'll simply become less self-deceptive and more understanding of what it means to be human—perhaps even more compassionate.

But for the ambitious among us, there is always the danger of turning self-deception into a dark art—or into what, in *Cutting Through Spiritual Materialism*, Chögyam Trungpa calls the "bureaucracy of ego"—where our ambition to matter as writers plows rudely in front of our intuition and casts aside the patience needed to work intuitively—which is to say, from an unknowing mind, from a place of doubt and uncertainty.

Indeed, one of the symptoms of ambitious writing is precisely its tone of knowingness and certainty. The more skilled the writer, the more dangerous the pitfalls of ambitious prose; the writer begins taking dictation from the prefrontal cortex—a rote skill unhappily enhanced by technology. Such knowingness infects the writing of many commercially successful writers, who—like all of us—have Google at their fingertips.

More importantly, what attaches to the knowing mind—as securely as a barnacle attaches to the hull of a boat—is a subtle arrogance. Arrogant writing is avaricious writing, in that it appropriates aspects of the world *for* itself—everything in sight just begs to be written about, gobbled up like fodder—and then arrogates *to* itself (tonally) all the credit for whatever significance it finds. This is the neurotic side of the artistic impulse to steal and transform. Our hunger to matter infuses our observations of the world with a harmful self-consciousness, and the meaning evaporates.

Fortunately, the world, as it is, is self-explanatory and complete. It does not need the writer to give it meaning. In order for the writer to bestow significance and wisdom on the world, he or she must first receive it *from* the world, and all received wisdom is built on the humiliating message that nothing we do or write is going to keep us from dying.

The refreshing thing about teaching beginners at the college level is that the vast majority of my students don't want to be writers; they just want an A. They are petri dishes of pure ambition, test-tube babies of the American ethos of success, and I can mess with them in any way I want. My strategy from the get-go is to reveal to them the emptiness of ambition and the value of not-knowing. First by insuring them a decent grade. And second by answering all their questions with the question "What do *you* think?" This guarantees that nothing in the room is *ever* certain or safe. Strange things will happen that shock and panic people.

It was hard to keep from laughing, the other day, when I noticed the alarmed expressions of students sitting across the table from me, as they watched the slinky blonde student to my left put her arm around me and begin to fondle my ear. In another workshop, a student—at my urging just before class—threw her essay at me and called me a useless old fart with nothing to teach, then stormed out of the room. Assigned exercises might go uncollected; assigned reading, undiscussed. Guidelines for behavior and attendance have no place at the table. To the dismay of my colleagues, neither do grades. And the students love it. They don't text; they engage. They laugh and cry. Freed up from concerns about their GPA, they move willingly toward meaning and authenticity, and thus they do work that they actually like—often for the first time in their college careers.

Ambition is the default environment in American education, from the top down; no wonder we come out dripping with it. The gift of failure in such an environment is that we get to experience, hopefully long before we meet our maker, the wisdom of the First Commandment: Thou shalt not value false idols and graven images over Me, your creator. To suffer significant failure is to be humbled, returned to the state of cluelessness and uncertainty with which we were born. We are forced to begin at the bottom, yet again. In this way, failure mimics a return to our soft and sturdy child-self, the one who knew only that the door to life had opened—and that anything was possible.

But there's a distinction between the innocent toddler we once were and the wiser child-self we encounter after failure: In the first instance we were presented with the challenge to survive; in the second, with the challenge to openly face death—the void. The first childhood demanded that we develop a protective ego and learn to plan, organize, and compete; the second demands of us a rigorous surrender to the world as it is, to what Trungpa, throughout his teachings on Buddhism, calls the "isness" of reality. Simone Weil calls this kind of surrender "attention without object"—without a motive. Somewhere on this second path lies the gift of authentic voice: authentic not because it is our *personal* voice, but because—transformed by failure—it is no longer *our* voice at all. Not a voice of free association but more accurately a voice free *of* association—stripped of ambition: a stark-naked, unashamed voice that may actually stand the test of time precisely because it no longer cares to be immortal. We may not attain such a voice until our final gasp, but we can aspire to it by failing in the deepest sense to aspire at all.

In the Hindu system of chakras, which I pay attention to when I teach, the ego is located in the solar plexus and associated with ambition, drive, and control. Interestingly, the sense assigned to the solar plexus—to ego—is sight. The ego is somehow connected to the eyes, a notion confirmed by the great Western mantra "I came, I saw, I conquered." The throat chakra, on the other hand, which is associated with self-expression of all kinds, is assigned the sense of hearing. In the void created by failure, there may be nothing to see, no construct we can visualize. But we can listen. And only then can we write.

I once saw an interview on PBS, in which a Mohawk chief, when asked what it felt like to be in charge of his tribe and tell everyone what to do, answered that if he told everyone what to do, he wouldn't be the chief. His job, he said, was to listen. The job of the writer is to listen. Our experience of failure might just confirm for us that writing and listening are one thing only. We call that one thing *voice*.

Writing About the Dead

*Association of Writing & Writing Programs Conference,
Washington, DC, February 2017*

A few weeks before my father died, I asked him to speculate about the possibility of an afterlife. He was eighty-six, a painter and sculptor by profession. Having grown up an only child in a devoutly Methodist household in the Midwest, he decided early in life to break from the church. Art became his religion and family, his solace. "The only afterlife we can hope for," he told me, "is to live on in the memory of others."

So, it came as a bit of a shock when, a few hours before he actually died, my father reached out to my mother and said, "Well, Winnie, I'll see you the next time around."

The next time around?

We don't know what happens after death. But the question, posed by this panel, of how to write about the dead confirms that we tend to think of the dead as somehow being able to listen in on the living. (Who among us has not imagined attending our own funeral?) If death is just a flimsy boundary curtain, no wonder it has the power to modify our assessment of the dead—whether for better or worse. And since we'll all be passing through that curtain, a process that reduces the best of us to a pitiful heap of spent desires and done deeds, none of which can be rescinded or redeemed, why disturb the ashes? Better to cut the dead some slack and think of them as free.

Which, of course, they are, until some nonfiction writer comes along seeking a deeper truth, or perhaps just their own personal identity, but in any case with an eye to resurrecting the dead person in question—usually a relative—and performing a postmortem meditation.

Clearly, the challenge for nonfiction writers *is* to resurrect the dead. I'm always telling students, "Give your dead grandmother a voice! Give her breath to speak again." Which they do—and sometimes convincingly.

But with whose breath does Grandma then speak?

There's the rub.

Writing about the dead is a form of time travel, and the unspoken rule of time travel is that you don't bring luggage from the present along on the journey. You must be careful not to mar the past with sharp-edged assessments from your privileged perspective. To have any hope of capturing dead relatives as they actually *were*, in a space free of the judgment that inevitably comes with the task of writing, the writer must assume an almost ghostly stance.

And this is where most of us fail. We can't get out of the way. Perhaps because the ego fears nothing as much as it fears mortality, we often fail to relinquish our preciously constructed identities (victim and survivor, to name two) as we resuscitate the dead. In failing to let go, we close ourselves off from any surprises the dead might reveal. For instance, that they had lives of their own before we appeared on the scene.

Let's say that I want to write a personal essay about my relationship with my artist father. I sit down and type what I hope is a true sentence: "Every morning of my childhood, right after breakfast my father would leave our house and walk the fifty yards to his studio at the edge of the pasture, where he would work at his easel until noon."

No sooner are the words out than I find myself typing: "He used the studio as much to get away from my mother as to paint."

And as I write that second sentence, I smugly reimagine my father escaping—at least until lunchtime—the domestic gravity tugging at his solitary-artist self. It is an image of him that arises in my mind as naturally as mist from a suddenly sunlit lake, but less from any verifiable struggle *within* my father than from an early fear of *mine* that the hamster wheel of domesticity was going to be *my* lot in life.

In other words, I have just interfered with the past *as it was for my father*, and in the process, created a fiction. In fact, my father loved his domestic life and embraced his treadmill routine. He'd seen firsthand the slaughter of war. He wanted peace. It was *I*, not he, who needed to break free of family and experience worldly chaos.

So, the problem becomes how to protect against dragging ego baggage into our accounts of the dead. How to see the dead more clearly—free of clever constructs and unconscious complexes. How to achieve charitable objectivity in our characterizations, especially of those who were rough-edged and abrasive while alive.

Some years ago, a young woman took my undergraduate creative writing workshop. She was larger-than-life and seemed both happy and fearless. Prompted, along with the other students, to write about the most painful experience of her life, she showed up when it was her turn to be workshopped with a six-page rough draft, which she read aloud to all of us. The situation of her essay was the sexual molestation by her stepfather, an almost nightly event for as long as it lasted, about which her mother remained in stubborn denial. It was a graphic account, inexpertly written but bravely detailed and boldly read. The narrative was sequential and devoid of judgment, resentment, or outrage, and it contained no clinical catchwords. Just five pages of disturbing narrative, followed by a single, crystal clear sentence at the top of page six, which read: "Before I was born, my mother was a traveler."

Listen to it again: "Before I was born, my mother was a traveler."

The sentence captured in a nutshell what turned out to be the real story of the essay—her mother's denial—and it hinted at what Carl Jung calls the shadow, which is sometimes described as the unfulfilled longings of the parent projected onto the child. The sentence, which she arrived at after a ton of detail, came to inform her entire essay in later drafts. In nine words, it contextualized (if it didn't excuse) the abuse and denial portrayed in the essay, and it did so by addressing her mother's *nature*. Not who her mother *should* have been in retrospect—a responsible adult—but who the mother was before the daughter's arrival on the scene.

Too often, when writing about our deceased parents, we forget that however much we might have been wished for and anticipated by our parents, our birth interrupted their lives in ways they could never have imagined. Their world was full of many other things than us before we were born. Including *infinite possibility*, something much diminished by parenthood.

Traveling back in time—as a memoirist—demands that we drop what Piaget called "the illusion of central position," an illusion innocently enjoyed by young children but too often clung to in adulthood—especially in America where, in James Baldwin's words in *The Fire Next Time*, "identity is almost impossible to achieve and people are perpetually attempting to find their feet on the shifting sands of status."

Even if you are writing about a dead parent only to find your own identity—even if, in the end, it *is* all about you—remember that it isn't, really. Not even *you* are about you. What's about you is the flow—or what the Blackfeet people call the flux. Identity—for the living and the dead—is a quantum phantom: nothing at all if you try to pin it down and own it. And like emotional states, identity is fluid. It flows around and into us when we are conceived and around and from us, to others, when we die.

On Discovery in Writing

Association of Writing & Writing Programs Conference, Washington, DC, February 2017

Legend has it that the young poet Rilke, whose mentor for a brief time was the famous sculptor Auguste Rodin, was sent by Rodin to a Paris zoo to write about one of the animals in captivity there. Rodin's prompt resulted in Rilke's brief but immortal poem "The Panther."

Clearly, Rodin meant to sharpen the quality of Rilke's attention—entice him to stare at something other than himself, probably. In like spirit, I send undergraduate writing students out across campus to find a stranger to stare at—someone eating in the dining hall or studying in the library. Invariably, the students experience themselves as stalkers—embarrassed, at first, to be invading the space of another person. Some even experience anxiety, which is perfect, since I mean by the prompt to sharpen their curiosity, a word whose Latin root *curiosus* means "careful" and "inquisitive."

Not so long ago, curiosity was a tool of the trade for an aspiring writer. It's what you did: You *stared* at people. Staring even had a certain cachet—perhaps the charisma of being conscious—and the stared-at often seemed to understand that the notebook in which you were writing or drawing constituted a permissible public record.

Since technology in the last few decades has come to interfere with the way we *observe* our world and hamper the way we *approach* each other, I often find myself warning students that for all the beauty of the iPhone, the world itself is ripe for the taking only in the *now*. "There will be no replay of the present moment," I tell them. To which they invariably roll their eyes, as if to say, *There he goes again!*

But then, when I suddenly slam my hand on the workshop table, the quality of their attention shifts. Besides numbing my hand for the next hour, the violent gesture produces a visible alertness in those sitting nearby—an alertness based in *feeling*. No longer is my preachy admonition to pay attention confined to their minds, where it was encountering all sorts of generational resistance; now the admonition resides in the tensed bowel or the fluttering heartbeat.

I mention this as a way of suggesting that the generative workshop prompt might best be aimed at the feeling rather than the intellectual aspects of our consciousness.

The word *prompt* comes from the Latin *promere*, "to take forward," "to bring up to date," or "to make available." The definition implies that, with prompting, a dormant mix of synaptic impulses will suddenly flicker to the front burner of our mind and coalesce into what we call an idea. We tend to think of an idea as the result of a process that begins and ends in the brain—in the head.

A student last semester told me that she had an idea for a story.

"Great," I said. "Did you bring it with you?"

"With me?" she asked.

"You said you have an idea. Where is it? In your backpack?"

I was messing with her, of course, but after some back-and-forth, we agreed that to *have* an idea is just a convenient bit of fiction. An idea doesn't actually *exist*. In fact, for an idea to exist it needs dimension, as when we commit the words describing the idea to paper.

Obviously, the very act of writing is an idea-grounding process. But how can we gear a succession of prompts to exploit this outcome—and by what system can we then assess the results?

For twenty years now, I have been guided as a writing teacher by the Hindu concept of kundalini energy, sometimes pictured as a coiled serpent lying dormant at the base of the spine, in what is called the root chakra. When aroused—when prompted—kundalini energy, experienced as an electric current, rises through discretely identified states of consciousness—chakras—toward the crown of the head. In the West, we call this felt phenomenon a shiver running up our spine.

To the Western mind, the image of a coiled serpent at the base of one's spine may seem ludicrous and unhelpful, at best. Chakras, with hard-to-pronounce Sanskrit names, don't physically exist; a surgeon couldn't find them any more than a neurosurgeon could slice open your brain and extract an intact idea.

But the concept of kundalini remains the most accurate way I know of to refer to the location of *feelings* in the human body.

Everything, if you boil it down enough, seems simplistic, of course, and kundalini is no exception. But, basically, there are seven primary chakras. The first four are the root chakra, located at the very base of the corpus and representing painful and often-*unconscious* feelings, like anxiety; the sacral chakra, in the region just below the navel, representing the *semiconscious* feelings we call libido; the solar plexus, representing our *conscious* willfulness; and the heart chakra, representing the *supraconscious* feeling of unconditional love. Then the throat represents expression; the third eye region, thought; and the crown chakra, all-knowing bliss. All these regions are connected along the spine via the central nervous system.

The first four chakras are worthy of a writing teacher's attention, because each comes complete with its own color, its own emotions, its own element, and its own sense function. With chakras as a guide, a teacher can actually locate where on the spectrum of consciousness a writer resides at any given point in a written work; and kundalini is an excellent tool that can assess blockage by exposing which chakras are missing from an essay or story. The progress of an essay can be charted in terms of the progress it makes (or doesn't) in its upward flow of consciousness, toward, say, its resolution.

Prompts can be aimed at any chakra, but the root chakra, where pain and anxiety lurk, is the best place to prod or poke the unconscious—that is, to awaken the serpent.

Listen to Ian McEwan exploring the role of pain as a writing prompt, in his amazing novel, *Nutshell*:

> I've heard it argued that long ago pain begat consciousness. To avoid serious damage a simple creature needs to evolve the whips and goads [. . .] of a felt experience. Not just a red warning light in the head—who's there to see it?—but a sting, an ache, a throb that *hurts*. Adversity forced awareness on us, and it works, it bites us when

we go too near the fire, when we love too hard. Those felt sensations are the beginning of the invention of the self. [. . .] God said, Let there be pain. And there was poetry. Eventually.

Eventually is the key word, of course. Pain awakens us, but the process of becoming conscious—becoming "realized," to put it in writing lingo—requires the journey upward through the lower chakras before "poetry" can appear as heart.

The color associated with the root chakra is indeed red—that good old attention-getting alarm. The element of the root chakra is earth, the same ground from which lightning springs. And like lightning, the root chakra is connected with the sense of smell. Think of that sweet smell of ozone before a lightning storm; and, indeed, the word *ozone* comes from the Greek *ozein,* meaning "to smell." Consciousness is awakened not with an opening of our eyes, as we might imagine, but with an opening of our nostrils—with breath.

You may note the word or concept *red* appearing in student writing about fear, anxiety, and pain; or you may encounter details linked to the color red (blood being the most obvious, but blushing, too, and anger—*seeing* red); or you might even *provoke* the appearance of red in a narrative, as I once did in an adult workshop when a writer began her generative response with an exquisite childhood memory of withdrawing her bare foot from some sticky lakeside mud.

"What color was your foot?" I asked, hopefully.

The woman, in her fifties, thought for a moment, then literally shivered in her seat when she remembered that her little toenails had been painted red. From the mud (the unconscious) she had pulled something red. And she knew it immediately—as did the reader, later—that this was going to be a dark and delicious story.

My time is up, so I'll leave you with the bare-bones prompt I use on the first day of my undergraduate nonfiction workshop, which is attended by sixteen students, most of whom have never met each other before—even while waiting for class to begin—and for whom this may be their first creative writing experience.

Without preamble of any kind, including introducing myself, I ask them to open their notebooks, close their eyes, take a few deep breaths, and then try to recall the most painful, most disturbing, most upsetting day of their lives. "First thought, best thought," I tell them, stealing the advice from the Zen master Shunryu Suzuki. And when they have that painful day in mind, I ask them to take the next ten minutes and write about what happened. When the ten minutes are up, they read out loud what they've written, and I feed back to them ways they can turn what they've written into a three-draft personal essay.

Try it. But be warned: You'll be handling sixteen nearly simultaneous lightning strikes right there at the workshop table, and the warning to pay strict attention in the moment will now apply to you, the teacher. Because you will have poked (a better word than *prompted*) sixteen heretofore-dormant kundalini serpents.

The Case for Serendipity in Dating After Sixty

Gray Love *Authors' Reading, Labyrinth Books, Princeton, NJ, March 2023*

In a very real sense, my personal essay titled "At Once," which appears last in this *Gray Love* anthology, is a total outlier. In the essay, I don't even consider the option of online dating—or for that matter, even mention the obvious vagaries of seeking and finding love in the seventh decade of life. What happens in the story just happens. Nothing special. Serendipity does all the work.

Serendipity is defined in the *Merriam-Webster* dictionary as "the faculty or phenomenon of finding valuable or agreeable things *not sought for*" (italics mine).

Betsy and I first met, as adults, at our forty-fifth high school reunion, in 2003, when we were sixty-three years old. We had barely spoken to each other during our teenage years, back in the '50s, and we were surprised suddenly to feel an intense mutual attraction. Neither of us had been seeking a partner. Betsy was married, and I was otherwise involved. Eleven years would pass, with no further contact between us, before yet another school reunion washed us up on a clean beach of opportunity. Betsy was now widowed. I was free. At age seventy-four, we were both acutely aware of how little time we had left. We moved in together and have lived happily ever after. Of course, no one lives "ever after," happily or otherwise, which adds urgency to the story.

But being included in this collection of dating stories, largely about online dating, has heightened my curiosity about what the process of seeking and finding love actually means to us humans. There's nothing particularly new about seeking a mate by advertising for one—mail-order brides in the nineteenth century come to mind. To object to the high-tech version of that search, which is here to stay, is to piss into the wind.

That said, I want to take this opportunity to piss into the wind: to use what I've learned about yogic energies and bodily consciousness in order to push back against the prevailing winds more explicitly than I do in my essay.

In what's already being called the age of AI, we spend large portions of our days consciously seeking and planfully obtaining data-driven information. We don't even have to leave the house to do this. Seek and ye shall find. The algorithms seem already to know what we want!

And when it comes to sex and finding a partner, we can simply order from a menu, as if buying ice cream after a movie. I'll take a cup of vanilla, please, some sprinkles, and a dollop of whipped cream. Oh, and I'll take a long-legged woman with auburn hair, who already has her PhD, loves sex, and actually enjoys cooking.

It's all so tidy: Work up an identity, as if applying for a job; articulate what you want and don't want in a potential mate; broadcast it; establish boundaries; imagine ideal bodies, minds, and proclivities. Revel in all the choices, pick a few, and ghost the rest until what you have in mind matches exactly the person that the algorithm offers you. Then maybe you can meet for a drink.

Sounds cool, certainly sounds risk-free, but risk-free is also, by definition, experience-free. The word *experience* is related to the Latin word *periculum*, which means "peril" or "risk." The feeling aroused by risk is anxiety, and we feel anxiety in the body—not the mind, not the organizing brain, certainly not the algorithm. We feel anxiety, often unconsciously, way down low, in the bowels. The sense most often associated with this region is smell. Risk-related anxiety wakes us up, causes us to sniff things out, alerts us to that slightly higher state of bodily consciousness we call desire or libido.

To be clear, desire is not the same thing as want, as in "I want a mate, I want a lover, I want a job." We feel desire almost as a surprise—distinct from want—in the sacral region of the body, the genital region. When first felt, desire is inarguable and blame-free, and as Carl Jung noted in "The Concept of Libido," "unchecked by any authority, moral or otherwise." It does not require, or yet feed on, anticipation, assessment, or judgment. It just happens to us. In this way, desire is nearly indistinguishable from the unsought-for agreeability of serendipity. The sense associated with desire is taste, which perhaps explains why the kiss is a reliable prelude to sex.

Luckily, desire survives the aging process, sometimes implausibly or even laughably. On the scale of bodily consciousness, desire is merely semiconscious, but it constitutes an essential ingredient of sentience—which is perhaps the only faculty left that distinguishes the human being from these emerging deep learning bots.

To use a dating app necessarily involves subverting our sensory apparatus by eliminating both the anxiety of meeting first in the flesh and the subsequent dawning surprise of desire. Dating apps happily replace the five sensory tools we've been born with—smell, taste, sight, touch, and hearing—with algorithms incapable of bodily sensation. Incapable, too, of the sixth sense, which is the sagacity or wisdom gained from pooling together information from the other five senses.

One shouldn't need to practice kundalini yoga or obtain a degree in neuroscience to understand where in the human body desire is felt. Yet two decades of teaching creative writing at the college level have revealed to me that when students are asked where in their body they feel desire, many of them point to the solar plexus or heart. Which is strange, since the solar plexus is pretty busy with the complexities of hunger, want, satiation, and digestion; and the heart is just a muscle that can't feel anything. It is perhaps no coincidence that many of these same students are prescribed cocktails of antidepressants that come with warnings of reduced libido.

In the scheme of seeking and finding—and, I would argue, keeping a partner—risk-inspired desire seems to be an essential ingredient, without which we are left with naked want. *Want*, and its partner *need*, simply addict us to the always-voracious corporate algorithm.

A number of online dating stories end in disappointment, and some end with the resolve never to go that route again. Often this requires embracing the kind of resolute solitude that resembles hopelessness, which I submit is the perfect destination. It is the Buddhist *shunyata*, as described by Chögyam Trungpa wherein, by accepting the void of hopelessness, one paradoxically opens a feeling of immense space, immense possibility. *Shunyata* tells us not that the game is over but rather that it has just begun. It invites serendipity.

The risk, then, for young and old, is to abandon want as the primary search engine and return to trusting our awareness in any given moment, trusting it to bump us off the curb of cautious, manipulative, nonsensory search into the sometimes-bruising traffic of unsought feeling. In other words, allowing desire to hit us, like a bus. Only then can we properly employ our higher consciousness in order to think twice, tweak our choices, and decide.

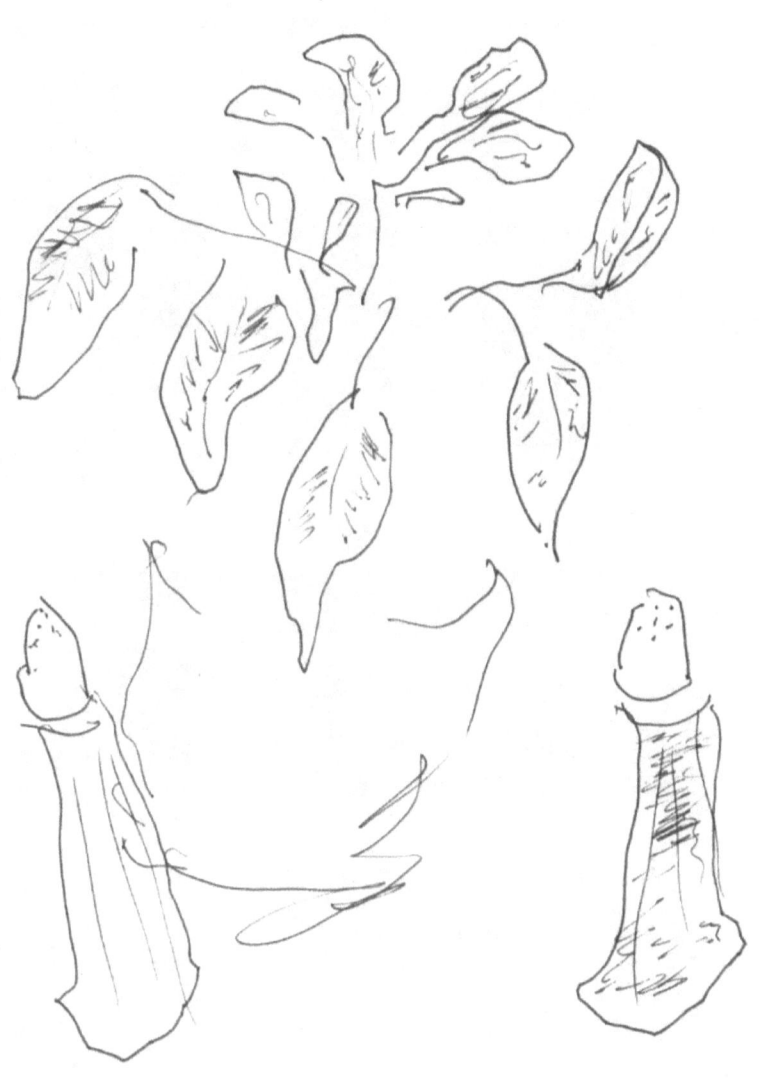

SELECTED
FICTION

A Question of Heart

When paleontologist John Fishman, working his site in the La Cumbre region of the Dominican Republic, found a heart-shaped gold locket trapped inside a twenty-seven-million-year-old chunk of amber, he kept the news to himself for a year. It was the only way he could think to unmask the perpetrators of the hoax. Going about his business as if nothing unusual had happened, he waited a full year (February to February), watching his colleagues daily for signs of pranksterish impatience. When asked, as he inevitably was each morning, "What's new?" he would set his mouth in a stiff smirk and mutter, "Same old, same old," then arch his eyebrows abruptly and peer over his glasses, searching for some hint that the perpetrator had finally exposed him- or herself.

At first, he suspected his latest recruit, a bright and much too clever young man named Alex. Then his attention turned to his rival at a nearby site, Dr. Lummley Pyle. For a while he imagined it might be that recently retired old Swede, Olaf Block, who had so much wanted to head the research here. In the end, though, he came to suspect (without a shred of evidence) his trusted younger associate, Dr. Anna Wooley.

It would have taken a professional of Anna's caliber to pull this off. Repeated tests conducted by Fishman in private had confirmed the amber's age, and there was no sign that it had been cut into or reheated or monkeyed with in any way since it had hardened eons ago. Polishing hadn't revealed even the natural fissures common in a specimen that size. In a test with polarized light, a display of rainbow colors cycled through the transparent amber without distortion. If Anna were indeed the culprit, she'd managed not to compromise the specimen's two tiny air bubbles, and the relative proportion of the various isotopes in the gasses contained therein confirmed beyond a doubt that the sample had formed in an earth atmosphere prevalent during—and only during—the Tertiary period of the Cenozoic era. Were it a fig wasp, a gall midge, or a frog trapped in that exemplary amber, Fishman would have validated the find immediately. But a gold locket? Come on.

Dr. Fishman finally confronted Anna Wooley on February 14—his sixtieth birthday—in his favorite restaurant in Puerto Plata, a dive frequented by artists and escorts and avoided by most of the scientific community. At a candlelit corner table for two, watched over by a gaudy plastic crucifix, John removed a small felt-covered jewelry box from his jacket pocket and placed it gently on the checkered tablecloth.

Anna's eyes lit up. "What's this?"

"Open it," said John, tapping the box lightly with his silt-caked fingernails.

"John . . . come on," said Anna, tucking in her chin suspiciously. But her left hand moved crab-like toward the gift, until her work-roughened fingers rested atop it.

"Go on," said John. "Open it."

Anna withdrew her hand, coyly.

The box sat mutely between them, a mysterious blue mound on a red-and-white-checkered field. John studied Anna's eyes. If she were the perpetrator, she certainly wouldn't want to open this box without first preparing a suitable response, which she seemed to be doing, stalling for time, probably trying to imagine how the rough specimen she'd tried to foist off on him a year ago looked now—sanded to within a millimeter of the locket itself, then polished and buffed like a jewel.

"You already know what it is," said John.

"I know what it *might* be, generically," said Anna. "I know this gesture from romantic movies. Does it come attached to a question, perhaps?"

Clever woman, thought John. "Yes, Anna, a big question."

"May I hear the question first?"

"Alright," said John, leaning closer to the candle, giving her one of his over-the-top-of-the-glasses looks, even though he was wearing contacts tonight.

"Let me guess," said Anna. "Does it begin with *w*?"

"Why, yes, it does," said John.

"Second letter *i* perhaps? As in *will* . . . ?"

"Ah . . . nope," said John, wondering in a fleeting way if this approach might prove to have been a mistake but still certain that she was the hoaxer, her confession imminent.

The waiter, Pedro, came over and stood by the table.

"Vino de mesa," said John, with uncharacteristic brusqueness. "Dos copas. Y guacamole, por favor."

Taking the hint to get lost, Pedro nodded and retreated quietly.

"It begins with *w,* but it isn't something like *will you marry me?*" said Anna.

John chuckled gleefully, nudged the box closer to her, and shook his head. For a split second, he thought he detected disappointment in her countenance, a subtle darkening from within—the opposite of a blush. But as suddenly as it had come, her inner cloud vanished and her bright eyes squinted conspiratorially.

"There's a present for you, too," she said, "in case you'd forgotten what day it is."

* * *

Anna and John had each been married—several times—to fellow academics: Anna, twice (first to a full professor and then to a graduate student); John, three times (to a full professor and two graduate students). According to Anna, her two marriages had begun in the same levelheaded way, with well-defined boundaries, but had turned out to be short-fused and explosive. She likened them to prolonged wrestling bouts in which she'd always managed to stay on top—intellectually, emotionally, physically. ("Men are a slippery subspecies of anaconda," she liked to say, "and need to be handled as such.") Both husbands had suffered breakdowns and both had attempted suicide—one by scratching his wrists with steel pushpins while standing in traffic in Harvard Square; the other by downing two bottles of acetaminophen tablets mashed up in 150-proof Jamaica rum. John's first wife, Martha, originally an associate of Lummley Pyle, had died in a mine collapse in the Western Cordillera range, burying forever her intention—expressed in a letter just a week before the accident—to leave John for Lummley. Wives number two and three had each bolted within eighteen months of their vows, shrieking their disaffection for everyone to hear. John never likened his three marriages to anything, keeping them wrapped instead in a kind of equation-proof mist of their own. ("Work and love don't mix," he often said, by way of explanation.)

Neither John nor Anna intended to marry again. They'd made that clear to all their associates and friends. Anna had confirmed it as recently as two months ago, when, on turning forty, she'd announced (to the entire staff) that she could see (from that significant peak) forty more years of *labor y soledad* bolstered by the respect of her colleagues, with whom, like John, she could share many—but not quite all—the aspects of her life. Her work in the field, she said, was child and husband enough, and she made it quite clear that gratifying her healthy sexual appetite was a simple matter of planning ahead, of picking and choosing, with the help of a calendar and a list—like her weekly dinner menu, which she shopped for on Mondays (with John) in Santiago.

* * *

The wine arrived in a carafe, followed by a plate of guacamole, chips, and salsa. John poured two glasses, passed one to Anna, and raised his own.

"Happy birthday, Dr. Fishman," said Anna, beating him to a toast. "How does it feel to complete six decades?"

John was jolted by the question, blindsided as he often was by the subject of age. He'd thought of sixty as the *beginning* of the sixth decade.

"It'll feel better when you open your gift, Dr. Wooley," said John, indicating the blue box with his pinky.

Anna made no move to open the box. "It's *your* birthday, John, not mine," she said, adjusting the fancy bow on the green ribbon that served as her neckpiece tonight.

"It's also Valentine's Day," said John, popping his eyebrows.

"Valentines are supposed to be anonymous," said Anna, jolting him again with another overlooked truth.

A pause ensued. At times like these, in the absence of matters scientific where his authority could be brought to bear, John found their professional relationship, with its rarely articulated but clearly understood and generally convenient hands-off policy, restrictive. He was going to want her again tonight—he could feel it coming on—like that time in the mine a year ago. Want her beyond all reason.

"Okay," he said, "if it's *my* birthday, where's *my* present?"

"You can't open it yet," said Anna.

"Oh, really?" said John, glancing at her purse, tucked between the napkin dispenser and the saltshaker.

"Don't be silly," she said. "It's not in there."

"Where, then?" John lifted his end of the tablecloth, pushed his chair back, peered beneath the table. Anna's bare knees shone in the dark, her water bottle, too, and her bright red toenails. But no package of any kind announced itself. He sat up again.

"Not there, either?" teased Anna, leaning into the candlelight, challenging him with her clear auburn eyes. "You'll just have to wait, I guess."

John wasn't going to beg, not even for the fun of it. He got Pedro's attention, ordered their usual combination of enchiladas, rice, and beans, then contented himself with little sips of red wine. *Let the ball be in her court*, he thought.

* * *

For five years now, John Fishman had enforced a rule. Anyone working his site—which collected and analyzed samples taken directly from the sorting tables of seven nearby mines—must make at least one trip into a working mine, using the simple tools of the miners themselves: a hammer, a chisel, a candle, and a burlap sack. He led these forays himself.

The outings consisted of crawling on gloved hands and padded knees, with one's back only inches from the ceiling of a crudely constructed mineshaft. For long stretches there was only room enough to slither on one's belly, sometimes through standing pools of chilly water. The route itself was un-ambiguous, following as it usually did a clearly visible lignite layer, deep inside some recently formed mountain in the fog-shrouded Cordillera Septentrional range. But the route, if well defined, was dicey nonetheless. Aside from the risk of cave-ins during the monsoon months, there was always the possibility that one of the staff might panic.

"If you want to play, you've got to pay," said John, when-ever new staff members objected to his rule. "You simply can-not learn the intrinsic value of a thing until you know how it's come by. You can't learn what you don't earn." That's how he had put it to Anna during her long first interview three years back. Anna had responded adamantly that she would never enter one of those mine shafts, not even to obtain the job. "I'm a tall, sub-stantial woman," she said. "If I got stuck, I'd freak, I'd just ab-solutely freak." John had quickly shifted the subject to the back burner—he'd had to. Not many paleontologists with Anna's cre-dentials worked with amber, and those who did often obtained their samples from among the collections of rich connoisseurs, allowing them to work and teach in the States. Anna's expressed interest was not in the contents of dusty specimen drawers but in amber that was rarely seen—fossilized in the very early Paleocene epoch, some sixty million years ago. John, secretly feeling lucky that Anna had even applied, took her adamant refusal as an inflexibility he could massage and soften with time.

Anna managed to defy John's rule for two years before he persuaded her at least to try. "Just you and me," he told her. "I'll talk you through it and be right there with you all the time. If you really can't do it, it'll be our secret. We'll bring a picnic lunch." He chose the Number 4 mine, a three-hundred-yard-long downsloping snake of a tunnel whose entrance was halfway up Mount Alma and a half-mile trek on foot from the service road. Eduardo, the head miner, had agreed to stand guard at the entrance, even though it was Sunday.

John tossed Eduardo the keys to the pickup. "Cuatro horas, Eduardo. Nada más." He shot Eduardo a look that signaled the seriousness of the time limit.

Eduardo nodded.

It was nine o'clock when they entered the shaft, John in the lead. They covered the first hundred yards without having to actually crawl even once. John lit a new candle at each station along the way, every thirty feet or so, depending on the curves. He kept up a constant monologue to distract Anna from what he imagined would be her growing apprehension, and he was somewhat puzzled when she told him to "shush" so she could enjoy the "ambience of the place."

A hundred yards in, the tunnel narrowed bluntly to a width of two feet and a height of three. John, knowing that Anna might begin to "freak" at the prospect of entering this smaller passage, said, "Here's where it starts to be fun. Just wait until you see the quality of the matrix along here. If you feel more comfortable going first . . . "

"No, no," she said, "you're the leader."

John took the canvas sample sack from around her neck, removed the chisel and hammer from her belt, and dropped the tools into the sack. Folding the sack in half, he wrapped the straps around and around, making a bundle of it. "Carry this in your hands," he said. "Always keep it in front of you. Same with the candle." He checked her clothing, zipped up her vest, and buttoned the top button for her.

"At the end of this little stretch, there's a comfy space," he said. "We'll take off the kneepads there and light new candles." He avoided meeting her eyes, not wanting to give permission for any kind of panic on her part. "We're off," he said, candle in one hand, sack in the other. "Follow me."

As he ascended the two steps that led to the narrower passage, he was surprised to find Anna right on his heels.

They crawled on a slight downslope for another fifty yards or so. John had not remembered this passage to be quite as tight as it now seemed. "How are you doing?" he called out. When Anna failed to respond, it occurred to him that he should have asked Eduardo to bring up the rear, although that would have left no one to go for help. If Anna were to freeze on this stretch, he'd have no way to get either of them turned around, no way to coax her backward. The thought of them both being trapped made him edgy. Instinctively, he made a move to sit up, jamming his mid-spine hard against a sharp rock. The pain brought him to his senses. He called out again, impatience evident in his voice.

"I'm fine!" yelled Anna. "Go on! Why are you stopping?"

Irritated that she seemed to be doing so well without him, John began crawling again, faster now, lighting the candles along the way but not stopping to point out variances in the matrix rock. Something was building inside him, some dread he couldn't quite put his finger on. When he reached the little chamber that marked the beginning of the third leg of the journey—the part where you had to slither on your belly—he drew himself into it and sat up quickly, breathing heavily. Anna crawled into the chamber, shoving his legs aside. She curled around and plopped down near his feet.

"Whew!" she said, removing a glove, wiping her sweaty brow, smiling at John. "You okay?"

John, noting her utterly calm demeanor, nodded. He took a deep breath, avoiding her eyes. His clothing felt tight at his chest and his throat was oddly constricted. There wasn't nearly enough air in here today.

"You sure?" asked Anna.

"Of course," snapped John, thinking maybe he should abort the venture right now. He'd left his watch on the dash of the pickup.

"Boy," said Anna, "there's some good stuff all along the way, isn't there?"

"Yeah," said John. He thrust his candle into the shaft ahead. The dimly illuminated space funneled abruptly into what looked like an impossible squeeze, and the slope of it, descending into the bowels of the mountain, seemed nearly vertiginous from here. He could hear water running downhill in the distance. He tried to imagine the route, but nothing stood out in his memory, no way stations. Was there even a place to get onto one's hands and knees for a bit? He thought not. He wondered what the water level was in the chamber at the end of the shaft.

"I want to get some samples," said Anna, pulling off her kneepads. "I hope there's going to be time. Shouldn't we get going?"

John thought of letting her take the lead, thinking that if she panicked he could talk her back—*pull* her back if necessary—but then he pictured more vividly having to squirm backward uphill. He imagined his pant cuffs catching, bunching up, wedging him in. The mere thought of it stole his breath away.

"Shit!" he said. The curse startled him, as if another man had uttered it.

"What?" said Anna, pulling on her glove.

"A cramp," said John, covering his lie by trying to straighten out in a space where there was no room to straighten. Realizing he'd better get a hold of himself immediately, make a leader-like move, muscle through this odd new dread, he lit two more candles and passed one to Anna. "Come on," he said, stuffing the lighter in his vest. Without meeting her eye, he squirmed head-first into the next passage.

He was perhaps two body lengths in—far enough to envision Anna squeezed in behind him, blocking his retreat—when he realized that he'd failed to remove his kneepads. That's when the panic hit. It began as a horrible feeling of inflation, a sense that his entire body was swelling, and it led to his imagining the immensity of the mountain above him, its *living* immensity, and from that to an image of the mountain sighing and settling just a touch, ignorant of his presence within it. A moan escaped his lips, followed by the word "Jesus." He struggled forward but his right kneepad caught. He started to hum a quick little tune, a musical invention that came from somewhere deep in his past—his childhood maybe—little beads of nonsense noise strung together in the dark. The beads grew into sustained bursts of sound, followed by quick gasps for air. Now his jacket was catching, restricting his shoulders, and his chest, belly, and thighs were sopping wet.

John tried to deflect his terror by remembering the way Anna had looked climbing into the pickup truck at dawn, her freshness. Unable to sustain the image, he wriggled backward frantically, whimpering and moaning, until Anna began punching the sole of his sneaker. "OhGodohJesusGod!" he heard himself say. It took all his wind to say it, but it seemed to help. He stared at the sample sack, which he'd let go of several yards ahead, then slowly began inching toward it, letting his kneepads slide to his ankles.

"It's okay!" he yelled to Anna. "You're doing fine! Don't look at the big picture, just focus on details! Details, only details!" He got hold of the sack, buried his face in it, and tried to think of a prayer. With eyes still closed, he began inching forward incrementally, candle in one hand, the sack pressed to his face in the other. In this manner he contained the fright for some time. The downward slope was forcing blood to his head and he pictured being struck by an embolism, paralyzed.

"Ohforfuckssake!" he shouted, the sound of his voice fleeing into the tunnel ahead and dying out grimly in the bowels of the earth.

* * *

With her elbows on the table, her wineglass in both hands, Anna seemed content not to speak. John took her unflinching gaze to be a sign of perfectly respectable birthday party adoration and didn't mind basking in it at all.

"My boss," said Anna, out of the blue.

"What?" said John.

"Technically, by a slim margin, you are my boss."

"Yes, I am," said John, "and it's a good thing, too."

"Do you believe in holidays?" she asked.

"You mean like religious holidays, or just days off?"

"I mean little burps in time where the normal rules don't apply."

"Holidays . . . " mused John. "Did you know that the inner layers of plywood are often composed of inferior material, sometimes causing a 'holiday' just beneath the surface that goes undetected until you put weight on it?"

Anna sighed. "I didn't know that, John."

"Do I *believe* in holidays?" asked John, realizing he'd just stepped on one of his own making.

"Do you believe holidays are really possible, that the rules one follows day-to-day can just be suspended for a given period, after which life simply returns to normal?"

"Happens all the time, doesn't it?" said John, pouring more wine for himself, Anna not ready yet. "Take Christmas. Work stops, families unite, stupid games get played, then everyone goes back to their normal lives."

"But do they?" said Anna. "Don't holidays bleed into the rest of life?"

"Depends on the will of the participants, I guess," said John. "I think most people compartmentalize pretty well, if they're adult about it." He eyed the blue box. "What are you getting at?"

"You compartmentalize," said Anna.

"I try to," said John, proudly.

* * *

When John felt his shoulders wedge in between two vertical tunnel supports, he opened his eyes, fully expecting to see the final chamber dead ahead. But he saw nothing. He blinked repeatedly. Still nothing. His candle was out. He peered into the unremitting blackness until his eyes ached. He pushed up with his hands, but there was no leeway above him—none. His elbows felt raw. One glove was missing. Forcing his left hand between his chest and the ground, he reached deep into the upper pocket of his vest. But the pocket was empty, the lighter gone.

"Anna!" he called, his voice cracking.

No response. He tried to look over his shoulder, tried to glimpse her light from behind, but nothing issued from that direction, not even a dim glow. Either his body was wedged so tightly in the shaft that no light could get through, or she wasn't close behind him anymore. He kicked his feet rapidly, hoping to signal her. Nothing.

"Anna!" he called, angry now, struggling frantically to get up, turn over, see something. Defeated, he collapsed and started to hum again. Then he made himself lie quietly, eyes closed. His hearing wasn't what it should be, and the deficiency increased his sense of isolation. Again, he thought of Anna stepping into the pickup truck, the aura of dawn on her cheek, the glint of first sun in her hair and eyes. The life in her face shone like a light in his mind. "Anna," he said, softly. Then he repeated her name, several times, like a mantra. He could hear his own breath, its uneasy rhythm amplified by the proximity of the walls. Water gurgled up ahead, or behind—he couldn't tell which. But he heard nothing else.

He felt in front of him for the sack, managed to unwrap it and remove the tools. Squirming backward a few inches, he located the upright timber and smacked it three times with the flat of his hammer. The sharp wooden sound was oddly reminiscent of surface activities—of sunlit endeavor. He waited for an answering signal, but none came. Again, he smacked the lumber—not so hard this time, careful not to disturb the support—then again and again and again. Nothing. Clearly, she must be far behind. He would have to get to the end, turn around, work his way back through here, meet her face-to-face in the tunnel. He envisioned her being hung up on something, saw himself having to squeeze past her in order to free up some article of clothing, imagined them being jammed together in this passage, pressed head-to-foot forever, like sardines in a can. He thought about her ankles, how he might remove her sneakers and socks, die with her bare feet in his hands.

Just then something slimy began to slither up his calf, toward the back of his knee. He kicked and thrashed, clutching his hammer, clawing at the ground. A high-pitched squeal of fear accompanied his effort. Wrenching forward, he burst between the narrow wooden uprights. He couldn't tell whether his eyes were open or shut, and he didn't care. It didn't matter anymore, as long as he didn't get bitten.

Suddenly, he felt himself sliding and then, just as suddenly, falling into open space.

* * *

The food arrived. John cupped his hand protectively over the little blue box. Pedro set down the steaming platters.

"Gracias, Pedro," said John. "Otro tambien."

"Claro," said Pedro, filling both their glasses, then indicating the inch or so left in the carafe.

John obligingly downed half his glass and held it out for the refill. "Might get a little drunk tonight," he chuckled, winking at Anna.

"Bueno," said Pedro. "Es luna llena hoy."

"Bueno," said Anna, raising her glass again. "Feliz cumpleaños, Señor Doctor, y muchos más."

"Thanks," said John.

They set about eating right away, mixing and mashing the enchiladas with the rice and beans and shredded lettuce, lifting the mixture off the plate, letting it cool, forking it into their mouths. Occasionally, they would jerk their heads in the direction of this or that restaurant patron, whom they either knew or didn't: a familiar escort, for instance, with her weird new client, or some timid tourist couple taking it all in.

After a while John tapped the blue box with the butt end of his knife. "Not even curious, are you," he said. "Got it all figured out?"

"No, I don't, actually. It's a little scary. I'm trying to ignore it."

John studied Anna's face for signs of deceit but found only puzzlement. He thought back to when he'd first put the box on the table, the way she'd moved spontaneously to open it, the light in her eyes when she'd first seen it.

"I'm not proposing to you, Anna," he said.

"Well, that's a relief," she said. "Pass the Tabasco."

"What if I were?" quipped John, feeling foolish that he'd humorlessly perceived her earlier mood to be one of disappointment.

"People who compartmentalize feelings are deluding themselves," said Anna.

John wondered what that had to do with his question. The candlewick was struggling to stay lit in its pool of wax, its flicker playing nicely in Anna's eyes. He waited for her to elaborate.

"You might think you can suspend feelings," said Anna, "but feelings *exist*. They're molten and viscous, like magma. And they leave traces."

"Maybe Christmas isn't the right example," said John. "Take Mardi Gras. You put on a mask, go out reveling, act like an asshole, drink too much, have sex with whomever, get it all out of your system . . . "

"And . . . ?" said Anna.

"Then you take off your mask, hang it above the mantelpiece next to your graduate diploma, and forget about it until next year. You acknowledge that you need to be different for a night, that there are forces you can't control, but you also acknowledge that for most of the year you must control them."

"What if something happens during your revelry? What if feelings emerge that you don't *want* to control anymore? What then?"

"You don't *let* them emerge," said John, sagely.

"But what if they do?"

John snorted, as if such a possibility were absurd. But he knew she had him. And he knew she knew he knew.

* * *

John could not have been a pretty sight, squatting in the corner of the terminal chamber, water up to his shoulders, blood dripping from his hair line, eyes squeezed shut, whimpering. But Anna certainly was. He'd never seen anyone as beautiful in his life—in dreams maybe, but maybe not even in dreams. He hadn't heard her coming and had no idea how much time had elapsed. What alerted him to her presence he couldn't have said. But when he opened his eyes and he saw her crouched in candlelight near the opening of the shaft, her tallness folded so gracefully, he was struck dumb by the iridescence of her skin. As she worked her way into the water and waded toward him, holding the candle before her, he struggled to stand, but his knees had locked and she had to lift him up with one arm.

"You're cut," she said. When he was steady enough to stand on his own, she fingered the thin hair at the top of his head, looking for the source of the blood. "It's not bad," she said. "A bleeder, that's all."

John raised his hand to her cheek, stroked it lightly, feeling the dawn still contained within it. "You made it," was all he could say. He nudged her stray hair back behind her ear and pulled at her earlobe gently, marveling at its bulbous warmth. He touched her other cheek and her other ear, and then with both hands stroked her temples. He ran his fingertips across her forehead and down the bridge of her nose, fanned them out onto her cheeks, brought them together at her lips, which pursed reflexively. Slowly he traced the line of her jaw. She held the candle absolutely still for this, both hands gripping it now. She didn't say a word. His fingers moved down the length of her throat, and behind, to the nape of her neck, dwelling awhile in the sweaty warmth of the declivity there, then exploring her moist hair where it bunched beneath a whalebone clip. His fingertips tingled with electricity, his eyes blurred with tears. Never had he experienced this kind of joy before. Gently forcing the candle aside, he drew her face to his. As she would describe it later, she allowed him to kiss her, and the kiss would last for some time. She allowed her lips to part and her tongue to play— even allowed his fingers to unbutton the top of her vest, unzip it halfway, and toy with her nipple beneath the sweat-soaked T-shirt. ("It seemed to calm you," she had noted.)

The long kiss and its accompanying caress would not lead to anything more complex just then. The water was bone-numbingly cold. There were samples to collect.

There followed a year of normal days.

* * *

"Answer me, John," said Anna. "What happens if irrepressible feelings emerge?"

John contemplated a twisted glob of melted cheese stuck in the tongs of his fork. He looked across the table at Anna, perusing her features, noting for the first time the possible significance of the bright bow at her throat and the suggestion of cleavage below. "You mean, what if continental plates collide somewhere deep within you?" he said, smiling at her. "Is that what you mean, Anna?"

"That's it," she said, smiling back. "Sedimentary beds of limestone get thrust upward, breaking and bending and shearing."

"And fossilized resin from ancient algaroba trees is exposed, no doubt—ancient amber," said John.

"It can happen," said Anna. "There *is* that danger."

"Maybe an impossibly rare specimen is even brought to light? A singularity trapped within that amber?" said John, almost tapping the blue box again but managing to control himself.

"Exactly!" said Anna.

"And would this rarity be treated as such by you—integrated into your overall understanding of behavioral fixity in the fossil record?"

Anna smiled, conceding that it would.

"And what is the principle of behavioral fixity, young lady?" asked John, drawing impatient circles in the air with his fork.

"'That the behavior of fossil organisms will be similar to that found in their present-day descendants.' That's a quote."

"Very good, Anna," said John, satisfied that she'd played right into his hand. It was she who had—

"John?"

"Yes?"

"You said this little box here comes attached to a question. If the question is not *Will you marry me?* or some semblance of same, what, pray tell, is it?"

Anna had a knack for cutting to the chase. John scooped up some more cheese with a tortilla chip, wondering how she'd wangled him back to square one. He chewed for a while, stared at the little box, and drank some more wine. He shook out his right hand like a magician—as if to clear it from his sleeve—and, after a prolonged hesitation, picked up the box.

Slowly, deliciously slowly, Anna extended her left hand across the table, palm up. They leaned closer to each other, until all that separated their faces was a warm and wavering shaft of incandescence.

"Are you ready for the question?" asked John, supporting her fingertips with his own. He brought the box close to his chin, but Anna kept her eyes on his mouth.

"Such seriosity," said Anna. "Yes. Ask me."

John took a breath, then began the question on an exhale: "What . . . "

Anna raised her eyebrows expectantly.

" . . . is . . . "

She stifled a giggle.

" . . . this thing . . . " said John, placing the little box in her hand.

" . . . called love?" asked Anna, opening the gift so, so, ever so slowly.

Walking Through Time

Molly couldn't put a sentence together, but that hardly mattered. When the semester ended, Professor Richard Hall had submitted her grade and waited until it cleared the registrar's office, making it official. He *did* wait. What happened then had been incubating all spring anyway, lurking in the organic confusion with which Molly would begin a sentence in the present tense and end it in the past, or vice versa. Her refusal to heed his suggestion that she be consistent in her use of verb tenses had begun to rub him the wrong way. A professor can get fed up, too, writing small in the margins and being disappointed by beauty.

"It's all very tiring, especially when you're as old as I am," he had explained to Molly, who was sitting at the far end of the workshop table, on a Thursday back in February—no one else in the classroom. The habitual suck-ups had departed, like the senior from Brooklyn who was going on to med school and was always asking, "How long should this story be?" Or the soph-omore from California who hovered around after each class, making sure to be the last to place her paper on the pile—hop-ing she'd be the first to be read.

Richard could see through all the student ruses, and he had made sure that Molly, the tense-shift girl, knew that he was running out of patience. He narrowed his eyes at her when he spoke—usually an effective strategy when dealing with recalci-trant students.

"It's exhausting to always be telling you to proof your work before turning it in, Molly. I don't want to give you C's, but I have no choice."

* * *

Even so, it seemed perfectly obvious, now that the semester was over, that Molly had been way ahead of him. He was sure of it. And now, as he waited for her, lonely and old in his academic office, with the door propped ajar and only a few days left before the end of finals, he felt even surer.

Sometimes he felt like screaming into the empty hallway, "Anybody! Come in, whoever you are, and let me know what the fuck is going on with young people these days." He was cer-tain that his students' lives depended on what he, their teacher, sent them into the world of their mind to accomplish, the ter-ritory of their heart to feel, and the country of their desire to stumble upon.

He hadn't noticed Molly's legs, at first. He knew she was tall, but even when she'd come near him the first time, in late January, smelling of soap and lavender shampoo—a perfectly spoiled brat who'd somehow convinced God to pour her a body and lend her a strut—even then, when she stepped closer and asked him whether he'd mind if she ignored his fiction prompt and instead wrote something of her own choosing—even *then* he hadn't seen her legs clearly. He'd said, "Okay," in the wake of her aroma, but only because (thinking back on it now) he must have realized even then that she wasn't asking for his permission. She'd probably known she'd show up at his office door in May, long before he'd ever learned how to read or write or discovered what to say *yes* with and why to say *no* to a student like her—a girl who was now no longer technically his student and who'd said on the first day of class that she liked his tangerine shirt ("the orange evidence of your desire," she called it) and who must have reached deep into him many eons before he first tasted fruit, or reached for the branch Eve called her arm, or taken from her hand the dry leaf and red apple of her poem. He'd been a lover once.

As if conjured by magic, Molly poked her head into the office. "Was this a good time now?"

"Perfect, Molly," said Richard. "Come in."

Wearing a short navy blue skirt and a sky blue blouse and carrying nothing in her hands, Molly slipped into the office and returned the door to its ajar position. Richard stood up and went to the door, studying the graceful way her calves tapered down to her ankles. She had the legs of a dancer. She wore light blue flip-flops.

"Listen," she said, "what you need is a white noise machine in this office. Everyone knows this is where we students come to cry."

"Is that so," said Richard, signaling her to step farther into the room.

"You must have perceived," she continued, "and maybe you still do, that when I sat in your line of sight all semester I had you in *my* sights. You think I can't spell, and I couldn't before I met you. But from now on I will. Remember when you gave me that lecture about giving me C's?"

"I do," said Richard.

"I'll bet you'll never forget how poignant and painful it was to watch me walk away that day, you being so old and unreachable and me so unteachable and young."

"That's very poetic, Molly," said Richard. "Here, let me close this door."

"Youth is all about simile," she said, not moving but lifting her left eyebrow humorously. "Metaphor is meaningless to us young people. We punctuate sentences with *like*."

Or something like that. It was late in the day.

She began to quote Ralph Waldo Emerson: "Consistency is the hobgoblin—"

But he cut her off by kicking the little rubber doorstop wedge with an uncharacteristic abruptness, almost clipping her ankles when shutting the office door. He never shut the door all the way with a living, breathing, active, current student because there was a boundary—he got that. But she wasn't his student anymore.

"Sit down in that chair, Molly, and cry for me. Teach me to reach across the years and obliterate tenses, too."

She laughed as she sat down, heaved a sigh, and looked up at him.

"Help me to understand," he said, "what you thought of the answer I gave to your question on the last day of class, 'Did the world end soon?'"

Her fellow students had laughed at her diction, but he'd taken her question seriously.

"*Will* it end soon, you mean?" he'd said. "The answer is yes. It *is* about to end, and the world I will never get to know—your world—is about to begin. Think of it as a horse race. All you horses are now in your starting gates. Your skittishness is gone, your reluctance to being harnessed has passed, and now there's this brief but drawn-out time when nothing at all is happening. Just this weird silence, right? This big question mark about the outcome. The gates are still closed, you horses are resigned to the imminent whip, your jockeys sit poised in their saddles, the crowd has grown hushed. The loudspeakers don't even squeak. You can hear a pin drop on the dirt track. *That's* how you can tell the world is about to end."

"Do you think Christ was coming back?" Molly asked him now.

"*Is* coming back, you mean?"

"Whatever," she said.

"Who knows?" he said, sitting down in his chair of authority. He suspected he was here to usher *someone* in, someone quite close by. He could feel Her—she who was about to begin. He sensed he was passing a baton. He felt like one of the last men to be filled with passionate mission, brimming and bursting all his life and now about to dissolve because it was impossible to contain the heartbreak in the world and be broken himself—surely he was one of the last old men standing who remembered Orwell and Huxley.

Richard didn't tell Molly that her slim ankles were putting him in the mood to slip through the walls of decorum. But he sensed that she already knew. Walls don't make a room; space makes a room. Walls are simply performance, and he was part of the space today.

Molly sat back and said that she had no idea what the genesis of her last story was, or where in the world it came from. She didn't, of course. Who ever did? She was being honest, he was sure.

A silence settled in between them.

Richard watched Molly like a puddle of water admiring the rain. Perspective was everything when you taught. A particular collection of moods had gathered within him—like a surface tension on the Great Plains, where lightning struggled to make babies out of dust and cactus, and where humans struggled now to make sense of why a snail has been assigned to pull the next queen's chariot, and where slowness would come to define love. No more locked eyes or love at first sight, like in the movies, but split-open hearts and people refusing to learn ever again to build a wall or a bomb, or to seek careers filled with Do, in a world that was aching for Be.

"It will all start all over again," he told Molly, answering her question more clearly, if a little late. "Your world will start again as something else."

"Tomorrow?" Molly asked.

"Tomorrow never comes," he said, risking the cliché.

"Soon?"

Richard shut his eyes, but no answer appeared on the back of his lids.

"What would a baby learn by growing up in such a world as this, anyway?" she asked, looking vaguely around Richard's office.

"It might learn how bone forms to complete its skull," he answered, without the slightest hesitation. "It would probably conclude that the reason the fontanel that we're born with closes over in our first year of life must be explored more deeply."

* * *

When he was a young man, Rick (as he was called back then) got hammered one October night and climbed the mast of a Portuguese freighter during a violent storm in the middle of the

Atlantic Ocean. High above the waves, he'd clung to the slippery railing of the crow's nest as it described a crashing arc amidst lightning and rain and twenty-foot swells. He rode the wet arc as if clinging to the tip of a huge, impossibly heavy metronome arm—*tick* this way, *tock* that. And then, suddenly, he was completely sober, fully awake to the terror within him.

Frozen with fear and clinging for dear life, he pictured the crew and twelve other passengers weathering the swells politely as they sat at the captain's table down below. They'd have no idea where he was, and the first mate, a bullfighter in his youth, was probably beginning to wonder where he'd gone on such a wild night.

Rick had been afraid of heights in those days, but there he was, somehow *at* the height.

He knew nothing of time, then, but here, fifty years later, here he somehow still was. He had no clue then how long his life would be and how many times he would have to scare himself ashen to learn once and for all that everything makes sense only when nothing does; that when one pays attention on a deep level, slowness settles onto the face of things, even the incessant clock, even the remembered life.

To know you're on time when you're late is to be real. The funeral procession in town just last week, which involved old men dressed in black suits emerging from limousines to hold up lines of traffic at the stoplight, might very well have delayed some ultimate and other collision, way in the future. He didn't mind waiting anymore. He felt full with waiting, even until the moon melted redly into the sun, and maybe even longer than that.

* * *

Richard caught Molly staring at him intensely. He considered standing up and kneeling on the floor before her, but he didn't. He just shifted his gaze to her bare knees, admiring how the quiet four-headed muscle above the femur curved around and partially encased her right kneecap. Exercise obviously worked for her and kept her sturdy, even if she were called upon to tend goal, he imagined.

"So?" he asked. "How may I help you, Molly?"

"You know . . ." she began.

But he didn't let her finish. He'd noticed by then how the flesh on her right wrist seemed full and flat between wrist bone and tendon, a smooth stretch of taut skin about as many centimeters wide as might make an inch and a half, and he just went ahead and touched her there, saying, "I do know, Molly, I do."

And then he said, "You have a beautiful wrist, Molly."

He suspected no one in all her twenty-two years had ever told her such a thing—no timid sophomore or drunken jock, not even her father or brother. "Your wrist," he said, thinking *pulse*, thinking *life*, testing if there was any left in him, teasing the spark in the tinder bowl of tantric potential with his tiny boy breath, his child hope, his impossibly foolish desire, which was born again and again of hopeless wonder and all-be-damned.

"What a time to be alive," he said out loud, removing his fingers from her wrist.

At which Molly started to smile, then suddenly to cry, and in her expressed confusion of feeling she met someone who wasn't afraid of him at all, who could see through her tears the hermit cave where he lived, without misunderstanding why he had no real craft or skill to teach her. Without making a big point of herself, or taking notes, she extended her left hand toward his face, his long horseface with its unblinkered eyes and its tempestuous brow made thick and wrinkled with years of forethought and function.

Brave it, he told himself, as her hand came near.

And he did not shy. He, the shy boy inside the old man, did not flinch from her gesture of love and compassion and her willingness to spread the gift of curved flesh that she now bared with her right hand—the hand nearest him, the one she'd reached out with but instead used now to unbutton her blouse and release her miraculous burden, which neither descended of its own weight nor shivered nor shrank in the conditioned air of the office. Nor did it wither under the brutal fluorescence from above. Her fingers then played with the hair on his right temple and seemed to remember that it once grew long, signaling protest and youth and pain, and that it once was brighter and blond, not dull and creaky, and that it had once worked over his ear in waves rather than struggled so sparsely gray and in a manner that would challenge an undertaker to make neat of now. She grew him backward into a place he thought he might never have been, to a garden he might never have smelled or tasted in the sweet soup of his youth, and she put him in the grasp of arms he might only have imagined, with a gentleness, a gift, a magical generosity of share and come-together and what's-mine-is-yours beyond the law.

She seemed to imply this: I will be old like you some day and you have been young like me, so it's okay if you take what I offer to you, a man who sits with people who cry and listens with less than a professional purpose and more like a priest who must of necessity be filled with as much grief as can be found in a bucket of blood.

"Don't worry, old man, take this," she didn't actually say, and it didn't actually feel anything like that when it happened. It seemed like it only now that he found himself dying again.

Oh, her left hand had reached out, and he could imagine its warmth on his right temple, could almost feel her fingers curl round past his ear to the back of his neck to pull him gently toward her breast and offer his forehead some rest upon its unfathomable softness. His mouth might then have opened, for he felt everything move within him—every sinew and twang of past consequence and chime he had longed for, along with the want that had preceded it so long ago.

But there emanated from the hallway beyond his closed office door an unusually portentous silence, which in itself constituted a space filled with suspicions about who might soon knock and interrupt what was going inappropriately on. But that would be wrong. Her grade was a fait accompli. The registrar had already posted it. There was nothing she could do to change it and nothing he could do to change any more than he had. It wasn't a matter of blame or bravado or bluster or bloom. It was what it simply was: He had given her a final grade of A. For willing inconsistency, for miraculous tense shifts, and for opening the gold box of Be.

Interrogation

When she came home in the evenings, Sally didn't tell her husband everything. It wasn't allowed. On occasion, at dinner, she would recite from her notes, but only in pertinent part (as the lawyers put it), sharing the substance of the afternoon sessions but few of the particulars. She would inject newfound phrases into her conversation, like *aggregate weight* and *OP* (Observation Point), and she enjoyed pointing out odd legal distinctions, like that between burglary in the fourth and fifth degrees. "So much of law seems to be about *possession*," she told her husband, Ben.

She dropped these tidbits at Ben's feet the way the family cat deposited dead mice at hers. Ben would listen, sort of, usually seeming already to know most of it. When she told him, for instance, that she'd discovered a new synonym for cocking a handgun—*racking the slide*—Ben informed her that the phrase was hardly new, and he went on to demonstrate on an invisible pistol just how it was done, even clicking his cheek to effect a ratcheting sound.

After two weeks—midway through the term—with less new jargon to report, Sally, known also as Grand Juror 13, grew laxer about her sworn oath not to repeat what transpired in the jury room. At times she just couldn't contain herself, like when she told Ben about the gunshot victim who had pulled up his sweatshirt and displayed his still-exposed intestines and his colostomy bag. She recounted how he'd told the jury that he'd simply been standing on the corner "conversating" when a stranger walked up and shot him.

"Hmmm," Ben had said, seeming genuinely impressed.

If, on any given day, the cases were cut-and-dried, she would describe the oppressive fluorescence and overheated stuffiness of the jury room itself. She drew a little diagram of the twenty-seat amphitheater and the small table where the two forepersons and the jury secretary sat, just so Ben could get the picture. She praised the court stenographers, even sketched a few of them for his amusement. She did what she thought was a hilarious imitation of Clara, the eccentric old woman who sat to her right, in seat number 12, telling in a squeaky voice how Clara (who wore sunglasses and a Yankees hat in the jury room) had once lived in the very same building where she and Ben now resided, at Riverside Drive and 116th Street, and how she'd been a fine arts instructor (Ben's department!) at Columbia in 1952.

But it wasn't until the end of the third week, just as the first guests began to arrive for their annual Saturday night holiday party, that Sally told her husband about Grand Juror 11. "I think you'd like him," she called out to Ben, as she rushed down the hall to press the buzzer.

If Ben hadn't picked up on the strange breathlessness of her declaration (and there was no evidence that he had), she herself had blushed about it at the time. It wasn't that anything inappropriate was happening between her and Juror 11. She hardly knew the man. It was more that she wasn't sure *what* was happening, and she didn't want her husband to become aware of her confusion or attempt to clear it up for her.

"Listen," she'd said to Juror 11, on the third day during the midafternoon break, "my name is Sally, and I just want to tell you that I wish I could get my husband, Ben, to wear hats the way you do." That's how she'd introduced herself! Juror 11 had handled this assault gracefully, asking if Ben was susceptible to skin cancer, but he hadn't offered his own name in return, or said whether he himself was susceptible. The subject of skin cancer (Ben *had* had a few removed) then had led, for some ridiculous reason, to Sally's description of her husband's wardrobe. "Ben has a *complete* disregard for appearances," said Sally. "A typical professor. He always dresses casually, like you, even for weddings and funerals."

"I have one suit to my name," said Juror 11.

"So does Ben!" she blurted.

"Mine's still got wine stains from 2001—hasn't been out of the closet since then."

"Ben's too!"

It was true. The two men seemed a lot alike, though Ben, sixty-five and ready to retire in June, was probably a little older. This man was what, fifty-eight? Sixty? Silvery hair to Ben's full head of white. No wedding ring. No briefcase. Always an interesting book in hand. Sneakers, linen pants (in December!), blue

L.L.Bean work shirts. Even his gold-rimmed glasses looked a bit like Ben's.

As she leafed through *The New York Times Book Review* on the morning after their party, Sally blushed again at the maddening way she'd dragged her husband—in her mind—into nearly every conversation with Juror 11. Why hadn't she asked him what had occasioned the wine stains on his suit in 2001? She watched Ben now, slouched at the far end of the sofa, her darling crossword-puzzler lost in chintz, his slippered feet plunked on the glass-top coffee table. He would doze off soon. Yet, if she were to go for a walk right now, he'd turn on the game. She was sure of it. Next year at this time they'd be gone from New York City and Columbia University—retired upstate. She'd head up there early; her hands would be digging in the earth this coming spring, no more indoor pots. Ben would putter about in the renovated garage, as he'd always wanted to do. Her sons could visit between semesters, each with his own room.

For supper, she and Ben consumed catered leftovers in the kitchen—bits of chicken and tofu, English cheddar, cold asparagus with a hint of garlic, day-old bread from Zabar's, and the last of the open Chablis. Rehashing the party, they assessed the state of various marriages, made note of the Rosens' grown-up children, the sound of Karen Winnow's solo flute, and the oddly eerie wind whistling off the river last night.

"So, who's this juror you've met?" said Ben, brushing crumbs from the counter and dumping them on his plate.

"Oh, nobody, really," said Sally. She shuttled some dishes toward the sink. "Just somebody with a brain in his head, which can't be said for everyone there, that's for sure."

"You sounded intrigued," said Ben. "I know when you're intrigued, you know."

"I'm intrigued by you," she said.

"Oh, rubbish," said Ben. "Pure rubbish." He stood up and stretched, then padded down the hall to his study and shut the door. Sally tidied up for the house cleaner, then ran herself a bath.

* * *

What did he do, even? She hadn't a clue. Always early, he sat at the far end of the long mahogany table in the jurors' lounge, near the open window. He never seemed hassled or rushed like most of the other jurors, seemed rather to enjoy being there. Sally had taken to arriving early herself, even with all the shopping for Hanukkah and Christmas, and for a week now, she'd boldly plopped herself down directly opposite the man. Each would read until one of them—Sally usually—spoke. "Good book?" she might ask.

That kind of thing.

She lit a red tapered candle and placed it on the white footstool by the bathroom scale. She tested the bathwater, then lowered herself into it, enjoying the way the bubbly liquid eased the gravitational pull on her breasts. Nicely buoyant beneath the suds, they seemed their old alluring selves again.

One day last week, she'd noticed that Juror 11 was reading a biography of Saint Augustine. "Is it good?" she'd asked. "I don't think I read the review."

The man had looked up from his reading with such penetrating tolerance that she'd felt compelled to avert her eyes.

Then he read aloud: "Our yearning anticipates landfall, throws hope as an anchor toward that shore."

The words had stunned then fled Sally's mind. She had expected this man, who dressed so carelessly, to share her husband's academic cynicism. Just then, Clara had entered the lounge room and taken a seat nearby.

Despite her warm bath, Sally felt flushed and cold at the same time. All that remained of Saint Augustine's words was an abstract message of hope that seemed dangerously New Agey. And how had she answered it? It made her sick to think about now. "I don't have a single spiritual bone in my body," she'd declared.

As the memory of her response took shape, the white-tiled bathroom walls began to close in. Feeling entombed, Sally had to force herself to remain immersed.

"To be spiritual means to be infused with spirit, doesn't it?" the man had said. "We're all infused with spirit. It's not a matter of choice."

"Even stones have spirit," chimed in Clara, her tiny voice competing with the sounds of traffic rising from the street below.

Sally had smiled at Juror 11, hoping for a knowing smile in return, for some hint of complicity, but she found none.

"*Especially* stones," he said.

Sally undid the clip fastening her now-wet hair, unwound her braid, and let her thick gray hair fall where it would. Cupping her hands, she scooped water to her face, washing away the beads of sweat that kept popping onto her forehead, then stroking back the hair at her temples. If she were kneeling at an oasis, she would do this, she thought. The rhythm of it, the simple sound of water splashing. Proof of her life on earth.

"My sister got all the spiritual genes," she'd said, hoping that Juror 11 would take that offering as an excuse for her density. But the man just raised his eyebrows, waiting for her to continue. Clara said nothing. No other jurors had arrived, no possible interruptions.

"When my father died, an owl got into the house," she'd eventually heard herself say. The words had left her mouth without permission.

"Where was the house?" asked Juror 11.

"In California. Not southern—northern."

"How old were you?"

"Oh, I wasn't young. His death wasn't unexpected. Nine years ago, I think."

"Were you there when he died?"

"I got there the next day."

"How did the owl get in?" said the man.

"Through a window. My father had a little shop attached to the house."

"What kind of owl?"

"A small one, like so," she said, her breath feeling insufficient for this interrogation.

"Let the record indicate that the witness is holding her hands, one above the other, about a foot apart," said the man.

Sally had laughed sharply, her sheer gratitude for the injection of humor causing her to exhale with an abandon that usually signaled the onset of tears.

"I almost caught it," she went on. "I used a broom and my father's heavy work gloves. It took all afternoon, but I finally got it to fly out the little window again. It pooped everywhere and left a lot of feathers around, beating its wings against the beams. What I'm saying is that my sister—the spiritual one—saved the feathers and gave me one after we buried my father. She thought the owl was an important visitation, that the feather was a sign."

"And you?" asked the man. "What did you think?"

"Pure rubbish," said Sally. "My sister was my father's favorite. Personally, I thought the owl's appearance was serendipitous at best."

"Did you keep the feather?" asked Clara.

"No."

Sally sank farther into the bathwater, her ears going under, her wet hair tugging gently at her scalp. It was Ben who'd thought the owl's appearance was "serendipitous at best."

"I was the bad sister," she'd said, "the atheist, the anti-war radical, the nut."

"The prodigal daughter?" suggested Juror 11.

"I guess so," said Sally, "except that I didn't go back home. I went to Berkeley and never looked back. Ben was teaching there. It's where I met him."

* * *

Sally hadn't wanted jury duty. She painted best during daylight hours. She'd begged off successfully twice before, until an unambiguous summons finally arrived, stamped MUST SERVE. She gave into it because she had no choice, but if the truth were known it wasn't such a hardship to serve three hours in the afternoon for four weeks. (Five hours, all told, including travel.) Juror 11 had put it this way: "I like being forced to be here. It's a section of town I never choose to visit on my own."

Which was precisely how Sally had come to think about it.

She felt around for the plug, drained a few inches from the tub, ran the hot for a full minute. The candle flame burned as steadily in the moist air as a child's night-light. Ben would be in bed by now, if he wasn't still on the Internet. They'd had separate passwords for years now, she and Ben, separate websites, separate laptops. Established in cyberspace, they were free now to pull up their urban roots. She could sell as many paintings on her newly designed website as in her gallery in Chelsea. Ben could always teach online.

Not that her roots were really in New York. "I have family in South Dakota," she'd said to Juror 11. "Distant family," she'd added. Ben had no use for her mother's side of the family—hated South Dakota, despised the Midwest.

"Distant family?" asked Juror 11.

"I never see them," she explained. "My cousin Margaret married a Sioux Indian. They had four kids who burned up in a trailer fire six years ago, in Rapid City. I kept their picture on the refrigerator—until that happened. Now I just send money to a children's fund. I never hear from Margaret. Her mother's long dead. Her husband's in prison. My mother was raised on a farm out there, but she never talked about it. Her history is as dim to me as the history of South Dakota itself."

"That's sad," said Juror 11.

"I know," said Sally.

"There was an ocean there, millions of years ago," said Juror 11.

"I know," said Sally. "Somehow that seems sad, too," she added.

Later, she mentioned that she'd been born in a small coastal town in California. "On the Pacific," she said, as if he didn't know.

All of a sudden, Sally didn't feel up to a second round of hot water. Pulling the plug, she sat up and took a deep breath, dispelling some unspecified unease. *Is there really only one week of jury duty left?* She hummed a few bars of "Silent Night," segueing artlessly into the "Hallelujah Chorus." The descending bathwater left an appealing tickle on her skin. Her knees, like smooth and veined islands, slowly mushroomed into substantial mountains of flesh. Her breasts regained their weight, sloping like warm dough toward her armpits. She cleaned her parts in the last few inches of water and listened to the bath drain away.

Feeling slightly faint, she stood carefully, reached for a fresh green towel, and wrapped herself twice. She turbaned her head in white.

After standing still on the red bath mat for a moment to be sure of her balance, she loosened then lowered the green towel—slowly, inch by inch, as if for someone's benefit. Before her, in the full-length mirror, stood a decidedly voluptuous woman. Lit by candles from below, she looked statuesque. Athena, maybe, or the woman on the old silver dollars—the heavier-faced one, pre-1923. Sally enhanced the mythic image with aloe lotion, watching herself as she applied it, drawing her hands up her sleek legs as if she were pulling on stockings. What man could resist this body, even now? Two grown men, having issued forth from it as infants, now inhabited the world. The youngest was developing a drug habit, according to his current girlfriend; his older brother was desperately clawing his way into the movie business, a world Ben detested. ("What is this intern stuff?" he'd demanded at Thanksgiving. "Those Hollywood creeps are rolling in it! Make them pay you! Start a union!")

Juror 11 had put it this way: "What is it that compels your son to be a movie director?"

Fluffing her damp still-auburn bush, Sally thought of allowing her imagination to go where it would make no sense to go. She could feel a pleasant effervescence building in that nether region, a sensation she'd long ago learned to channel into her best paintings and, for lighter diversion, into sex with the man most available to her. There might still be life changes ahead; she knew that. But she was too far out on the branch for any major forks; her life could not sustain a weighty new passion. The marital compact she'd made at age twenty-two, she would keep into old age, even unto death. There had been some hard bumps in her marriage, of course, but she'd grown used to whatever doubts they'd aroused, the way the old maple in the pasture upstate had grown used to the barbed wire some farmer had stapled to it decades ago. Over time, her strong will, her sheer refusal to entertain what her imagination even now suggested she entertain, had simply overgrown and eaten up all doubt. Desire survived in her like an itch, never absent but never intolerable, either.

* * *

She first pronounced his name on Monday, the sixteenth day of her service as a juror.

"He's an intriguing man," said Clara.

"Tobias?" said Sally, looking up from her Christmas list.

Clara jerked her thumb at the empty juror's seat on her right, and nodded.

"Yes," said Sally, "I guess he is." *Tobias*. Having aired the name, she pondered the sound of it. Not just another one-syllable thud, like *Ben*.

Clara then made a shushing gesture with her lips and pointed to the front of the room. A young assistant district attorney, dressed smartly in a beige suit, had entered and was positioning herself behind the witness table. She now reintroduced herself to the grand jury, saying she wished to reopen a case they'd heard last week.

"You may remember," she instructed, "that you gave this case the code word MACE. Of course, your recollection is what decides these things. Do the members of the grand jury recollect that code word? Seeing nods from the jurors, it seems they do."

The case involved an attempted rape in an elevator, one that had gone awry when the alleged perpetrator had ostensibly sprayed himself in the face with his chosen weapon. Testimony had been elicited the week before regarding the quality of the "perp's" erection—both before and after the botched attack.

Sally had noticed Juror 11—Tobias—silently convulsed with suppressed laughter. He'd had to leave the room.

"What do you find so intriguing about Tobias?" whispered Sally.

"Shhhh," said Clara.

Tobias showed up in time to help indict the mace rapist. But he spent the entire midafternoon break pacing the outer hallway, talking on a cell phone. At the vending machines, Sally pressed Clara for details, as if they were schoolgirls. But Clara did not elaborate on the word *intriguing*.

"Where does he come from?" she asked, instead. "Where does he go? Is he a spy for City Hall? An undercover jury spy?"

"I'll bet he is," said Sally.

"I *never* eat M&M'S," said Clara, poking buttons "D" and "5," and watching excitedly as a plastic bag filled with the candies was nudged by a mechanical arm from its shelf into the receptacle below.

"I never eat Fritos, either," said Sally, inserting three quarters and punching "E" and "2." Fritos, she'd noticed, were Tobias's favorite, and she managed to pass him her unfinished bag before the session resumed. At five o'clock, Tobias donned his hat and coat and left without so much as a wave goodbye.

On Tuesday, Sally arrived early to find the young Asian woman, who sat all the way on the other side of the jury room, sitting directly opposite Tobias in the lounge. They were sharing sushi from the same plastic containers, even dipping into the same wasabi-and-soy-sauce mixture. Sally, beyond all reason, felt faint at the sight of them and spent several precious minutes gripping the sink in the steamed-up ladies' room. Emerging from the toilet, she took the chair next to Tobias's. This woman hadn't offered a single question to a witness during the entire proceedings, hadn't said a word to another juror for weeks. She'd voted to indict every single drug case, even when most of the mothers in the room had refused (on principle), and here she was, suddenly a font of information about places to see in Thailand! Her tiny, unsupported tits poked at her pink cashmere sweater, and she swung her crossed leg under the table—stimulating herself, if anyone ever was, though you'd never know it by looking at her impassive face.

Time was draining away!

At the first chance, Sally revealed to Tobias that she and Ben had been to Thailand just last year, that she'd stood at the foot of the Emerald Buddha, ridden the river at night in Bangkok.

Wednesday smelled like snow, until the sun came out. There were barely enough jurors for a quorum: only sixteen of twenty-three, including Tobias, who'd arrived with no time to spare and who, during the break, sustained an intense discussion about the state of the world with another older man. (Ben would have loved it.) Sally, sitting directly opposite Tobias, again, watched the two of them go at it. They talked in the same way that old men play tennis—not so much competitive as eager, perhaps even grateful, to play. They agreed on nearly everything: their odd silence about the ongoing drought; the unseemly warm December days; the obligations of a benevolent ruler in an age of division. Their agreement only enhanced their fervor. Then, as quickly as they'd taken it up, they dropped the discussion, filled their plastic bottles at the water fountain, and reentered the jury room.

"What's new?" was all Tobias had said to Sally as he squeezed past her chair.

What's new? she asked herself.

* * *

Thursday was the day. Sally shopped at Rizzoli on Broadway during the noon hour; she found the dictionary her oldest son had said he needed and bought Ben the latest T. C. Boyle. Pausing at the section labeled "Spirituality," she spied an odd little book of translated haiku by Basho. Flirting with the idea of buying a token present for Tobias, she opened it and read:

> Learn about a pine from a pine
> and about a bamboo from a bamboo.

It seemed a bit pedestrian, and weren't there too many syllables? Or not enough? She perused other titles, but they all seemed rather inaccessible. Alan Watts—she knew his work. She'd purchased *Cloud-hidden, Whereabouts Unknown* at the City Lights Bookstore while still an undergraduate. She could even now envision the sunlit nook where such titles were to be found. Would the section have been called "Spirituality" back then? Hadn't everything been political? Had she even read Alan Watts? She hadn't chosen Berkeley to be "cloud-hidden" but to be involved. Art and politics had meshed nicely, in those days. From his assistant professor's pulpit, Ben had spoken sagely of the need for integrity and risk.

And Juror 11? How would he take to being given a present, anyway? It wouldn't be appropriate.

* * *

Sally wolfed down a banana before descending the steps to the subway, wolfed another upon exiting at the Borough Hall stop.

Tobias was there when she got to the ninth floor of 100 Centre Street, sitting in his usual chair, alone.

"Well!" she said breathlessly, taking her seat opposite his. "I see I'm not the only one who's early today!"

As she put her coat, scarf, and bag on the next chair, she felt the blood rushing into her wind-chilled cheeks. "What a day. Busy, busy, busy." When she sat down, she realized there was nothing at all on the long mahogany table between them. "No book today, Tobias?" she asked, greatly relieved to have finally called him by his name.

"No book. And you can call me Toby."

Sally felt a stab of regret. She should have bought him the Basho.

There followed a moment of rare silence in which the two of them simply sat looking at each other. Snared by the stillness, Sally held her breath. Thinking about it later, she would realize that almost anything could have happened just then. The space for something to happen had been *huge*. In her memory of it, the event would expand in time from perhaps a fraction of a second into several seconds, the moment becoming elastic with the bulk of possibility. Within it, their hands might have touched in the center of the table, or their ankles brushed beneath it; their fingers entwined atop it, or their lips met after leaning over it. In movies, fully dressed people had sex on tables like this, the woman's panties yanked roughly to the side, ripped even, to facilitate insertion.

But, in the long run, it was the image of Toby's quiet gaze that Sally allowed herself. She would come to feel that she'd managed to communicate all her longing to him. Not a longing for him, exactly, but a longing that had been born because of him: longing *as* longing. She would never tire of revisiting this . . . what? This single tick of the clock?

Yet it was she who broke it off.

"Want to see what I got Ben?" she asked. Five of their ten private minutes were wasted showing Toby the T. C. Boyle novel, and then the dictionary. Five whole minutes before she finally asked Toby what she'd planned to ask him from the get-go.

"Where would you travel right now if you had your druthers?" she said.

"Tibet," he said, so quickly that it shocked her.

It would have been pathetic if she'd said, "Me too," or something similar. All her life she'd wanted to visit Tibet (not the spiritual Tibet; the *place* Tibet, the mountains), but she didn't say so just yet.

"Why Tibet?" she asked.

"Because that seems to be where the flame was kept," said Toby.

"Are you a Buddhist, Toby?" she asked.

"No," he said, "just another interested party. And you?"

"Ben is Jewish," she said. "Culturally speaking. He's non-practicing. Our last name is Waldster."

Toby waited.

"I was born Sally Harper Winston. Protestant, Your Honor."

"Let it be so recorded," said Toby.

"I've always wanted to see Tibet," she said. "But Ben isn't interested. His specialty is the Renaissance. We only went to Bangkok because Columbia sent him there to lecture."

"Why not go alone then?"

"Because I think he's afraid he'll lose me to the world."

What she'd meant to say was that Ben was worried for her safety. She must have said it that way a million times before—to friends. That it had come out this other way scared her, but she let it stand, the way she sometimes just went with a quirky brushstroke on the canvas. Toby was nodding now, as if her unintentional implication that Ben *could* actually lose her to the world (or to other people in it?) somehow made sense. In this permissive atmosphere, the ridiculous notion began to snowball, looming suddenly as a distinct possibility. Years of objection to it vanished.

Three other jurors had arrived. More were filing in from the hall. The jury warden, entering from an adjoining office, nodded hello to Toby on his way to the men's room. Everyone seemed looser today, it being the next-to-last day of the term. Sally wanted desperately to ask Toby about the flame being kept in Tibet, but with all the mingling, the room had taken on the strained ambience of a cocktail party. To pursue a subject of such consequence seemed futile.

The session began on time. Three indictments went down without a hitch—two burglaries and one spousal abuse.

At the midafternoon break, Sally saw the Thai woman pass a business card to Toby. He pocketed it then shook her hand. Clara horned in next, chatting with Sally until the session resumed.

A case involving two counts of armed robbery, and additional charges of weapons possession and assault, sent the post-break work into overtime. At exactly five o'clock, though, Toby gathered his coat and hat onto his lap. Reaching across Clara, he passed Sally a folded piece of yellow paper. He gave Clara's arm an affectionate squeeze, nodded goodbye to both women, stood up, and quietly left the jury room.

A juror in the front row had just raised his hand. The assistant district attorney was approaching him. Sally put Toby's note in her purse, without reading it. She avoided Clara's eyes. When the session ended, she said, "See you tomorrow, Clara," then headed straight for the elevators. It wasn't until she'd crossed through the dark little park and come to the lighted area where Franklin Street meets Lafayette that Sally took out the note and read Toby's scrawly handwriting:

Sally,
Regarding Tibet: I hear October's best.
Toby.

After stopping by Rizzoli Bookstore once more, Sally showed up early again on Friday. She was not really surprised to find an empty jurors' lounge. She'd half planned to give the Basho to Clara, anyway. Although she'd dressed nicely in matched green corduroys, she'd also planned to wear them to dinner, so nothing was lost by it. Clara showed up with a large box of chocolates, which she shared with all the jurors. Sally chose an orange-flavored heart.

The grand jury was called to order by the warden, who thanked everyone for their service, and then dismissed them on the spot.

It wasn't even dark outside, much too early to head home. Sally walked north, wending her way west in random increments, coming finally to Greenwich Village. She sat by the window in Caffe Reggio and ordered a cappuccino and a glass of water. Smoothing the wrinkled yellow notepaper on the table, she read Toby's words again. Then, opening her notebook, she tried to sketch his face from memory, glasses and all, without looking at the page. The result was a portrait of Ben.

* * *

At dinner with the Rosens that night, Sam Rosen was going on about his oldest daughter's honeymoon in Europe the previous summer—how they'd found a charming room in Hotel Danieli in Venice, and how they'd spent a romantic week in Positano on the Amalfi Coast. He turned to Ben and said, "But you two have been to Positano, haven't you? Or was it Ravello?"

"I, for one," said Sally, "have decided on Tibet." Her impatience with even the idea of the Amalfi Coast was unmistakable.

An awkward silence ensued but was ended when Ben informed Sam that, indeed, he and Sally had seen *both* Positano and Ravello. "I actually bumped into Gore Vidal at the Villa Cimbrone," he added shamelessly.

"Who on earth doesn't adore the Dalai Lama!" Beth Rosen sighed, touching Sally's hand.

"Well," said Sam, "the guy is certainly at the top of his game these days. Hollywood's behind him. How many bestselling books?"

"Sad," said Beth, "what's happened over there—in Tibet."

"Yes, it is," said Ben. "All the art is gone, I'm sure. But we still have half of Europe to see, don't we, Sally?"

"Half the world, I suppose," said Sally. She knew how to meet Ben's eye, and she did it now. "But Tibet's at the top of my list."

"Well," said Ben, pressing his weight against the unyielding chairback.

"So, Ben!" said Beth, raising both arms and shaking her bracelets, like a rodeo clown distracting a bull from a downed rider. "Tell us about your moviemaking son! What's *he* been up to lately?"

When Sally reiterated her intention to go to Tibet, Ben said that he'd think twice about that, if he were her.

"China's demolished all the temples, anyway," he said. "It's an unstable region of the world."

"I'm going in October," Sally announced.

Several seconds passed before Ben, having readjusted his posture, noted that October would be the height of the foliage season during their first autumn upstate.

"There will be other autumns upstate," said Sally. "Tell Beth about our moviemaking son."

The Query

Nancy could shatter store-bought lumber with the heel of her hand, but during our first thesis conference, in early autumn, when she had searched her phone for a photo of her dog, her fingers resembled those of a child. She was slight of build but alive with intensity, her aquiline nose protruding sharply and with romance between two no-nonsense eyes. Her face, which was both flat and round, lent her the demeanor of an Elizabethan mask and made her expression seem timeless in an odd sort of way. Despite her size, her aura bristled with kick and strike. She'd earned a black belt at age thirteen.

Now Nancy shut the door behind her and stood there in a long black winter coat, buttoned to the collar, waiting for me to indicate where she should sit. I pointed to the chair that sits at a ninety-degree angle to mine. She removed her backpack, the kind I myself carry between class and office.

"I asked you to come in," I began, when she'd sat down, "because you mentioned in class that you haven't been sleeping."

When you teach, it's your privilege to ask probing questions and to learn all you can about a college student, even if college counselors consider it their rice bowl.

"That's right," she said. "I lie awake half the night thinking."

"I wanted to be sure it wasn't because of the personal essay I've asked you to go deeper with. Or if it does have to do with the essay, to be sure that we keep the pain in front of us, you and I, in a productive way."

"My parents are both Buddhists," she said.

"I see," I said. But I didn't, just yet. I reached for the porcelain container my wife had purchased that week so that I could bring good coffee to work. I poured two cups, each half full.

"These cups get hot," I said, "and you need this stupid rubber sleeve to hold them safely."

"Better than wasting trees with cardboard sleeves, like Starbucks does," Nancy offered.

"I suppose," I answered. "Do you think that what you just said is a Buddhist response?"

"What?" Nancy asked.

"Does the urge not to harm trees have its origins in Buddhist thought?"

"It might," she said, pushing out her lips to signal that she was thinking it over—or that she was about to chop me in the throat. I couldn't tell which.

"Maybe not," I said. "Have you ever heard a tree scream when it's hit with an axe?"

"God, no!" she said. "But I can break three two-by-fours with one blow of my hand."

"They don't scream when you do that?"

"They go 'Ouch!'" she said, laughing.

I laughed, too. "I bet they do."

We sat in silence for a bit, which gave Nancy the opportunity to take off her winter coat, fold it in half, smooth it, and lay it neatly on the floor next to her backpack. She settled back and crossed her legs with the care another woman might have brought to the task of arranging flowers.

"So why?" I said.

"Why what?" she said. "About sleep, you mean?"

"If you like . . . sure. About sleep or sleeplessness."

"Is that what you meant? Do you want me to talk about sleep?"

She knew better than to ask me this. I waited for her to remember that I expect nothing from students and that I will always throw the responsibility for the answer back on them. We were at an impasse. I had fought a black belt to a standstill.

"I think it's because I have a lot on my plate," she said.

"Have you tried breaking the plate?"

She laughed. "No. But I broke two pieces of china when I was a kid, and my mother has never forgiven me. They were part of a set. I was carrying all eight of them at once, and two just slipped through my wet fingers. I caught the rest."

"Yes, you did."

"How do you know?"

"Because you just said you did. Go ahead."

"Where was I?"

"You were carrying your own plate—as an adult—and you were thinking that you had a lot on it. Or maybe you have seven invisible plates under the one you're carrying now and that's what's making your own plate feel so heavy."

"Meaning?"

"Yes, it might have something to do with meaning. What's on your plate? The one on top."

Nancy looked at me, then at my bookshelf, as if something there might clue her in about how to answer me. I followed the direction of her gaze to an eclectic blur of titles.

"What do you see on that shelf, Nancy?" I asked.

"I was just looking at the books. I see you have one about Switzerland."

"Have you been there?" I asked.

"No."

"What do you think it looks like there?" I asked.

"Big, I'd say. Steep."

"What color comes to mind?"

"White. Snow."

"You are very beautiful, Nancy," I said.

"What do you mean?"

"You are a beautiful person, and you have great courage, the way you've directed your energies. What does that feel like?"

"To be beautiful?"

"To be so focused with your energies—to be so directed and intense?"

"I don't know."

"Is it scary sometimes?"

"Yes, actually."

"Why?"

"Because I don't always know what's next."

"Have you run out of black belts to earn?"

"Yes. There's only so many degrees at my level."

"Understood, but maybe there's another level beyond belts . . . ?"

"Well, there's teaching," she said. "I could teach."

My sciatic nerve had begun to throb. This was my fifth conference of the afternoon. I reached across my body and with my right hand took hold of my left armrest. I did a gentle twist.

Then I did one the other way. I took a deep breath and let it out. I felt a dull click emanating from my spine, a muffled sound, like the croaking of a white pine in a winter wind. The muscles in that region of my back relaxed, and the pain that had been shooting across my left buttock receded.

An air of ease blossomed between Nancy and me as I sat back in my chair. Silence creates a negative pressure that, in turn, feeds the open space in which we grow. That's how we become who and what we are. Space is always alive, which is why we breathe it in, and why emptiness and loneliness are so thrilling and scary in their need to be filled up.

"Teach?" I asked, as if we were talking idly about the weather. I kept my eyes averted so that whatever she said next would occur spontaneously without any help from me. I listened. In the distance I heard a siren, probably coming from the west, a wail so filled with grief I had to finger the crease of my pants to keep from crying. So much pain in the background of our days.

"I could teach martial arts," said Nancy.

"I'm sure you could," I said. And then I said, "But why?"

"Why?"

"Yes, why? Think about it for a minute. Why do you want to teach something if you are so good at doing it yourself?"

I looked directly at her now, etching my question on her brow. It looked brand-new on her skin.

"It isn't the money, obviously," she said. Her smile bumped up the corners of her eyes, and her brow softened. "Little kids, three times a week over the summer."

I nodded.

"Just getting the belts—I don't know why—it isn't enough for me," she offered.

"You're very accomplished," I said.

"But once I've done it, it's done," she said. "I need something else—a goal maybe?"

"What kind of goal?

"Life goals. You've heard of them, right?"

"Aren't goals better left to soccer or hockey?" I asked. "What happens when you reach your goals, what then?"

"You die?" she said. "Just kidding. Just kidding. You set a new goal, I guess. You adjust."

"So the goal is always out there, in front of you? For the picking?"

"Of course. Way out there sometimes."

"Always outside of you?"

"Yeah. Out there. Sometimes long-term, sometimes short."

"Never just organically within you?"

Nancy shrugged.

"Who would keep track of these achieved goals, Nancy?"

"I guess I would."

"How would you know when the goal was reached? Where would you store the proof? In a trophy cabinet with your black belts?"

"Ha ha. Maybe in a journal?"

"Maybe," I said. I *had* suggested to her class that keeping a journal was a way of storing memory jogs, useful when you got old.

"You know, Professor, you ask a lot of questions. Haven't you ever read a self-help book?" She glanced again at the bookshelves.

"It's my job to ask questions. It'll be your job, too, when you teach."

"*If* I teach, you mean. I'm not sure yet."

"How will you be sure?"

"See! Another question!"

"A question implies an answer. It stops the predictable narrative. Recocks the starting gun."

"Really? Does it really?"

"See! Look how your question just chiseled its way into our conversation. Now you're querying the question, digging deeper to get an answer."

"What if there is no answer?"

"Then the question becomes the answer. Permit me one more, Nancy."

"One more what?" she asked.

"One more question."

"Okay, one more. I have to get to the dining room."

"Where in your body do you *feel* it when you teach kids?"

"In my body?"

"Yes, the part of you that isn't legs and arms and head. Your body, where you feel things before your brain turns them into emotions."

Nancy glanced at the ceiling, as if seeking help, then lifted her small hands from her lap, slowly, as if dowsing for the feeling I had asked her to locate. I watched them linger at the level of her belly, then rise up past her belly and settle softly on the region of her heart.

"Here," she said. "I feel a lightness here when I teach."

"Yes," I said. "You do."

Near Genius

Waking from his nap, Professor Poe Jackson sat up frantically, as if snakes had invaded the office sofa. His chest felt painfully constricted, and his heart swelled with a raucous commotion. In his dream, James Joyce and Ernest Hemingway were dining together in a restaurant. As he approached their table, he noticed an empty chair awaiting him. Suddenly realizing, in the dream, that Joyce and Hemingway were dead, he looked over his shoulder to see where he was. The rest of the dining room was empty, the waiters and customers gone. Beyond the huge doors through which he'd entered, nothing but white.

A wave of dizziness jellied Poe's muscles as he clung to the arm of the sofa. The dizziness was something new; the palpitations were not. To subdue them, his daughter Carrie, a Buddhist, had instructed him to breathe purposefully—to shut his eyes and imagine with each round of breath that he was inhaling and exhaling the entire universe. The technique usually worked, and Poe obeyed Carrie's instructions again now, only he kept his eyes open for fear of revisiting his dream. *Universe in . . . universe out.* His breath whistled in his nostrils like wind passing through reeds in a swamp.

A streak of April light blasted through the leafless red maple that loomed above the north end of Campus Walk. Abandoning his visualization of the universe as a nonspecific immensity, Poe turned his attention to the amazing old tree. Its wild array of forked branches suggested the infinite complexity of life, but its overall shape, governed as it was by its quest for light, seemed serenely simple, uplifting, and of a piece. The tree had reddened with pre-foliage buds in recent days. Greening wouldn't occur for at least a week. Poe would be eternally grateful for just one more week.

"I'll give up eggs," he said out loud, understanding immediately how pathetic that would sound to a god.

Several minutes passed. The pounding in his chest subsided, and the dizziness grew less pronounced. The phone rang. Once . . . twice (his wife, Betty, always rang once, then dialed again, so it wasn't her) . . . three times . . . four . . . In the absence of a fifth ring, Poe remembered that he had a student appointment in five minutes. It would be his second obligation of the day. The first had been his awful meeting that morning with the new dean of faculty, Carol Hillburn. Dean Hillburn had spoken of the refreshing influx of "new blood" into the faculty and staff—at least three times. She'd used the impending renovation of Baker Hall to evoke the unpleasantness that lay ahead for "*all* professors, Poe, young *and* old." At one point, she'd clenched her fist victoriously as she marveled at the faculty diversity in the year 2001. Poe had ridden out the meeting patiently, nodding mostly. Dean Hillburn was deadly; there was no other word.

An aspirin bottle sat on the edge of his oak desk, just two arm's lengths away. Poe pushed himself up from the sofa and stood with all his weight on his heels, so that if he were suddenly struck dead, he'd fall backward onto the sofa, rather than head-first into the desk. Shuffling forward in stocking feet, he reached for his pills, shook loose three tablets, and popped them into his mouth. He chewed the little pills, making a bitter mash with his saliva, then swallowed. Better than bypass surgery.

Gripping the desk, he made his way around to the high-backed leather swivel chair—a present from his oldest son, Harry, on his, Poe's, seventieth birthday, two years ago. "The Emeritus Chair," Harry had dubbed it, though Poe had yet to retire. Seated, he felt a return of optimism, bolstered by the fact that he'd thinned his blood, but bolstered, too, by anticipation. The student he was scheduled to see, William Kettle, was one of the most promising young writers he'd encountered in his entire teaching career. The first thing Kettle ever said to him (this was four years ago now) was that Hemingway didn't really know how to write and that he was scared people would find out. "My stuff is better," he'd said.

Professor Poe had *loved* the arrogance of that. Of course, he'd dutifully given Kettle several good reasons why he might be a bit off in his assessment of the famous man. But Kettle had insisted: "Come on, Professor, put Hemingway next to Proust—no contest."

"Make your case in writing," Poe had told him, and Kettle had done just that, in an essay titled "Hemingway and Me," about Kettle's growing up an adopted Black child, with a di-vorced white father who had worshipped Hemingway, spoken like Hemingway, and eventually killed himself like Hemingway.

Very few of Poe's undergraduate students had enough raw talent to command attention the way Kettle did. Some were in-tuitively brilliant, but the problem always boiled down to sus-tained effort. What drives *anyone* to write? Whence the hunger?

Most young aspirants in this age of prosperity were cursed with an abundance of career alternatives and thus destined for a life of bewildered lethargy—a vagueness of purpose they'd later attribute to writer's block.

Kettle was different—rim-lit with anger. That's what Poe liked about him. It was primal stuff, born of fear, perhaps, and in need of transformation, just as Poe's had been when he first came to the university after serving in Vietnam. For him the anger had come from growing up in Miami, Oklahoma, at the end of the Depression: His fear of duplicating his father's desperate obscurity, combined with his own anger at his obscurity as a veteran, had sustained him throughout his adult life in New York City. That anger—never explicit—had fueled each one of his five novels.

Kettle's anger, on the other hand, seemed to come from being too *much* in the public eye—his father having been a prominent Washington lawyer. Prep school educated, wealthy, he'd never even had to think of going into combat, never wanted for anything, probably—except, perhaps, a different skin color. Poe suspected that Kettle didn't want to be trapped in his skin; he feared a racial destiny. Racial issues rarely surfaced overtly in his stories, but the unspoken pain of racism—being seen, yet unseen—often drove his protagonists to dramatic self-definition and gave them their edgy voices.

Kettle was a quiet sort, tall, heavyset and sad eyed. He bore his weight with style and had developed a kind of easy slope-shouldered gait that seemed, to Poe, a cross between street swagger and the kind of professorial arrogance you saw on the walkways of Trinity College, in Dublin. He would clutch his books to his chest with one arm, as Poe himself did, and seemed always to have something of importance on his mind.

When the phone rang again, Poe answered it immediately.

"Poe here," he said, coughing up a flake of aspirin that had lodged in the back of his throat.

"Hello, Professor." It was Kettle. "I'm on my cell, can you hear me?"

"It's two o'clock," said Poe. "Where are you?" Poe was hell on students who were late. Hell on cell phones, too.

"Something's come up," said Kettle. "I can't make it."

"You found out about it just now?" said Poe. Merciless. You had to be merciless to teach.

"Can I call you right back?" said Kettle.

"Alright, William, but I don't have all day."

Poe hung up. A flock of starlings suddenly rose up past his window and landed all at once in the leafless maple. A brittle chatter accompanied their move, its volume increasing to a crescendo of complaint, then fading out. Poe watched the manic birds hopping sideways along the branches. They did this every year, energized by some collective inner wind. And he'd been here every year to see them—sabbatical years in Ireland excluded. Different birds, of course, but still the same species—just like the waves of students over the decades.

Classes would be over next week, the class of 2001 graduating in May. Kettle had chosen Iowa for graduate work. Two years in Iowa, then Europe, maybe. Poe imagined Kettle returning to this university someday, perhaps to teach, perhaps just to find his old teacher. Who would he find sitting at this desk?

Minutes passed. The professor was on his feet now, hovering over the phone. What had he left to say to this kid? What words of encouragement, which of warning, which of hope? He took a deep breath, fighting a renewed constriction in his chest. He managed to fill his lungs several times, making him aware of his taut musculature and the dreadful creaking dullness of his bones. He tried humming to distract himself.

When the phone rang again, Poe wasn't so quick to pick it up. He couldn't talk to Betty just yet, though it would please him to hear her voice. He could use a laugh to take his mind off things. She always giggled so readily at the way he answered the phone when he knew it was her on the other end: *Stately, plump Buck Mulligan here,* he might say. Or perhaps he'd begin by reciting an odd ditty from this or that literary work to see if she could guess its source: *The cock crew / The sky was blue,* for instance.

Picking up on the third ring, the professor turned and sat one buttock on the edge of his desk, so that he could look out over Campus Walk. As he waited for the caller to announce himself, he realized he was looking at William Kettle two floors down, sitting with his back against the red maple—cell phone in his right hand, his left arm around a girl's shoulder.

"It's me again."

It took a few seconds for Poe to marry what he was seeing with the voice on the phone. "Hello, William."

"Sorry about that. I've been so damn busy, can't even catch my breath."

"Right, well, it's that time of year, William. Exams and all." Poe hunched his shoulders, tried to shake off a trembling in his neck.

"Yeah . . . Listen, I just can't make it in today. I've got—"

"Excuses are for the man who needs them, William."

"What I was thinking was . . . " Poe watched as Kettle adjusted his position, crossing his legs and making a lap for his girl's head. "What was it you wanted to see me about today? I mean, can we do it over the phone right now?"

"Do what, William?"

"Talk."

"Alright," said Poe, suddenly aware of some deep urgency within himself. He was off the desk now, moving closer to the window, his eyes locked on the scene below. The room seemed cold in spite of the direct sunlight. He'd initiated this meeting with Kettle, but he wanted his student to show some interest.

"What would you like to talk about, William?"

"Nothing, really, Professor. I thought you had something in mind."

"How about the future?" suggested Poe.

"What about it?" asked William.

"What's it going to hold for you?"

"How do you mean?"

Poe could see Kettle gesturing to the girl to be patient. "What's it going to be for *you*, William?"

"The future? How can I know that?"

"What do you *want* it to be?"

"I don't know . . . Successful, I guess. I want to make it as a writer. I know that much. You know that about me." The girl poked Kettle's shoulder. "And, I've got a girlfriend. She's a keeper. I know that, too."

Poe widened his stance at the window and locked his knees. There seemed to be a huge difference between the temperature of his brow and the perspiration that had suddenly accumulated on it. He swiped at the cool moisture with the back of his hand. Switching the phone to his right ear, he shook out his left arm, trying to rid it of a painful pulsation and tightness. He wanted to warn Kettle that he must give writing his all. It was not a good sign that his student had decided against making an appearance today. It didn't bode well. You had to be single-minded to be a writer. Had he not made this clear to him, quoting someone, he knew not who: *Genius is the agreement not to love*?

"Why do you ask?" said Kettle.

"Why do I ask?"

"Yes." Kettle was stroking his girlfriend's close-cropped blonde hair.

"Curiosity, William."

"Curiosity?"

"How are you going to protect the writer part of yourself?"

"From what, Professor?"

"From competing interests."

"Such as?"

"Such as life's many distractions."

"Like?"

"Things that take the place of writing, William. Booze. Women." The dizziness was back. Words fled from his mouth, effortlessly. "Marriage. Kids. To name a few."

"Don't worry about me," said Kettle. "And, anyway, hey, look at you, Professor. You managed. You did okay, in your day."

Poe suddenly imagined it was *him* down there, *his* back to the maple, Betty's head on his lap. He pictured the grass growing tall around the tree, then the leaves turning and falling all around them, then the snow drifting over. That was it, wasn't it? Life builds and builds, and it gets harder and harder to shovel out from under who you love.

"Okay is not enough, William. It's not enough just to manage."

"Alright," said Kettle.

"Inspiration's only half the game. You have to focus on nothing else."

"I know," said Kettle. "I know, it's hard work."

"The work never stops—you need to write until you get to the heart of it."

"I know. You've said."

"Over and over again, you must do it again and again."

"Okay."

"I never actually—" said Poe, pausing to take a breath.

"Never actually . . . ?" said Kettle after a moment.

"Heart," said Poe.

"What?" said Kettle.

The professor had meant to say that he'd never been able to give writing all his heart. That he'd never climbed out from under the lived life or the teaching, never seen his way clear to do the really great work. That's how he'd say it, if Kettle would just show up in person and help him to a chair. He wanted to elaborate right *now*—everything so clear right *now*—but, as he opened his mouth to speak, he heard his knees hit the metal radiator cover and watched helplessly as the windowpane—still speckled with winter soot and water stains—came rushing at him. When his cheekbone hit the cool glass, he heard it crack and watched a thin silver line slice through the image of Kettle and his girl down there. The sizzle of splitting glass made Poe want to giggle and weep at the same time, but the breath to do either was gone. The sound had quickly merged into sunlight, sharp and stitched like distant lightning, and the clatter of the phone hitting the floor came to him as the dull sound of thunder on the Southern Plains. Just as he'd once imagined it, as a child gazing out from his bedroom at a lightning storm—that it would come for him, eventually, just like this.

Elk Meditation

Coming to the edge of the forest, where the wide plains and open sky lie unfurled before me, I bugle into the soft evening air: *Hear me. Find me again in my echoing voice.* Then I wait until I see her head emerge from an area of tall grass that has heretofore disguised a dip in the wavelike land. As she draws slowly nearer, her neck and shoulders become visible and soon her long, lovely legs.

She stops some distance away, and we stare at each other for a long while, perhaps not quite believing our luck. When she turns her head to gaze at the western horizon, where the richest light lingers, I glance toward the north to get my bearings, and then I peer into the already darkened east, where foretelling happens.

I can smell the dryness of the grass as it welcomes the developing dew. The fragrance of new growth mingles in my nostrils with the rich and layered odor of forest. Both aromas pull at me equally, engaging memories of the sowing and reaping of my life, and confirming the rooted sturdiness of my desire.

I feel solid where I stand.

A hawk cries overhead. The first bat shoots past. A mosquito makes its busy purpose known.

I will not need to bugle again. Once is enough. It is a condition of trust that what's trusted feels inevitable.

Softly, and with great elegance, she collapses in the grass and waits. I resist the invitation her acquiescence implies, feigning, I suppose, indifference: a more masculine state of mind.

His is a ruined world, I imagine her thinking.

I look around me once more then move with studied authority toward the place where she sits. She looks not at me but shyly at her folded legs, which seem from here both subdued and wildly alive. I know there is nothing to say. No need, even, to whisper.

The forest watches us like a concerned chaperone six leaps and one bound behind me, but there is no argument from that direction. I own the wide-open world, and it fills me with bravery to know it. Already some newness is occurring within me.

Soon I am standing beside her, a subtle engorgement in my groin sending a crescendo of ripples through my body, beckoning my heart and mind to join in. Kneeling in the grass, I feel my whole being conspiring to produce my velvety array. The violet dusk implores my antlers to convey the complexity of my episodic life: a story of many endings, to be sure, but spiked arrivals, too.

I am here, am I not?

I read in her averted gaze that she has awoken to my return without fear. Old bulls do not normally intimidate the cows. And I can tell from her shyness that she needs to hear from one who is not threatened by the apparent unsteadiness of the horizon on gray days—or by the vibration that occurs in spring, when seduction has value again.

Of course, the land around us has been gobbled up and claimed since our last encounter, as has the intervening time. The ongoing revolution we call existence has seen to that. But the edge of a forest remains an edge no matter where one draws the line, and she must have sensed that it was from the edge—and only the edge—that I would appear.

We do not speak about our marriages or our children, or about anything in the past. Dawn will come when we are done, and with it the all-too-common day.

The Algebra of Desire

It all came to a head on a midday drive to the New Moon Mall, along that stretch of two-lane road bounded on both sides by acres and acres of scorched corn. Sent by my wife on an urgent errand (and having taken the side road as a shortcut to accommodate her urgency), I instead came upon a red-and-white-striped construction barrier blocking the right lane. Beyond the barrier, a huge multitoothed grinding wheel was churning up old pavement. Six people of indeterminate gender were jackhammering the centerline with a desperate intensity, causing a sickly gray cloud of dust to fall in thick sheets upon a fleet of support vehicles. A ghostly plexus of throbbing cables and hoses writhed in the dust, as if in concert with the excruciating din emanating from the site.

When a tattooed flag lady wearing a silver hard hat and wraparound sunglasses suddenly materialized at my open car window and told me to stay right where I was until the opposing line of traffic could be waved through, I almost lost it. It was already the hottest July on record in Johnson County, Iowa, and the sun was boring mercilessly into the interior of my un-air-conditioned Toyota. The prospect of roasting interminably in the noonday sun combined with the echo of my wife's admonition not to "dawdle" in the supermarket aisles must, now that I think of it, have intensified the already unbearable tedium of my domestic life—a tedium that had grown more pronounced with the absence, every summer, of my graduate students.

In quiet desperation, I reached blindly into the glove box for some music. The cover of the CD I came up with pictured Lucinda Williams in the act of pulling some article of clothing over her head. As I stared at the orange-tinted photograph of the singer—probably snapped with a point-and-shoot—a mysterious image from the past insinuated itself into my conscious mind. Slowly it became 1972 again, and I was watching a young woman toss her car keys onto a motel dresser. In the slatted sunlight pouring through the blinds, she removed her tank top, revealing her uplifted breasts and smooth belly. A pair of low-slung jeans clung precariously to her somewhat angular hips, and her navel floated above her beltline like a daisy all alone in a field.

Not a lot of air-conditioning in those days and no digital alternative to boredom. Nothing much to do. but work hard and play. Me turned thirty-two and thinking I should be a great writer by then—filled up to here with gas and ready to go, but somehow needing a jump start. Still needing a prompt.

You can't know what I'm talking about, except as the muse applies to you. But in my case her name was Angie, and she drove a baby blue '68 Chevy Impala with a false-bottom gas tank, which is how she ferried the white powder to distributors in the countryside. I would invite her to my motel room or visit her house after a day's work at the circus, or during my meal breaks. I'd just amble across the street from the big top area—which straddled the state line between Missouri and Kansas—and there she'd be in her rented lime-green ranch, perched on the arm of an easy chair, say, alongside two of the nicest Black guys you could ever hope to meet. Soft-spoken dudes lounging on the sofa with sawed-off shotguns on their laps, watching re-runs of *My Three Sons* on TV.

Angie had adopted a male Doberman named Three—a snarly dog that, before he got to know me, once put his open mouth against my crotch and made me stand on tiptoe against the bathroom wall next to the medicine cabinet. Only pot could pacify the beast. It made him smile in his sleep.

Angie liked me because I was not of her world. She was my teacher, I suppose, and I imagine she knew it. And I was hers, thinking back. I would read her long passages of crazy prose from stuff that was still in vogue at the time, like *Naked Lunch* and *Tropic of Cancer*. Some nights, we just sat with a beer on the patio under a bare 100-watt bulb that attracted so many in-sects you'd have thought it was a nightclub. One evening she got me to recite from a beat-up old paperback of e. e. cummings poems. She liked the obscure ones that made no sense if you expected them to.

"There you go, Billy," she told me when I read her favorite poem. "Learn to write like that."

One day (it must have been a Monday, when the circus was dark), she took me with her on a shopping trip to a downtown leather store. She bought herself a purse then browsed the men's section, where she picked a belt off the rack and selected a buckle from a box full of buckle shapes: a bronze snake biting its own tail. She stuffed both items into her new purse and walked right past the cash register without paying. Outside, on the sidewalk, she removed the belt and presented it to me in full view of the salesgirl, who was staring at us through the window—smoking a cigarette and looking amused. The belt was nearly two-inches wide, and when I used it on Angie's pale buttocks that night, an imprint of square-shaped waves carved deep into the leather remained briefly on her skin. When I put my open palm gently on the welts, Angie whispered, "That's it, Billy. That's how."

She was long-legged, slightly pigeon-toed, and naturally blonde. She laughed the way a child does, with no distance between impulse and result. I trusted her completely and very much appreciated the bodyguards, with whom I sometimes played Crazy Eights before turning in. I didn't love Angie. I wouldn't have known how. But I romanced her a lot on hot and memorably slippery nights in the un-air-conditioned master bedroom of the anonymous home where she probably kept the neighbors awake with her high-pitched expressions of pleasure.

And then one day, after my two-month gig with the circus was done—when I'd stowed away the high wire rig, and the elephant and I had pulled up the last of the perimeter stakes—my training as a child and my schooling as a young man, not to mention the expectations of my wife back east, called me home to a less adventurous reality, one that involved a hopelessly sick child.

There have been many times, across decades of dutiful marriage, when I thought of Angie and tried to imagine my life had I remained a fixture in her world, a bit of furniture in the architectural plan of a woman so in charge of her own nature you couldn't even tell she was running the show. Where might it have gone, such a life? Try as I might, I could never conjure up an ending.

We would not have grown old, I think.

To be clear, I didn't go right home when the circus was done. On what I assumed would be our last evening together, I told Angie that I regretted selling my 750 cc Norton Commando. "I could have taught you to ride," I said, "photographed you going flat-out on some desert—naked, with your hair streaming out behind."

"Like a comet!" she said. "I like that."

I confessed that I had also imagined hopping on behind her and caressing her naked nipples in the wind.

"Really?" she asked, teasingly.

"Really," I said.

"You swear?"

"I swear."

Her smile widened effortlessly. "W-e-l-l-l-l . . . ?" she said enticingly.

Three days later, we were in Death Valley, resting for the night in a crazy little last-chance "resort" that some born-again goat had hammered together atop cinder blocks in the sand. I remember a cactus-shaped headboard studded on top with "needles" made of finishing nails. You could rent handcuffs at the counter.

The next day, I took pictures of Comet Angie creating a contrail of dust on a flat expanse of the Mojave. Before we left, I hopped on behind her, and, just as the first raindrops in years fell, Angie cranked up the borrowed bike until the needle hit 90, then dropped her wrist and slowed way down so I could finish the fantasy from behind.

By then, America was well into its headlong stumble. All those loyal, hoodwinked kids, too confused to resist the war. It was never the same after that. Lies and conspiracies had corroded the whole idea of democracy, and what happened was that people came along who never knew the truth and hence didn't care. And very soon everyone had forgotten the history, or gotten it wrong, and when the drought kicked in and the fires began, people started pouring more war on the flames.

There are lots of Okies in this country now, millions and millions more than in the Great Depression, but California is full this time around. And we still haven't come clean about how the whole mess began—with our treatment of the Indians.

But I've let myself drift. I apologize for that. It's what happens when you sit on the porch too much and watch too many sunsets. You realize that you didn't say what you could have said when the world needed your voice. It all starts gushing out too late.

* * *

By the time the flag lady—that tub of scalded misery wearing a silver hard hat—finally waved the traffic through, I was more than a little pissed, but I looked diligently straight ahead and swung out into the left lane as instructed, even gave her a little nod of thanks, acknowledging that she'd simply been doing her job. There was always the possibility that she wasn't a flag lady at all but Ganesh in disguise. Ganesh (as I repeatedly warn my students when they complain of writer's block) is both the remover and the *placer* of obstacles, which makes him a sneaky little deity, built like a linebacker and just about as fast on his feet. Take a detour to avoid him, and there he'll be, right in front of you again, in the shape of a doe or an adder—or even a possum pretending to be splatter on the centerline. Sometimes he'll turn into a woman; he likes to dress up, being a child of his mother alone. He plays a drum. Always there's a mouse or two about.

Mice make quick the task of scurry, which is how Ganesh sends the message that things are about to change.

And change they soon did: The flag lady grew tiny in my side-view mirror, and the stream of traffic behind me finally obscured her altogether.

Half a mile farther along, after cruising like a race car driver constrained by a yellow flag—and enveloped all the while in the sweet odor of benzene—I snaked back into the right-hand lane, still in the lead. I floored it with great pleasure, my old Toyota. The hot summer air whomped and sucked at my four open windows, sounding like the lungs of Jonah being brought back into service. I felt grateful for the turbulence, and within my gratitude I sensed that maybe there was something else to be done, other than the errand I'd set out to do before being detained: that my destination might change, or had changed, and that my attachment to duty might shift. But, clearly, I would need to recognize the opportunity as it presented itself—snatch it from thin air and plunk it right down on the page, so to speak.

I glanced again at Lucinda, whose voice had remained sleeved in the CD cover while I waited at the barricade, but who was still lying face up on the passenger seat—my two-dimensional copilot, so to speak—a woman who clearly spelled trouble but seemed simultaneously (as she pulled her shimmery whatever over her head) like an angel about to sprout wings.

And because I said out loud to her, "*That's* what I need—an angel," there appeared in the most unlikely place on earth—in the vast desert of the future that the road had become—a shimmering oasis up ahead. The name of the establishment, it soon became apparent, was the Apricot Fountain Café.

I resisted the quixotic lure at first, unable to formulate a legitimate reason to pull over and stop, especially after being delayed for so long on the errand my wife had sent me to accomplish. I didn't need a restroom. I had crackers in the car and all the sad tunes of my audio friends. And I could buy water at the mall. *No need to stop*, I told myself.

But then, inexplicably, my right arm buckled at the elbow, its collapse causing the steering wheel to swivel the Toyota's front wheels a few degrees. My right foot responded to the change of plan like a drummer's, and I began thumping the brake with my toe. Suddenly, I was orchestrating a diminishing wind. I had lost the lead. More ambitious people flew past me, and a few even honked in anger. I heard loose gravel being rearranged in hard dirt by tires whose pressure had increased to near bursting. Pretty soon, I was reaching for the ignition key and turning it toward me.

The faithful engine gurgled and spit, shuddered, and died.

As I sat there, ignition key in hand, heat accumulating like lava on the floor of the car, and me just staring through the windshield at a bright-orange arrow reading GARDEN IN BACK, I realized that when it came to my errand—and my marriage—all bets were off.

* * *

When I think back on it now, I'm hard-pressed to explain how there could have been a cool breeze in the walled-in garden behind the café. Or how, if there really was a breeze, it could have remained so conscious of me as I moved along the uneven stone path toward the one table with an open umbrella. Not a human in sight. A few sparrows, a butterfly, a catbird complaining about its name. Blossoms everywhere. Some bees.

The self-consuming sun was still high in the sky, still as belligerent about growing old as any of us would be if we were locked into a barely discernible orbit, with everything else dependent on our light.

I got what the sun was up to, calling attention to itself above the garden, and I sympathized with its murderous need to loose its broil onto someone else. But at the same time, as the cool breeze ushered me to my chair, I felt enormously humble in that green and gentle space, within which I could hear no hint of traffic, no throttling or zooming, no purpose at all.

A collection of soothing molecules clustered around me like a mob of waiters clamoring to serve a celebrity. I pulled the cushioned wicker chair away from the hot metal table and settled into it as one might ease into a cool tub. I felt like a child in its embrace. My spine clicked and cracked. My head rolled slowly in both directions. All the knotted nonsense a neck can become gave way to a mysterious and patient rebraiding of nerves. I felt new to this life, I swear. The pink and blue impatiens near my shaded table bobbed their heads. A Japanese maple postured at the edge of a dusty mosaic of shards.

How can one's entire, weary reality just crumble in a matter of minutes? Where is Babylon today? What city was that, and when? Who *are* we when we're simply present to this life, served by a carefully negligent breeze?

Once, a long time ago, in Rome, I was standing at a bus stop, clueless about everything that would soon occur in my life. As the bus pulled up, I happened to notice an almost featureless face half buried in a patch of dirt at my feet, a timeworn sculpture lying in the shadow of the Roman Forum, too unremarkable to have been resurrected and put on display. The bus pulled away without me.

But I got where I was going, didn't I?

The cool molecules eventually dispersed and moved everywhere else, without taking my order. In their departure I read a quiet admonition to decide. I looked around the garden, taking it all in, including the new bamboo shoots growing in the corner where the fence abutted a cement-block tool shed. Ants worked the world at my feet, single file lines of ambitious citizens carrying burdens away and coming back for more.

* * *

When Angie and I were returning from my fantasy in the desert to her lime-green ranch in Kansas City, she said, "We can do it right now, right here."

We were sipping Cokes and eating blueberry pie in a Utah diner, listening to poor dead Janis Joplin on the jukebox. A few lean folk and some sugared-up children occupied the nearby booths. Outside, our borrowed motorcycle leaned like a drunken horse on its kickstand, the front wheel nodding sleepily in the sun.

"Do *what* right now?" I asked, dropping my fork and shaking a Marlboro loose from its box, putting the last few bites of pie on hold. I snapped open my Zippo, flicked the flint, and sucked in the sizzling narcotic delay. Dumb as a post about what Angie was up to.

"We can do it right now," said Angie. "In the ladies' room. Behind the bushes. Out back. I don't care. Let's make a baby and see what it means."

I looked away and thought of my ailing son back east, how just yesterday my wife had described on the phone what the doctor had said: Daily doses of digitalis might work for only a few more months. Nothing I hadn't expected but still hard to hear, coming from his mother.

"It means another mouth to feed, Angie," I said, "and I already have one."

"You're missing the point," she said.

"Am I?" I asked, looking over my sunglasses, as if I knew more about life than she did.

I hadn't told Angie about my son's condition. Our time together had felt safely parenthetical. I didn't want that to change. If something's parenthetical, it can remain obscure—an aspect of the narrative you might choose to remove in the edit. An allusion with which the reader can do what he or she wishes, but for which the writer need not necessarily account. In those days they called children afflicted with Down syndrome "mongoloid idiots." It was hard news to hear from a doctor and even harder news to communicate to friends, and when it came to telling those people with whom you just wanted to live wild and be free that your life could never be wild and free again, well, that was just too sad for anyone's ears. Not to mention having to describe to them the then-inoperable heart condition that in my son's case accompanied the syndrome, and how the very word *inoperable* felt paradoxically like a solution. I loved my doomed and gleeful child—my truest teacher, all things told—but it was a love bent permanently on the anvil of shame.

I hadn't told anyone at the circus, either. We were a small crew and just worked hard and laughed a lot. Made good money. Sent it home. The elephant knew, but that's another story.

"You can live any way you want, you know," said Angie. "It's up to you. Come on, let's do it. I can feel a boy's spirit knocking."

I sensed that she was talking about mine.

* * *

No waiter appeared in the garden of the Apricot Fountain Café. Since I'd gone unnoticed, I felt no obligation to stay. But as I followed the path back toward the parking area, I noticed a jog on my left, a gentle elbow of reach paved with white pebbles, which led to a shiny-black screen door. I heard my sandals shuffle to a stop, and the sound they made alerted the café's darkened interior to my presence. The tinny ring of cheap silverware being racked in a dishwasher hung longer than usual in the air. A mouse probably stopped what it was doing. I smelled condiments and coffee and maybe a happening sandwich of some kind. I could tell it all in advance. That's how I determined it was real.

I waited for a moment, considering my deepest and most precious needs, and in doing so I gave my needs power over anything my fear might stipulate or my will override. I took a few steps along the crunchy white-pebbled jog, and I opened the black screen door. Crossing the threshold, I found myself standing in a room as empty of humanity as the garden had been—except for a young woman seated in the far corner with her back turned, almost exactly as I would have imagined her. I pulled the screen door shut behind me, quite firmly, bracing myself as my prescience about what I would find in that room ballooned like an airbag into a jolt of reality.

To be honest, I hadn't foreseen that she would have dark hair. Perhaps I'd half expected to see Angie herself sitting there. Nor had I anticipated the stunning chiastic balance suggested by the woman's hunched-up right shoulder. Propped on one elbow, she seemed to be reading a book. I waited for her to turn and notice me, to confirm my presence in that place, that day. But it wasn't up to her.

* * *

Singing along with Joplin, Angie looked past me, out the window.

I said no to making a baby, of course, right there at the table. What kind of man would have done otherwise?

"Am I not a good lay?" she asked. "I've got a shitload of money. Our lives would play out like a dream, like when you have no idea what's coming next: no expectations, no rules, just all-out *go*. And sex. Can you *imagine* that? And you can write about it any way you want. I won't mind."

"You mean like 'let's live suddenly'?" I asked, quoting her favorite e. e. cummings line.

"Yeah, but even more sudden than that. That poem's already been written, Billy. Write it new for me. You know what I mean?"

"Yes, I do," I said.

And I must confess, I procrastinated for two more days, until we'd returned the motorcycle and it was time for me to go to the airport. I told her that I had long yearned for and could well imagine such a life.

But it wasn't true. To fully imagine anything, you must play it out on the page. To live that freely, you must be willing to expose your imagination to the death that awaits everything. Over and over again. The story always fails. It's never quite right and never enough, and it always dies to give the next story room. Even if it's good, it dies. Yet if you don't actually go there with your imagination, the story can't ever have lived, either.

Once again—when the taxi came—I told her no.

To be fair to my younger self, I'd had no experience to compare the death of a child to—no heartbreak, yet. No big failure.

* * *

I couldn't just stand there in the back room of the café like some old idiot who'd forgotten why his wife sent him to the store. Nothing was going to change what I'd already ventured into, even if I were to spin on my heels and flee. You start down one path—it becomes the path you're on. The choices your characters make become the choices they made; those choices determine what the truth you set out to find will be.

But I did try to delay the temptation. I walked straight to the men's room in back. Standing at the toilet, I waited for the piss to come, but the piss belonged to the heat of the day. I told myself that I could just as easily ignore the woman whose back I so much admired, and as I checked in the mirror for chin stubble and nose hair, I decided to do just that: I would walk right on by. Right past her table, into what seemed to be the main room of the café, then right out the front door to my car.

I flushed the toilet, in case someone might wonder why I hadn't. Leaving the men's room, I walked determinedly along the little aisle created by some pushed-together tables. An oil painting of a gathering dust storm hung on the wall behind where she sat. I dragged out the time like a dream-walking man wearing buckets of cement on his feet, staring at the artist's composition of the storm, noting the textured roil of the dust.

From a distance of several feet, I observed the sheen of her long black hair, perceiving in it a thrilling waterfall of expression and noting the sweet ease with which each strand negotiated the terrain of her beautiful back without once splashing onto her magical bare shoulders. The flow stopped abruptly, scissored neatly at the point where her slim waist turned to hip.

I stood stock-still beside her now, as helpless as a fighter who's just been dealt the penultimate punch. Dizzy with anticipation of what was already happening, I gazed in her direction as if looking back from tomorrow. She lifted her head from her hand, and I read in the soft eagerness of her expression a longing almost equivalent to mine. Her eyes were as dark and deep as the outer reaches of an expanding universe. In them I detected myriad plot twists and infinite endings. Gaseous whirls of meaning began to organize and stream toward a single point, alluding to the origin of everything and reminding me how to begin.

Her smile widened effortlessly as we stared at each other.

"W-e-l-l-l-l . . . ?" she said enticingly, offering an open palm toward the empty seat across from her.

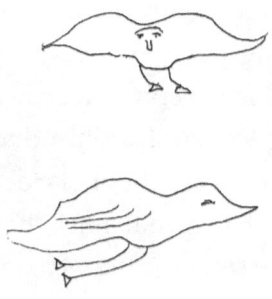

The Grand Ceremony

The posture in itself is the grand ceremony.
—Zen saying

As I reentered the world of human communion, after a brief period of contemplation in the soft hills of memory, I noticed a young woman standing at the glass bakery case, near the entrance to the crowded restaurant. She stood quietly next to a cardboard hostess, who announced from both sides of her silhouette self, "Please take a seat."

I nearly flinched in my effort not to stare at the newcomer. She was looking for an empty chair in the busy place. My heart began jiggling and tapping, like a weasel caught in a box. After scanning the room, the young woman approached my small table and without a word sat down directly across from me. She placed a soft winter hat on the bleached-wood tabletop.

In earlier times, the hat would have been called a toque, from which stored information I instinctively extracted nine connotations of chime and gong. A toccata resulted in my not-unmusical groin, and I felt deeply touched by the silent message with which the young woman had introduced herself. Clearly, her presence was neither casual nor accidental. My breath returned to normal, which helped to hush the weasel in my chest.

In my long absence from the big city, during which I'd been exposed to fields and lakes, I'd come to treasure the soft stillness life has to offer, so it was perfectly natural that I would notice how her hair fell golden and straight along the slide of her cheek, settling gently against the scalene weave of her neck, like wheat laid down by the wind. Her hair would have caressed her spine, I'm sure, had she not been wearing a light winter overcoat—or had I been wizard enough to perform such naked imaginings from a more elastic perspective.

The serenity evident in the young woman's face surprised me, confirming yet again that anticipation is constructed almost entirely of precedent, blinding us to the reality we might actually find. I soon recognized the trap and quickly ceased having diddle with my mind. I took up residence instead on the second floor of self and read into the appropriate dimensions of her nose and mouth, and into the lie of her eyes and the smoothness of her brow, a timeliness supported not so invisibly as you might think by the Mozart that happened to be playing at the moment—as well as the dissonant echo of crowd, of course. The space she was cupped in felt rendered and right.

Suddenly, I heard a shriek from a teenager sitting two tables away. She screamed at her friend, "Ben Affleck can't act worth a fuck!" and slapped both her hands on the table. Her friend responded, "No shit, girlfriend!" and they both squealed like pricked pigs.

I allowed the squealing to settle into the past tense, waiting until it became the known value at the table. The commotion was what it perfectly was, and it would soon become the swarm and substance that connected our eyes—mine and those of the young woman who had just sat down with me.

It was quick, what happened between us, quick as a photon, even across a yardstick of reach—a brief agreement: The level of meaning we would pursue with each other from that moment on would be the level each moment had to offer. Smiling at the shrill language coming from the nearby table, I sent an etheric suggestion that we absorb anything the idiot girls and mindless crowd could emit, and that we ride the ambience happily, whatever it might turn into in the full and final version of our upcoming meal.

We said nothing.

She looked at my bread plate, piled three high with a choice of whole wheat, French, and rye, and then glanced at my squeezed-open gold-foil butter pat.

I thought, *How stupid to have started without her.* But since we had never met before this, I carried the guilt only briefly.

I buttered another bite of hard crust and ate it with all my attention. I granted her the space a hunter allows a deer when first he spots it, a space I would liken to disbelief—the kind that bursts forth from pure boredom, rupturing the stillness, but without belligerence. Disbelief is simply a thrice-folded glimpse of the present, during which all bodily senses shut down, leaving only the shudder you feel from the collision of coincidence and fate within the darkness of the folds. That's how opportunity blossoms—origami-like—a process my better nature says don't disturb. On this particular evening, my opportunity came when the young woman asked me what was good on the menu. She asked this while holding a menu in her hand.

(I am old, by the way. Have I mentioned that?)

So, it fell on me to answer her question, to declare what was good on the menu, which felt intimidating because so much these days simply isn't good or happy for the creatures being harvested, or promising for human karma.

But, *Fuck it*, I thought. "Shrimp," I said. "The shrimp salad is great."

While I buttered another break of bread, she ordered the goat cheese and red beet salad, which I could have told her was drenched in balsamic vinegar and which she, being Danish, wouldn't like. Did I just say Danish? Sorry. I am suddenly narrating in a nonlinear way. But, in fact, I think I'd guessed her heritage by then.

I could have leaned across the table and embraced her with ease.

* * *

Our waitress in this establishment was an Irish gift of grace—round-faced and rosy-cheeked. I enjoyed the uninterrupted way her left triceps participated in the sharp flex of her elbow when she lifted my empty coffee cup from the table. She had thanked me several times for my patience, as if patience were currency. Which of course it is. I had already issued some when she spilled the coffee and then more when she forgot my water. I have a good supply of patience, which I keep handy in the depths of my ear. I access it simply by pulling the earlobe. I learned this trick from Buddha.

Would you like to know how and when?

Okay, but don't forget where we were. Just remind me that my shrimp salad has not yet arrived, and that the young woman (whose name, I will prematurely divulge, is Emma) has not yet regretted her own choice of salad, nor come to envy my shrimp, nor asked me if I'd like to join her at her apartment, in a search of her bookshelves for something good to read.

Just remind me that we still haven't yet left the restaurant or watched the dawn together, okay?

* * *

Some decades ago, near the end of the Vietnam War, I visited the Metropolitan Museum of Art and aimlessly wandered into a quiet room, where a huge bronze statue of the Buddha had been put on display. I took a seat on a mahogany bench, directly in front of the ancient figure. There was no one else in the room. Buddha sat cross-legged on a broad wooden pedestal, vaguely gazing in my direction—peering *along* my direction, is more like it, staring blindly through me, through the walls we call "museum," and perhaps even through the million walls that we recognize in photographs as the Tri-State Area. Buddha was somewhere else, you might say, and it made me feel very young (which I was) and very, very powerful (which I wasn't) sitting there on a shiny wooden bench at the Met, alone with Buddha. Any old idiot with bourbon and riot on his mind would have felt equally manly in that room.

I was thinking something like, *This is Buddha! This is important.* And from that thought came another, more logical thought—a conclusion: *If Buddha and I are here in this room alone together, this moment must contain significance.*

Just as my ego was about to explode with some mustardy conceit, a little man dressed in monk's clothing and wearing sandals came strutting into the room. Never before had I seen such posture—and never have I since. It went beyond what the military can teach for ceremonial processions but evoked ceremony of another kind. We tend to think of size in terms of height and weight, but this man, who could have been no taller than an American boy and who could have weighed no more than a collie, had entered the room with the double impact of a bull and a mouse. He seemed both huge and slight, giant and child. He was so wispy I could have coughed him from the room with my Marlboro breath, yet so sturdy and grounded that I couldn't have budged him with a tank. He was, I realize now, totally *present*.

He stopped in his tracks and gazed with complete astonishment at the statue of Buddha looming over him. Instantly, he stood even straighter, like a string puppet jerked from above. His feet nearly rose off the floor. He looked at the Buddha with an amazement I could hardly believe, since, surely, he had intended to encounter this very Buddha in this very room. But then, strangely, I began to believe his surprise. It felt authentic and complete; his focus on the statue made the artwork seem new—gave the greenish bronze a sheen that I hadn't even sensed while sitting there alone. The Buddha seemed almost to notice him. So riveted was I by the posture and daring of this monk— the intensity of his discovery, the power of his totally unlikely surprise, and his obvious joy—that I could only hold my breath. He began pacing around the statue, swinging his shoulders like a samurai and exaggerating the length of his stride—stepping big, but without even a hint of sandal slap on the marble floor— and all the while smiling! His balance was exquisite. He walked around the statue a second time, pulling at his earlobes—both at the same time—tugging them hard and stretching them with a good deal of visible ouch in his eyes. He went around the statue three times in all and then, without so much as a glance back at me—his only audience—the little man left the room.

Exhausted, I slumped on the bench, like a coach who's just watched his team lose the game. The monk had stolen my sense of significance. I felt chastised, remote, excluded, alone, and invisible. I became a blob of slough. I nearly drowned in the puddle of me, almost choked on my own bewilderment. I was nobody.

When the puddle evaporated and the bench became dry, I looked up from my hunched-over misery at the bronze likeness of Buddha. He seemed not to have noticed a thing. Clearly, he couldn't have cared less. He was long gone. The monk was gone. And in the space created by their departure—and my own—I finally noticed the Buddha's long, droopy ears.

I *saw* his ears.

I knew then that I had far to go in the way I looked at things.

* * *

As I return to Emma, whose tranquility is about to be upset by the arrival of my shrimp salad, I am reminded of the impossibly slim distance between emptiness and what will happen in that emptiness next. Patience, like a surreal number, requires living very, very close to zero. So many people struggle with it, which is why I now keep mine in my ear.

Did you know it only takes ten pounds of pressure to remove the human ear? I often cover mine in public.

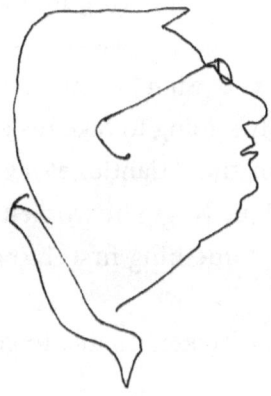

The Sounding

When Packer got the news that Joe Riley had died, the name didn't ring a bell at all. The call came from a video technician who introduced himself as Stan somebody, and who spoke with a presumptive familiarity typical of the new breed of film people.

"I've got bad news, Jacob," the guy said. No one who knew Packer well ever called him Jacob. Only Jake or Packer.

Guessing that Joe Riley must have been a grip or electrician, Packer said, "Sorry to hear it. Was he sick?" Learning that he was, Packer said, "Oh," with a touch more sympathy in his voice. Then he asked about Joe Riley's family, having no idea what family, if any, there'd been.

"They're doing okay," said Stan. "There's going be a little get-together at Sound Seven this Sunday, at five. Some food and a chance to say a few words."

"Right," said Packer, remembering now that Joe Riley had been a sound mixer.

"Nothing formal," said Stan. "You know Joe, he'd have frowned on it. The family's going to take his ashes out on Monday and scatter them in the Atlantic, along with his favorite tape recorder—that antique Nagra he worked with. We thought somebody ought to say something first. I know he worked for you way back when."

"Way back, yes," said Packer, unable to come up with anything more specific.

"Don't get me wrong," said Stan, "I know Joe had his problems. But he tried, right?"

Suddenly, Packer could picture the soundman: a thick-bodied, perpetually hungover curmudgeon, hunkered down in the dark behind his portable mixing table, peering out toward the working set. Nicotine-stained fingers and a bad complexion. A wife who'd died of cancer years ago; he remembered her now, too: a pretty woman, jet-black hair framing a milk-white face. Green eyes. But Packer could not for the life of him remember a single exchange he'd had with Riley.

"He thought the world of you," said Stan.

"And I of him," said Packer, tapping his pen impatiently on the kitchen counter, trying to think of some logical reason not to attend on Sunday—another funeral maybe.

"So, Jacob . . . Sunday, at five?" said Stan. "You'll be glad to hear that your name always came up whenever Joe reminisced about the old days. He used to say, 'Now there was a guy who didn't give a shit what *anybody* thought.'"

* * *

Fifteen minutes after hanging up, Jake Packer considered calling back Stan whatever-his-name-was and making it clear that his attendance would not be possible, due to a prior commitment. He poured himself a second cup of coffee and took it into his small office, the same little room off the hallway that his daughter had used, every other weekend, when she was little. He sat down at his desk determined to make the call, but when he flipped open his organizer to see how he might shift another appointment into that Sunday slot, the reality of his schedule became uncomfortably clear. There were no appointments to shift.

A decade ago (or was it more like fifteen years now?) this month-at-a-glance calendar would have been ridiculously insufficient to hold his busy schedule. Its pages would have overflowed with appointments—interviews, conference calls, casting sessions, preproduction meetings, location scouts, screenings. Christ, he'd have needed an entire calendar just for what went on *after* hours. In those days, working out of rented production facilities and propelled by what had become an obligatory mix of alcohol and cocaine, Packer's days had developed a compelling wavelike rhythm. Weeks gathered into months, months into years. Movie after movie after movie—the proof of it right there on videocassettes—third shelf up, next to the TV. He had aspired to capture that compelling period in a memoir, someday. Until a few years ago he'd been making notes—maybe five years now?

Today, as he studied the thirty-one little calendar boxes allotted for October, Packer found only two entries: a tentative meeting with a young screenwriter, on the sixteenth; and on the twentieth, "Abigail at 8?" The monthly dinner with his lawyer-daughter was never a sure thing.

Packer toyed with the idea of inviting Abigail to Joe Riley's memorial service, thinking she might get a kick out of seeing her sixty-year-old dad in the company of people who'd worked for him in the past. But then he remembered that she and her longtime boyfriend (a man he had yet to meet) would be in the Berkshires all week, visiting her mother.

His thoughts soon drifted to various lady friends (people might even *expect* to see him with a babe), but the thought of having to introduce whichever one it might be to people whose names he might no longer remember gave him pause. Anyway, being obligated to speak, he would need the freedom to work the crowd alone in order to glean some specifics about Joe. He'd want to make even a spontaneous eulogy lively, of course.

The idea of showing up alone and unprepared began to excite Packer. Perhaps he didn't even have to mention Joe, specifically. He could use some unrelated anecdote, then extrapolate an overarching life-death theme and deliver it to the assemblage of people. As a producer he'd learned to wing it in just that way. You did what you could to prepare—*define the project, hire the best, keep a tight rein*—but what separated the men from the boys was the way you dealt with the unexpected.

Yes. Of course, he would attend. It was only right.

* * *

On Wednesday, Packer took his fringed suede jacket to the cleaners, at Seventy-Seventh and Broadway. On Thursday he got new heels for his cowboy boots. Friday and Saturday saw him rise early and organize the file folders and old shoeboxes filled with ancient bar napkins and scribbled notes from which he planned to cull his memoir. He even managed to write a lively paragraph about his first meeting with Sherry Lansing, before she became the president of 20th Century Fox. And he followed that with an email to a literary agent whose card he still carried in his wallet. Late Saturday, he picked up his jacket.

On Sunday morning, Packer took a long walk in Riverside Park, hoping the exercise would inspire at least the gist of his eulogy for Joe Riley. But it wasn't until late that afternoon, while riding on the downtown number 1 train, that Jake Packer remembered the old bull elephant he'd seen on some nature show years earlier. He attributed the sudden memory to the herdlike behavior of his fellow passengers, as they exited at Lincoln Center. As he stood aside, letting people pass, Packer knew he had his eulogy.

The old bull elephant had been trying to find space at a water hole. Younger bulls ignored his efforts. They closed ranks, squeezing him farther and farther away from the water, and they took their time to drink their fill. The old bull didn't have it in him to fight, so he stood there on the outside of the group, awaiting his turn to drink. The herd moved on, and shortly thereafter the old bull died. The herd returned the following year and found the old bull's bleached bones lying scattered on the ground. There ensued a ritual of mourning in which even the young bulls participated. They picked up the old bull's bones with their trunks, and swaying to and fro, they sniffed the bones and waved them about in unmistakable gestures of grief.

Packer charged up the escalator at Columbus Circle and stepped out into the bright October light. He felt only slightly breathless, and very glad to be alive. What a day! *Grief. Grief at what is lost.* Wasn't that to be the message, today? Had not Joe Riley, toward the end of his life, been ignored and shoved aside in like fashion? Wasn't the old curmudgeon soundman being remembered this afternoon in the same belated way as the old elephant?

Tourists were everywhere about, bent against the wind. Packer yanked the brim of his white cowboy hat down over his eyes, gripping it between thumb and forefinger, as he walked west on Sixtieth Street. It was his signature hat—the one he'd plunked down six hundred bucks for, at Billy Martin's western shop, in 1979. Brought out of retirement for this occasion, it appeared weathered—like Packer's face—but weathered was good. What younger man could have conjured up the analogy of an old bull elephant? Just yesterday, Packer had stitched an eagle feather to the hatband. Catching sight of his reflection in a shop window, he had to admit the hat looked pretty sharp on his silvery head. And his new outsize sunglasses gave him the look of a man who was still in touch with power.

Packer crossed Ninth Avenue, the heels of his alligator boots clacking nicely on the pavement. The low sun cast long, angular shadows, adding to the Sunday feel of the place. Without the usual workday pedestrian traffic to blur the scene, the brick facades on the east side of the avenue looked downright Hopperesque. Packer couldn't help thinking that a second unit camera crew would earn its keep, capturing this mood. But for what movie?

Turning south, Packer walked to Fifty-Fifth Street, then headed west again toward Tenth. The wind was gusting heavily now, the river only two long blocks away. When he reached the corner, he stood for a few moments, trying to get his bearings. From here, he could see the building that was once Fox Stage 54. What a hassle they'd had getting permits to dig into bedrock beneath the stage in order to house the refrigeration units for *The Exorcist*.

With ten minutes left to kill, he walked south a few more blocks. A bright display of autumn color beckoned at the western terminus of Fifty-Second. Detouring in that direction would give him more time to mull over the theme of elephants.

He began walking briskly across the avenue, as a line of cars bore down on him. Quickening his pace, he made it to the opposite curb just as a gust of wind lifted the cowboy hat off his head and sent it tumbling back onto the avenue. A black limo swerved to miss the hat, but a sporty red Toyota drove right over it, catching it up in its undercarriage, dragging it north. The driver, his baseball cap askew, remained oblivious. Packer watched as the car proceeded uptown, leaving in its wake a pulsing, amplified bass, and the syncopated mantra "Muthafuckabitch . . . muthafuckabitch . . . muthafuckabitch."

* * *

Packer stood alone in the wide elevator of 540 Tenth, wanting his hat back. He wondered how his sunglasses would play indoors without it. Reflected in the stainless steel interior, his visage looked positively extraterrestrial. He took a deep breath and decided to remove the shades at his first encounter with another human being. He was not unaware that this was foolish behavior on his part, but neither did he wish to make an entrance without a prop—something to make people declare, "Whoa! A producer!"

The elevator door opened directly onto the huge fifth-floor loft occupied by Sound Seven. Packer had never been in the place before and suddenly wished he hadn't come. A wall of opaque north-facing windows failed miserably to register what kind of day it was outside. Fluorescent ceiling strips cast a weak pall on a dismal collection of cardboard boxes stacked floor to ceiling on steel shelves. To the left, a slapped-together office space gave the only indication that this was a place of business.

Packer heard voices coming from somewhere beyond the shelves. He moved into the loft as if transported on a dolly.

We all come to this, he thought. That's how he would begin the eulogy. Passing between the shelves, he came to an open area, bounded at either end by two green metal columns and separated from the wall of windows by a black backdrop. An odd array of chairs littered the space, some already claimed by overcoats and parcels.

A long-limbed skinny woman—East Indian, maybe—sat in the front, with the Sunday *Times* on her lap. She stared impassively at Packer. Ash-dark bags tugged at her lower eyelids, a vitamin deficiency, perhaps.

A small round table, draped in black and placed ceremonially in front of the chairs, displayed a framed 8 × 10 color photograph of a man seated in a rocker—Joe Riley, no doubt about it. Next to the photo stood a metal urn, and next to that a vintage reel-to-reel Nagra tape recorder.

No speaker's dais anywhere in sight.

A technician of some kind appeared from behind a wall, multiple keys dangling from his belt. The man nodded as he passed. "Food's this way," he said.

Packer, forcing himself not to turn and run, followed the man to another open area where about twenty people stood gathered on the far side of a long worktable covered with brown kraft paper. At one end of the table, plastic plates heaped with corrugated potato chips, sliced pickles, deli meats, and processed cheese balanced a drink selection of Gallo wine, diet soda, and a jug or two of water.

Packer didn't recognize a soul. But when he heard his name called, he said "Hey!" to the bearded man walking toward him. He stuck out his right hand and removed his sunglasses with his left.

The fellow wasn't young—it couldn't be Stan—and he didn't introduce himself. There was no hugging, thank God, but his handshake seemed sincere. "God, Packer, I haven't seen you in ages. Where have you been keeping yourself?"

Packer edged closer to the table and took a chip. "Been busy," he said. "Always something cooking."

The man leaned closer, lowered his voice. "You know what I was thinking about just the other day? Remember *Urban Angels*? Did we really snort blow off the tablecloth every fucking night in the Brittany du Soir? I mean, what the fuck were we thinking! What were *they* thinking?" The guy was laughing, emitting an odor of cheap wine. "That old, white-haired waiter, Battaglio? Kept trying to brush off the food crumbs, but we wouldn't let him because the coke was still on it? You started sucking on the tablecloth, made a big show of eating it. Remember? Hey, Packer, I want you to meet my new wife. Where is she?"

Packer looked around obligingly and caught sight of two young women, one of whom seemed to be awaiting her cue. She was upon them in no time, teeth agleam.

"Jake Packer, this is Teresa Longley. She kept her own name."

"Good for you, Teresa," said Packer, feeling a congenial warmth running from her hand directly into his veins.

"Pack's in hiding, Teresa."

"Really!" said Teresa. "I've heard so much about you. It must be hard to hide."

"He's writing a book," said the man. "Going to expose us all."

"Really!" said Teresa.

A skinny young man—probably Stan—was announcing something to the group, but Packer missed what was being said.

"You knew Riley pretty well, didn't you," said Packer to Teresa's husband.

"Been at that book for awhile now, right?" said the guy. "Weren't you—"

"A while," said Packer.

Teresa touched Packer's arm, smiling sympathetically. "You can't just dash off a book, George!"

George Miller! The assistant director! Packer had hated this guy, might even have fired him once. "When was the last time you saw Riley, George?" asked Packer.

"I can't wait to read about the shit we did," said George. "Teach these kids what fun used to be."

"Did *you* know Riley at all, Teresa?" asked Packer.

"Never met him," said Teresa. "Sad, huh? I was just talking to his daughter. She's so strong about it!"

People were beginning to drift toward the chairs now, herded by the fellow with the keys.

"Can't wait to read it, Pack," said George. "Spell my name right."

Packer moved with the others toward the chairs. He wanted water, but there wasn't time—not even time to grab an anecdote or two. People took their seats. Packer watched as family members settled into the front row, then he went up to the only young woman among them and extended his hand.

"Jake Packer," he said. "I worked with your father. I'm so sorry."

"I'm Carol, Mr. Packer." Carol remained seated and didn't entirely engage Packer with her eyes. She seemed exhausted.

"Whenever you're ready . . . " said Packer, figuring that the timing of this affair would become apparent as it went along. He released her hand and moved off to the side. He stood there, with his back to the shelves, waiting. No one looked his way. Family members began speaking from their seated positions. A woman whom Packer took to be Riley's sister spoke first. The high ceilings, and perhaps the cardboard boxes, absorbed the sound of her voice, as if she were speaking underwater.

From where Packer stood, he could see Joe Riley staring out from the color photograph. Perhaps the poor light enhanced the effect, but Joe's face had clearly mellowed. Gone was the wrinkled brow, the scowl, the downturned mouth. Gone the pale-yellow hair. His rosy face, framed by a mantle of pure white hair, seemed almost cherubic. Wide open blue eyes and an un-affected smile spoke of a man who'd made peace with the world.

Carol spoke next. She talked about how her father had been such a good dad—how, even though he'd been away a lot when she was young, he had loved her. How it had been hard on him when her mother died. How he'd grown closer to Carol in his last years. Her favorite memory, she said, was and would always be the time when he came to see the high school gymnastic event that won her a college scholarship.

"He cried when I won," said Carol. She stood up, walked to the little table, and touched the urn. With a tilt of her head she said, "Goodbye, Dad." As she turned back to her seat, a sob escaped her mouth, and in it Packer heard not anguish but relief.

Two more people seated in front addressed their sorrow to the backdrop. Then the East Indian woman stood up, turned to the group, and began to recite "The Road Not Taken," by Robert Frost. Packer eased his way around the corner of the shelf, then tiptoed backward into the shadows.

* * *

Going down, he rode alone again in the elevator. *Better to leave some things unsaid,* he thought. A security guard, watching the Jets game, nodded as Packer walked by. Somebody had just scored, and the roar of the crowd echoed in Packer's ears, even after he'd exited the building and started up Tenth. The sun was down. High purple clouds sat motionless in a pale sky.

The wind had died completely, but a new chill inhabited the air. Packer turned up his collar, pulled the suede against his neck.

It felt good to be out of there, good just to walk. He'd misunderstood his mission, perhaps, but as with all such unsatisfactory events, he'd come away with a greater sympathy for the dynamics of human grief. And in the process, he'd discovered an uplifting metaphor of mammalian regret. Surely it would surface again in his memoir.

He considered hailing a cab but decided against it. He wasn't ready to go home. He crossed the avenue and continued walking north, past a building that he was sure used to be the old Stage 54, right past the long-gone Slate Restaurant, and past that after-hours club with the hookers—what the hell was the name of it?

If the number 11 bus came along, he'd hop it, he thought.

But the bus did not come along. Soon, Packer found himself walking in the poorly lit region between the projects and the service side of Lincoln Center. Two teenagers, half a block away, were tossing a white Frisbee back and forth across the avenue. A small group of idle spectators stood in the gloomy dusk, backlit by the bare bulbs at the entrance to the project.

Packer removed his hands from his pockets, letting his arms swing freely. He lengthened his stride and added a touch of swagger to his gait, just in case anybody had a mind to mess with him.

One of the teenagers sailed the white Frisbee high into the air. It wobbled at the peak of its flight, then came tumbling straight down to the pavement. It didn't bounce. It didn't roll. A tall kid ran toward it, leaped into the air, then landed on the thing with both feet. He stooped and picked it up and punched it back into shape with his right fist. It wasn't a Frisbee. It was Packer's cowboy hat.

Spinning twice, like a discus thrower, the kid heaved the hat back across the avenue, where it skidded between two parked cars and came to rest against the curb. The other kid retrieved it, held it to his nose, and sniffed it.

"Hey!" he yelled. "It stink, yo!" Then he flattened it into a frisbee again and heaved it back to the first kid. Shrieks of laughter accompanied its flight, which took it all the way across the avenue, depositing it gracefully on the sidewalk, ten yards ahead.

Packer kept walking, barely broke his stride, as the first kid ran over and scooped it up again. Holding the brim between thumb and forefinger, the boy took a whiff himself. Swaying first this way, then that, he made an elaborate show of holding the hat at arm's length then waved it about, exactly like an elephant with a bone, in a wild, unmistakable gesture of glee.

How to Paint Be

Last year, when I still felt young, I saw a girl behaving oddly. I would call her "Chestnut," for the two-syllable simplicity of it, but the truth is that when she removed her contacts, her pupils caught the slanted sun in a lighter, more hickory kind of way. At twenty-three, she was possessed of sassy youth and had a way of walking that some might describe as free or mistake as child-ish—bent forward slightly at the waist, as if she couldn't wait to get from one toy to the next. She may have been both free and childish, or maybe neither of these things, but what struck my observing nature right off was the way she tested the texture of the sawdust on the barroom floor with the sole of her unbuck-led sandal. It made me miss my aim at the dartboard.

Could an old man like me—a cynical renderer of the paint-erly kind—have been tripped up by such a simple gesture? Or was there something more primitive behind it all? Perhaps it was simply the way she overfilled her blue jeans, which made curious the work of interpreting what she might look like on a model stand. I do have an artist's eye and full of find it is, even now, as I await her unlikely return, in this rough-hewn bar on Frederick Douglass Street, in this pathetic little town called Desire.

* * *

I told Hickory during our first-ever conversation that I have a theory: With enough agitation—and if left out to dry—red lead will become white gold in a matter of days. "The toast will brown, and time will go on hold," I said, turning my water glass ninety degrees in order to make solid the soft ground of idea.

She didn't smile right away from across the wobbly table near the jukebox, the place where I always sit and rarely invite interruption. But neither did she disturb the manner in which her chin sat planted on the palm of her upturned hand. She stared at me with knowing and with no small amount of trust for someone so young. No guile or disguise in her eyes, no shift of anxiety or rift of worry. Just the kind of quiet appreciation for slant that I've been pursuing the world over for decades, with butterfly net, tambourine, and rifle. Hunting involves the craft of cunning, and I don't move around much anymore to accomplish it, having set my sights lower—adjusting for the downhill aspect of twenty-first-century American life.

And why not? I am soon to die. With each tick, closer I come, and you, dear friend, who would listen on the stool next to mine, you, too. The clock has begun to move again, second hand, minute, and hour. Spin me around and you'll find the footprints she left on my back. Check my left cheek for an imprint of soft kiss—the only feel I retain of the immortality she promised me.

She called herself restless, right off the bat, which means I was duly forewarned. I readily admit as much. But you can't simply look away from a creature that time has kept hidden from you, that only fear has prevented you from exposing as real. In Chile, a three-legged piggy is full of import and smile, and it implies some inner stability for the one who sees it. If you saw one in the wild you wouldn't shoot it, would you? You would treat it with kindness and woo.

If you doubt me, magnify the rubber band exactly as it falls on the wood at your feet. Multiply its subtle implicates by whatever results in eleven. You will discover the scattered-together evidence of a slackening time in a relaxing universe, where water will soon be the major concern.

* * *

I used to drink a lot and get high in Santa Fe, particularly during the winter after the Shah of Iran fled into exile. That season, a violent prison break sent desperate characters (or so the rumors had it at the time) into the New Mexican hills. The sound of vigilante gunfire echoed off canyon and rock, shaking even the sword of Orion, which hung just inches out of reach at that altitude. I myself remained unarmed. The frigid night air sucked shut my lungs and froze the scent of pinyon into my nostrils— way back in that place where mind meets throat.

I did a pretty good imitation of Saint Peter without his book or keys, in those days. The time came when I was forced to watch without speaking. Without even tasting a crumb of the food only enlightened people with money can enjoy. I was then invited to a candlelight service on Christmas Eve. I found myself, that year, unable to stand with the others when they rose up in church to sing, but the ones nearest and dearest to me looked down from such a height as to understand my delay and my suspicion of the lecture-hall arrangement of pews.

Straight vodka has the aftertaste of cardboard and glue, and it makes muddle of mind and feels like dizzy in the depths of your temples. Past midnight, I would listen with longing to a staticky transistor radio, sometimes to a voice named Larry King, before he became bony and called himself a show on TV. He still smoked cigarettes, hadn't yet had a heart attack, and seemed to care what his guests really said, all of which gave him a radio voice.

In those days, in those hills, the wind howled like ten thousand wolves. I imagined a movie script about killers and rapists hiding in the darkened main house on Camino Militar, which was owned at that time by an oilman who'd heard I could paint and who'd loaned me his guesthouse to thrive in—or to ease his conscience, as I now suppose. I painted nothing. When he was off speculating with engineers in South America, I stole logs and kindling from his cordwood pile. I checked each log for gunpowder first, a precaution I'd learned from a Mexican pal, who knew the ways of white men—my people.

* * *

Hickory *was* restless, and I had been forewarned, as I've already noted. Her arrival in my life meant I was done hunting, of course. I didn't know this—in the sense of being sure—until my knees began to tremble at any given sight of her. The newborn calf in me would poke through the costume I wore, which consisted of a black cape with cold metal shoulders, a vest composed of breastplate and mail, and the dull sculpt of a glass-bottomed pewter mug clutched in my hand. The mug contained only water and a dash of chlorine. For three decades I'd drunk nothing else.

Hickory liked good whiskey. No one, she made clear, was going to get away with calling her Baby or Sweetheart or Kid. But when the goat in me bleated, "Beautiful," she told me I could call her by that name anytime because the word meant something coming from me.

"Why?" I wondered aloud.

"Because you see who I really am," she whispered.

"I do," I said. "I do."

And that was it. I'd never gone to my knees in all my time at altars, but now it was time, and I did. Before that, I'd stolen a banana from Buddha and twice said "I do" at the altar ends of red-carpeted aisles. Buddha hadn't minded, since the occasion was an art opening, where I was being treated as the newest thing or something-or-other less famous.

Back then, I'd heard only rumors of failure.

* * *

Hickory brought war and jumble to my heart. I suddenly wanted to live longer, to be there to see her put on the costume of true self—the tall woman I could sense pushing up from within her short frame. I'd begun to imagine the tall and short of her, in other words, and how she would deal with the concept of medium.

It's hard sometimes to watch the slowness with which humans develop character. I've come to admire it as a constantly thickening forgetfulness. In order for what we've learned at any young moment to be fully digested and claimed as our own, it must all be misremembered and utterly forgotten, then encountered again during a desperate drought—with terrible fear and a tragic need to give up. Only in this state of mind can green be seen afresh; it emerges from the red of confuse, but through a process the individual steps of which not much can be spoken. It can take years, and the seeker can die in the interim.

Many have.

About those who survive, one can never be sure why.

Here's an example of what I assumed Hickory still didn't know, rendered as dialogue (we'd been talking about Charlie Chaplin):

"What's so funny about being slapped in the face?" she asked me.

"The anticipation of being slapped twice," I said, without hesitation.

"Twice makes it funny?" she asked.

"Anything more, and you'll have to shelve it as tragedy," I answered.

* * *

Once on the steps out back, she touched me the way a picnic blanket tests the ground it must settle upon: ballooning out, deciding slowly, interpreting the possible presence of snakes or twigs or mounds of clotted growth. Her fingers separated and stretched and hovered just above my left hand, and her mouth-lips opened quietly, like a nylon blouse being unbuttoned by a gentle breeze from the east. Her hand settled lightly on mine. Nothing more. Then she bent forward.

On any of the rest of us, the bare flesh of the waist—the way it wraps around to the spine and spreads like water across the soft plateau of sacrum, promising to wash up and over buttocks still hidden by belt and jeans—is a sight we could do without. But when Hickory reached across my legs to fondle a blue iris, the gentleman in me—the stranger who knows better, the old man who's seen all this so many times before, in so many versions of wrestle and paw, and who has felt so many times drawn to it, like the child he once was when he saw his mother undress, and who later accomplished so many versions of thrill that never got written about or captured on canvas and now can't be described with anywhere near the clarity they deserve—this same old man's entirely present and ongoing self wanted to reach out and stroke that smooth skin, but his hand, in fact, did not.

Not then, and cannot now.

I was once young and brave. The perception of others meant nothing to me, or maybe it meant everything, and thus made me feel bold. In either case, I am a coward now. I do not want to be told I'm a dirty old man. Just wait until you, dear friend, come to this arid stretch of plain that distinguishes green pastures (where dong could grow lazily and long for no reason at all) from the obligatory foothills of stumble and rock leading to the ultimate, icy climb. To make love with but words and occasional improvisations of finger in the dust and ash left by younger customers, many of whom have realness and prime written into their postures, and who display a proper faith in the safety of drink—well, I was no longer a part of that crowd, or else I would have been a contender for Hickory's heart.

* * *

But I can dream, dear friend, and I did last night. Not one of those lust-burdened dreams of my youth that would leave spurt and release on the sheet, but a dream enforced by such confidence and care and wise delay in the timing of the sex, that my cartilage and flesh became bone in a whole new way and the time between wish and accomplish, between urge and move-in, with regard to our kiss and my entry, stretched into a pure accumulation of mutual consent that paid no mind to what a young mouth might taste of old in the physical world but rather to what ageless lips and tongues could create with imagination and geothermal originality. It wasn't even strange that she was blonde in the dream when we kissed, and it made perfect sense when she seemed to think about what the kiss actually felt like and whether it was proper. Her vexed thought became visibly comforted by my complete lack of anxiety about the verdict her vexation might produce. Her thought became a space in which I could believe the tired three words she wanted so badly to hear from me but feared so profoundly to utter. My pecker throbbed more than boned, at first, but she soon watered me large against her skin. I said, *Why not*, almost actually speaking out loud, and she shrugged with a deep persistence, until I finally noticed the tiny, scattered letters in the soft declivity above her left clavi-cle and kissed them into the arrangement she needed so much to say, and I needed now so much to hear. Were her thunder rigged and her lightning braced in a waking state, I could never have loved her so.

* * *

The last time I saw Hickory—months ago—she asked me, like a little girl speaking to her father from another room, whether I'd somehow been offended when she'd told me that she'd smoked a joint with some new guy she met out back. Her purpose had not been, she explained, to upset me, but simply to remark that it was good pot and seemed safe in comparison to the shit that was floating around in Ziploc bags these days.

She could have stabbed me with the busted broom handle that for some reason leans uselessly in the hallway leading to the garden—plunged its splintered tip deep into the gap between my shoulder blades—and it wouldn't have chilled my spine the way her new sense of apology did.

In response, I spoke language to her that felt planned: blustery bravado that I'd lifted from rumor of street; spitted clichés borrowed from stuff you could see on Netflix. It all came from some serious and deadly place in my gut, and it tasted like refined sugar on my tongue. Not hair-trigger reflex, not quick-draw construction, not strike-me-dead lightning grasped from thin air, just things like *Who the fuck do you think I am, a priest*? And *Do you think I was born yesterday, for shit's sake, that I'd be upset by* that?

Suddenly, it felt as if everything good I'd become in the stumble of old age had dissolved in a toxic dusk of dull self-rehearsal. I had unveiled a decomposed pile of Was. I wanted her to know that I'd been there with drugs and done that already, wanted her to be in awe of my first toke, back in the day, when pot was called tea and none of us knew how to sex it or grow it. I wanted her to visualize me as careless and immortal, me and my friends all shining in the newness of an anger we didn't and never would understand, all of us joyously assessing the risk of a "gateway" drug and the prospect of toppling an empire—playing like we knew what was ahead with regard to the stuff we would later sit around denying the effects of, like booze and blow, smack and mescaline, and blessed opium.

I had been the king of risk in my day, and I wanted to reign again—shine in Hickory's dark eyes—make her smile and say, *That's so cool!* Only then could I tell her with any authority, *Don't waste your life.* The legs that had grown sturdy under me before I met her, the wise self that had grown tired of Game, those same legs now had no belief in themselves, no trust in tri-pedal stability, no faith in the Ghost. They perceived only loneliness in the two-legged happiness of the crowd getting high all around. Those legs no longer danced with the new girl in town but instead weaved their way over to the chairs along the wall, and sat down to tap my feet.

Hickory followed and sat in the chair beside me, slumped sympathetically, just to my left.

"You don't know who I am," I told her.

But she did. She knew who I was and the condition I am repeatedly in, and the first condition she laid down was this:

Never again tell me what I don't know.

And the second condition was this:

Never again tell me what I already know.

"And if I have to repeat myself," she announced, standing up to leave with the boy who had good shit, "you'll have to shelve our friendship as tragic."

Where Humans Will Surface Next

It wasn't until his fourth marriage ended in divorce that Jeesum understood the beauty of an egg.

Between marriages—those periods when he was on his own, as he thought of them—his diet had consisted mostly of eggs. Indeed, eggs were all he knew how to cook, all his father had known how to cook, and his grandfather before that. Soft-boiled, hard-boiled, poached, deviled, sunny-side up, over easy, scrambled, omelets, frittatas, quiche—he had cracked open thousands and thousands of eggs, even eaten them raw in his younger, more ambitious days. Yet, in seven decades of life he'd never really *studied* one.

It took an oddly colored egg, on a lonely Saturday night, to alert him to the peculiar shape of an egg—and to what it really meant. It was one of eight that he had just boiled for ten minutes then cooled under the cold water tap in his studio apartment, with its single window overlooking the railroad tracks in Livingston, Montana. It was the eighth egg he'd dried that night—all with a single paper towel. He might never have noticed the egg had it not been encircled with shaded bands of varying widths that resembled the gossamer rings of Jupiter.

He stared at it now, watching it roll slowly toward him all on its own, as if it were sneaking away from the rest of the eggs he'd placed on the cutting board next to the sink. When the egg came to a stop at Jeesum's fingertips, he suddenly perceived the pleasure (or the pain—he didn't know which) that the hen must have felt producing the egg; he intuited in its integumentary rings the evidence of each push-and-pause needed to produce the egg's eventual release into the nest box. He wondered idly if it had been for the hen what taking a healthy shit was for him. Then he realized that even to wonder what it must have been like to lay an egg was probably a sign that he was destined to suffer the agony of imagining what life must have been like for the latest of his wives, being married to him. The lonely egg had provoked in him a new kind of sympathy. Suddenly he saw the segmented process as a wondrous whole, a fully shelled event—a miracle.

And just as suddenly, he felt free.

Alone, in a poor section of town, in a studio apartment, but on his own again, and free.

The egg sat quietly apart from the other seven, and Jeesum understood that even if the seven other eggs had repelled the eighth with some as-yet-undiscovered ostracizing force, the eighth egg was not alone in the universe—that would have been way too sad—it was just alone in relation to the seven: a solitary bit of clarity sitting off by itself, yet maintaining a gravitational relationship to everything else.

It was all he could do to keep from weeping. He did not want the fluorescent light fixtures, which he reviled so much, to see him weep. Not until he understood what the tears meant—whether they signaled defeat or victory, or if they even issued forth from anything meaningful at all.

He studied the speckled, dark-brown "poles" of the egg, a balanced opposition that seemed somehow significant. He turned the egg over slowly to inspect the two light-brown rings—yes, they were lighter, more halo-like—that separated the dark poles from the even darker, more jungle-like equator of the egg. Had this been a planet viewed from afar, those rings would have signified regions that contained less growth and more open plains, circumferences of warmth and light, maybe even water. He traveled the length and breadth of planet Egg in his mind, north to south, east to west. He held the poles of Egg between his thumb and forefinger and revolved the planet, watching day turn into night and back into day again. He tilted Egg to give it seasons; he varied the tilt to create wobble and provide wind. Then he set Egg aside and, choosing three of the seven remaining eggs, he placed them in a small stainless steel dish and put them in the refrigerator next to a small glass bottle of orange juice, for his breakfast. Turning back to the sink, he noticed the remaining four eggs on the cutting board, with Egg sitting off to the side.

That was it. He understood in a flash that the Fifth World was now within naked-eye view of the previous four, and that the time for its sustenance and nurturing had come.

Jeesum spoke to the four walls of the kitchen. He prayed to the pale-blue ceiling and the lime-green linoleum floor, and he spoke from his heart at last.

SELECTED

POEMS

TO MY SON, CHELSEY

(b. 3 May 1970, d. 22 November 1971)

Sunday morning littlechild,
who didn't speak but sang, who
would never learn but knew,
who couldn't quite clap but made
the absolute whispercrash
of two hands missing:
Hey, Chelsey,
sitting aimless
in the wintercity sun,
to all our tedious, tunestuck souls
you were such a dynamite song.

CONVERGENCE

The old man stooped
and seemed to harden there,
transfixed by the gaiety
of the child. His crescent posture
smacked of fairy tale, like when
the moon gives shelter
to a star.

But then the boy
arched back,
rose on his toes,
threw up his little arms
in helpless glee,
and as their faces touched,
two lives merged into a single
destiny: one soul
with so much time to go
and no time left
at all.

CHILDHOOD

Rosy-fingered, it begins,
all ahead full steam.
So much unknown!
Those teachers! Ask.
Listen. Disagree, no, no.
What if? And then what?
Why? But how? How? How?
What then?
Cap guns and Popsicles
and in the evening,
applesauce sprinkled with cinnamon.

Later, I feared I might be a bastard,
but no such luck. Nothing to excuse
my boner on the bus, my nasty plans
at night, my contriving for weeks
to feel my babysitter's tit.

Once, when I had a fever,
I compressed the whole of Jupiter
between my thumb and forefinger—
reduced its entire mass into nothing
but touch, with enough space left
to feel the throb.

GONE IN ROME

I am with the lizard
on the wall,
who eyes the cat
arched atop the Roman gate, who's
hissing at the stupid little dog,
who's pissing on a pine
from Africa.

Michelangelo heaves a sigh,
while from marble porches
emperors applaud,
and mourning doves,
with no opinions of their own,
make nests in locks
of Caesar's hair.

QUELLO CHE VEDO IN ITALIA

I see the sea, and the brown hills kneeling
at the shore. Clusters of daisies shiver
whitely near a rivulet in the sun.

Minutes ago, I saw a hermit crab
evade two heartless signoras planning
a tasty pasta dish. Crabs can see, I'm sure,

and perhaps with compassion, like me,
as I watch a woman with useless legs
crawl from the water onto the dry beach,

a primordial creature elbowing
her entire body toward a yellow
towel, slicing a frightful trench across

my ritual sadness—she, as brave
as the first fish to dare the open air.
Why should I lose heart when I can still pace

this foreign shore, a restless tiger
in a cosmic cell, this shell of ceaseless blue
pinned to heaven with forgotten moons.

A COUPLE ON VACATION IN ITALY

A middle-aged man is flailing at a bee
that won't quit buzzing his croissant.
His wife has seen this willful behavior
before. She stands up from the table,
steps to the edge of the terrace, looks out
at the sea.

Eventually the man cedes his breakfast
to the bee, throws down his cloth napkin,
joins his wife at the metal railing. She spins away,
drawn, it would seem, to a clump of purple
bougainvillea clinging to an overhead trellis.
Her husband,

left to stare at the sea alone, seems not to know
what to look for out there. After scanning
the empty horizon several times, he tries again
to approach his wife. She greets him stiff-armed,
offering an orange blossom for him to smell.
He takes it,

sniffs it, begins to speak, but before he can utter
a sound, she has retrieved her purse from the table,
and is walking off the terrace by herself, sandals softly
slapping the paved path. Blossom in hand, the man
turns and studies the horizon once more,
struck this time

by the thin, undeniable line where the sky separates
from the sea.

SPIRAL STAIRS

In a troubled time,
when the roof gave way,
I hit the stairs.
Rusty nails screeched loose
and bone-dry rafters
splintered.

I, in desperation,
spiraled round and round.
What's up?
What's down?
My soul had no idea.
A basement is the summit
in a storm.

Then you appear, somehow hailed,
diaphanous
in the gloom, and we are lifted above,
the rubble and set down
in a far field
where we dream our love awake
then shield our eyes.
Licked with lion tongues,
we climb out born.

THRILLS

An unimpeded inkling
swells in me,
vigorous and pulsed,
as if a firefly
had snuck beneath my belt.

All things outside me
suddenly pertain, all roads
spoke inward to a shining hub.

Those lovers there, entwined
along the wall, kiss for me,
because of me, and the white cat
licks its chest in studied
ignorance, while my heart pounds
with the promise of your love.

And who am I to stand
untippable against this molten flow
and wade waist-deep in fire
to pursue illicit you?

I've left my cautious cane hanging
on the ancient chair. Lava isn't lava
if it's cold.

ANIMA DREAM

The Queen is dead,
laid out beside the tracks.
A dagger drops,
the turtle moves
on cue.
You are ravishing, my dear,
just as you are.
Lie still
until she dies
inside of you.

The artist is the King,
but he's dead too. He rests
his head on handkerchiefs
to keep the ticks away.
Petty art for pity's sake,
and cocktail time.
No, not now,
thank you.

Who is this woman
waiting for the train, her
guidebooks packed,
her lingerie arranged?
I didn't hear a stop announced,
but no one's here to hear
but me, no one to help me choose.
I am the engine
and caboose.

ON THE BEACH IN SPERLONGA, ITALY

On an empty seashore in Italy, a fisherman
works the narrow inlet just north of town.
His apparatus is a simple steel frame suspended
by four chains linked to a bleached-white rope
that runs through a pulley and down to his fist.
Hanging from the frame, a circular net suddenly
turns conical when it slaps the surface.

The water is new with each try, the empty net
almost always a surprise. The sun balances atop
the Abruzzo Range. Angular seabirds, done for the day,
head home. In New York City it isn't even rush hour yet.
Am I so badly ruined that I should think of this?

On some impulse, or none, the fisherman hoists
the frame. Empty yet again, the net dribbles sea water,
as if trying to catch its breath. A seagull screams, *What gives!*
The man's grip loosens, the frame falls once more,
the bleached rope slackens.

Imagine what is going on underneath: fish adrift,
subject like the rest of us to some mysterious current.
Evasion isn't even the point. Here we go:
The net rises again. *Aha!* A little silver one, glinting
like chrome and flopping in the evening light.

But not enough. Not nearly enough. Not even
when compared with emptiness.

AWAITING SPRING

A bold insinuation of warmth:
fog blanketing the snowbound land.
My blood remains congealed,
but the trees know how to deal with this,
coaxing their sap
with comic gesturing,
shunning this cold valley
I am rooted in,
this feeble slope.

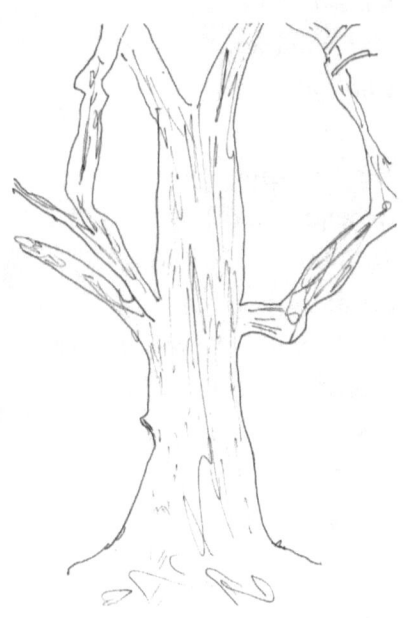

IMMORTALITY

I never see the snake,
only its skin.
Year after year it's there,
held fast by grass along its length
and wedged between two rocks
beside the well.

Six feet of crinkled, opaque history,
lifeless jaws agape.
Blind eyes bulging
with the agony of change.

This is who I was,
not who I am,
and who I was can't know
who I will be.

How pleasing it is
to be renewed!
To slither free of sweaty
certainty, to ditch
the evidence of mortal cells,
cast off the scales of age,
absorb the sun—
to feel the pulse of granite
as one's own.

CHANGE

The darkest wave washed over me today,
whether wind or water, I couldn't tell.
Maybe smoke.

It's been five months tomorrow since she left.
Why do I still wait for her to knock?
She won't knock.

You have lived too long in fear, expecting
war, even during this extended peace.
Neglect her.

Soldier on with a different point of view.
And stop referring always to yourself:
the weak I.

From the hill, tinder in a little box.
Watch the fire reflected in the lake, and eye
the far shore.

ENVY

A very small house set in a pasture. A child
would have drawn it as a face: two shutterless
windows for the eyes; for the nose, a bright-red
front door. Above the door, a peaked roof
suggestive of a clownish frown. Cedar
siding, a brick chimney, if I recall,
and I remember well how heartbreakingly
alone it seemed.

I never set foot on the land,
or in the place, though it remained empty
for the eleven-year duration of my second
marriage, and never went up for sale.

But I slowed down every time I passed it,
its glass-paned eyes beckoning me during
my ritual back-and-forth on the busy rural road
that stretched between our more elegant,
well-furnished house and the town
where I could shop for something organic.

That little house knew why I envied it,
understood long before I did, that its
emptiness silently mirrored my own.

CONTINGENCIES

If this is it,
me left too long alone
to study gauze
and glossy charts
of human innards taped
to pale green walls,
and if it comes to pass
that the doctor appears,
her starched white smock
stifling all hope of desire, her
expression stricken
with a hopeless grin, and if,
if,
prompted by the data, she
should blurt the awful news,
I'd hardly bat an eye,
I bet.

For I have thought ahead
to this, to cautions I could
cast away and past exhilarations
reinvent. How many shapes
abandon takes! Folded pleasures
now, of course, just creased and musty
uniforms crying out for air,
yet, still,

if Death held out its hand today,
I'd don those madcap, reckless rags
and resurrect my wild desires.

I would, in my last days,
stand hatless in the sun.

THE IMPOSSIBLE LOVE OF CRAZY HORSE

This is my work, the Fire.
Listen,
I am touching it,
the Stone.

Here's where we begin: in the dark
center of what wraps around
and holds
without a knot.

Gravity is the condition of fire,
flame, the escape.
We cannot be,
but *I* am, and *you* are. Let our flames
entwine.

Remember the seven spokes
that fix my vision of this world:
West, North, East, and South,
Grandfather Sky, Grandmother Earth,
and the Heart,

so that when I am blind
you can visit me.

AMERICAN VALENTINE, 1993

Huggy wuggy, now we care
all inclusively.
Huggy wuggy, now we dare
to love effusively.

United here beneath our banner
of mutuality,
we'll exercise in every manner
humanality.

Look at you and look at me,
filled with so much love!
We have Rights and we are Free,
by edict from Above!

A weary mantra, don't you think,
for a species in our state,
blindly surging toward the brink,
betraying a deeper hate.

Is this perhaps the way of things,
the way mankind will end,
believing what the mirror brings,
thinking we're our friends?

Interest groups among us stalk,
Gender, Hue, and Creed.
Hat in hand, of Rights we talk,
each of personal need.

But it's not just sex and race and class
we should be speaking of.
Let's start looking *through* the glass
at abdicated love.

Here's the ethic still unfound,
unprocessed legally:
The Earth comes first, this place,
our ground,
which bears us regally.

What rights have we without the Mother,
from whom all privilege springs?
There isn't going to be another:
no more offerings.

It sounds so much like ancient chants,
like Native ritual,
but, really, it's our only chance:
Stop growing. Sit. Be still.

MEMORIAL DAY, 1993

A day to kill for, not a cloud around.
Far behind the marching band,
shiny horses clop the center line that leads
us creaky old civilians out of town,

out there where graves declare the day,
though not just yet, no not quite yet.
Let's pause awhile and watch
along this simple country road,

let's snatch a blade of grass and ponder
this ritual day. Men have fallen in their tracks
for us, slaughtered so that we might enjoy
in peace our precious strollered children, all

ballooned and straining at their strings,
all agog at pretty flags festooned with gold.
And then along come thirty underprivileged teens
from the migrants' side of town, slouching

in green-and-white-striped sweats, until suddenly
they snap to, and sixty sneakers slap the pavement,
as their leader calls out cadence: *Hup, two, three, four,
we won't let you close the door.* And I am broken by this.

In tears behind my shades, I hear the rural
pastures sigh, and see the sky burn blue
with brand-new dreams, and know the streams
are free again to make no sense at all.

THE TWO OF THEM

The two of them, in their eighties, have shrunk
from view beneath the dashboard. Seemingly
driverless, their car shows up right on time,
he not one to make his hosts worry, she
just along for the ride, you might say, her life
popping out at her now, deer-like from the foggy
way she sees the world: A spreading oak is a ballerina,
in her mind.

And he attending to her wants all weekend, seeking
her opinion, still leashed to who she was, to what
he thinks he holds.

On Sunday, when rush hour is over, we belt them in.
They wave through rolled-up windows.
The accelerator screams while
the clutch takes forever to catch,
and like astronauts they lurch away, spewing
driveway stones, just as I, their firstborn errant son,
once did.

This evening, two cardinals have settled
in the cedar tree. She dressed in orange, bobbing
on a branch, he cloaked in red, one limb above,
from where, unbeknownst to her,
he can drink her in.

TRIAGE

I

With me, the ache is anonymity:
a life spent in the belly of the whale.
But you, your hand conducts
a symphony of pain. Arched palm down
above the table,
it reappoints a fork,
smooths out the butter knife,
counter-clocks the gold-rimmed plate
a few degrees.
Things must be just so.
I know, I've heard,
you're married to a cheat.

II

Talk around the table turns to change,
to yet another century whipping past
the sun. "And so much killing still going on,"
you say. "We haven't learned a thing."
The guests all nod, tut-tut, of course,
though no one says a word.
A nefarious weight descends, a few
polite coughs require another sip of wine.
I, your husband, don't let on, but know
quite well that you'd prefer to rescue
what is left for you
and ignore the doomed.

MY FATHER, NOVEMBER 2, 1995

What's left in November anyway?
Crows.
A few muted colors, an hour less light.

On October 2, when the wind died down,
the hospital staff raised a brand-new flag,
and he walked away from them on his own.
"A hopeful sign," he said. But we both knew.

A month later, I sat watching him watch
the end come on, from the bed we'd set up
in the dining room. Beyond the window,
a leafless maple was allowing shards
of unadulterated autumn light
to stab his eyes, making him flinch, as if,
against all odds, he'd not seen death coming.

FOR THE DYING MOTHER OF NINE
PUPPIES

Kenya heard your message
in a dry spell, then packed and left
for India. Only the well holds
anybody's interest anymore. Dry, dry,
the land is sere and dry, the dogs
cry in the house, even in the human
house,
dry.

Proud-necked giraffes, first of the four-footed
to glimpse the sun and last to see it set,
grow dizzy with the spinning days and curse
their pregnancies. Father, we watched elands
thieve the woman's cactus from her garden.
Thine, Thine, the well's not ours,
it's Thine.

Cobra didn't really mean it, Mother.
Wary and withdrawn, poised as if to gulp,
not bite, he must have thought of you as milk.
Oh, Mother, the cracked earth still emanates
the heat at dawn, we know you're here, we know
you're here, you're
gone.

JOHN WALKER LINDH, CAPTURED

I let the hands of strangers lift me down.
I've seen the photograph shown round the world:
A ragged beard frames my soot-caked face,
my gaunt-cheeked, stunned expression
is glassy-eyed with thirst.
I was thinking: *My hair stinks, my palms*
will bleed. What will Mother say?

I once lived on high in California.
When I was a boy and couldn't sleep,
I played in my pajamas with plastic
soldiers in the upstairs hallway.
One night, I rumpled the runner rug
into a mountainous terrain, turned out
the sconce light, hunkered way down, until my cheek
brushed the desert floor. Eleven American marines
stood stiffly poised for combat in a threadbare
valley. My three-legged metal horse sniffed
the wind. Tanks and heavy weaponry fell silent.
Light—blessed moonlight in my mind—
washed across the battlefield from beneath
my parents' bedroom door. In that cold, insufficient
glow, I conjured an unseen underdog, poor
but courageous fools who had yet to appear
and rise up against this Goliath force. What
was the point of story—of glory—if no one
took David's role?

Oh, God, look at my forsaken visionary stare!

Without water, the mind outstrips itself, sheds
its attachment to the heart. I'd forgotten
my given name and who I was. When they found me
hiding among the Taliban dead, a marine let me sip
from his own canteen.

ALONE ON NEW YEAR'S EVE

Having been forgotten
by the world,
I have forgotten it.
The old year crept out
without a bleat.
Where is everybody?
The television knows.

Nothing's changed.
The spurned moon wanes
yet again. The black Hudson skulks
along the city's edge, its frigid current
concealing a deep discomfort
in the land. I am afraid,
as midnight nears,
of being engulfed
in loneliness.

So I flee (fly)
to another time,
when you waited up for me,
still surprised by us.

A SQUIRREL EATING IN THE PARK

Furious preparation led to this:
Lips lifted, teeth bared, a single
peanut revolving like corn
on the cob between two fast-moving,
four-fingered paws.

No thumbs. Black toenails,
sharper and more evolved
than a rat's.
Pure muscle, sheathed in
sleek fur.

Done, he shifts sideways
on the iron railing, his balls
tucked up tight
beneath an upright fluffy tail.

He eyes me now and waits,
as if I might know which hunger
will beset him next.

ON WEST EIGHTY-FIFTH STREET

I passed an almost-dead man
on the street today.
His blood had turned an icy blue
beneath his whiskey-reddened skin.

Scuffed black shoes, laces untied,
no socks. Bulging purple ankles,
avocado-soft and bent, as if he'd
somehow jumped from too far up.

What has become of me?

I'm the kind of man who stops
for fallen baby birds, stoops for spiders
struggling in the tub. Yet, too,
this creep in brand-new Reeboks,

rushing past, his eyes intent upon the slush,
his warm Armani coat flying out behind.

NEW YORK CITY, APRIL 7, 2003

Seven dark starlings huddle
  in a tree, fluffed up
   against the insult
     of wet snow.
Paired kindergartners, harnessed
   like workhorses,
    march out of step underneath.
The birds' chaotic chatter fades,
   bus tires hiss the pavement,
   a gust of wind,
     a shudder of wings,
  gone.

DIMNESS

Strange, what candlelight reveals,
and disallows. As your sharp, hawk-like
features soften, traces of a more hesitant
persona appear. Despite your scented
earlobe, I sniff poverty mixed with a hint
of heather, and I sense a ritual doubt.

Silence pursues the path that the wavering
candle flame takes, swirling between us
like a genie, until our fingertips touch.
Earlier, you were so full of yourself,
hot words spilling from your lips, even
as I tongued them back to you.

Quiet now. You were about to say
that we've met before, been compelled before,
through endless incarnations to confront
each other in this life, in this dive called
Perpetuity. But don't, in light of this.

FLESH AGAIN

Just a glimpse, at first,
her bare white thighs amidst
a forest of well-clothed legs—
blue jeans, utility pants, corduroys.

Wintry in the subway car,
but not for her, this burst of April
radiance that melts my frosty mood
and reminds me and other passengers,

who also gawk at the two bright
saplings making their way to the doors,
that one need only follow her
through the turnstiles and up,

up, up the stairs to find once more
the blinding light of spring.

SHE APPROACHED

in a dream,
emerging from a shadowed room.
Stick with her, a soft voice said.
Years later, when I'd long since
stopped looking, she materialized
next to me during dinner at a retreat.
When the dessert arrived,
she leaned toward me and whispered,
Despair is born of desire.

So I let her in.

One last sail on the moon-tugged tide,
I told myself, as if Odysseus could really
go to sea again and not get hurt.
That night, we lay sideways
on a king-size bed in some Vermont motel,
smearing half-bitten strawberries dipped
in chocolate on our genitals,
kissing until our lips began to swell
and laughing at the pump-like
sucking sound and sweaty belly slaps
of helpless sex.

What a wild, unpredictable ride!
So, of course, she moved in.
But she could change like a cloud: diaphanous
and angelic one moment,

then wind-whipped and dark as thunder
the next. Even when stared at, not one shape
for very long.

I finally let her go, at her bidding.

She came back for some things one evening—
a book bag she'd left beneath my bed,
her boxed set of Coltrane CDs, and an old
Raggedy Ann doll from the closet.
I saw her out, my throat suddenly dry as hay,
and watched her dissolve into the shadows
of the street-lit New York City night.

NO LIMITS

This night there are no limits to what may be given.
—Rumi, *Unseen Rain: Quatrains of Rumi*

This night there are no limits
to what may be given, to what God will
let us distill from this. Begin by removing
the eye that commands us, the walls
that contain us, the bucket that fills our cup.
Dispossess us of memory, certainty,
foresight, and hope. Leave no food
on the threshold for expectation, and shoot
on sight any light that appears.

Between us there stands
only this question: *Are you prepared for never again,
for just this once?*
Perhaps you knew before you were asked. I'm
not so sure I did. Moving about in the pitch-black,
are you tempted (as I am tempted now) to betray
the grace gratuitously, to believe, to exaggerate,
to swear your love to death?

Let's wait.
The floor is clear enough to dance.
No obstacles to this, save the chance
of missing one another in the dark.

SHUT UP

What if I spoke up and said,
I love you?
Would the generator quit,
the lights dim,
the magnetism cease?
This otherworldly pull,
this chi we share, seems
born of silence and nurtured
on wordlessness, as heedless
of meaning as the never-worshipped
oxygen we breathe.

What more do we want, and why?
All of Creation meant nothing,
until we gave it a name.

PSYCHOANALYSIS
(WITH HELP FROM THE OED)

Don't fix me! she scrawled on a sticky note
attached to the ceramic teapot she'd broken
in the sink before leaving for work that morning.
She was a sensitive woman,
given to moods, which prompted me to ponder
what she might
more deeply have meant.

Don't make me firm or stable, perhaps? Don't fasten
or secure me? Neither decide nor settle, nor repair
the parts of me that are broken? Implant me not
in your mind or memory, don't gaze at me directly
or steadily, or attract or hold or single me out
with your eyes?

Perhaps she meant to threaten: If you ever place
me definitely or permanently,
or establish my station or determine my exact nature,
or refer me to a definite place or time, or rigidify
my features, or prepare me as your food or drink
(thus depriving me of my fluidity and volatility),
if you even once congeal me, or go so far as to punish,
kill, silence, or deal with me, or secure my support
fraudulently
(esp. by bribery);

or were you ever to arrange the results of this race,
or inject me with a narcotic, or make my colors
fast and permanent, or assimilate any of my essences
by forming a nongaseous compound, or castrate
or spay me, or otherwise arrest the development
of my language and literature, or determine the incidence
of my liability, or take up my position (my dilemma,
my predicament),
I swear I will . . .
what?

Stars become fixed only at great distances.
Everything else struggles to form,
even her name.

DEPARTURE

Dressed and ready for the day,
you poke your head in and smile
goodbye. At my desk, I am determined to work,
but something other there is with you
this morning, perhaps the tilt of your head,
or the way your lips part wordlessly,
or maybe it's the part of you already
out the door.

I stand up and kiss you, knowing, as we have discussed
so often, that this cannot last between us,
this Spring-Autumn love affair.
Look at us, you've said, *we're pathetic.*
And I know this. Pigeons inhabit the window ledge
with greater confidence than we hold hands
in public, and it's amusing, isn't it,
that you call us "fuck-mates" to your young friends.

I hold you tighter than a proper boyfriend might.
Your lips taste like cherry this morning,
the lemon balm used up. For a moment, I feel awkward,
half-dressed and barefoot, while you're decked out
in leather and taller than me in heels. It's so stupid,
isn't it, to get this close to leaving, only to be summoned,
once again, by something stronger than our plans for the day:
This desirous curiosity that drops us to the rug,

reduces us to what we probably only are, makes new
the undoing of a button, the unzipping of a fly,
the struggle to disentangle our clothes.

And me, still trying to remember the stanza I'd
half written when you so rudely interrupted me, still
reminding myself that this whatever-it-is
cannot conceivably last—thinking of death, and how
much impossibly more you mean to me than anything
I can think of *doing*—and soon I'm not feeling
the rug burns on my knees, no longer hearing
the computer fan, or believing for even a second
that what has died in others
will ever die in us.

EVIDENCE

When the life they'd had collapsed, he took it well.
Like most men, he knew to ride the rubble down.
Where she'd gone, how she'd fared, he often wondered.
He hadn't seen it coming, or registered
her last words, or taken particular note
of her uncharacteristic failure
to glance back and wave before disappearing
that last time. Nothing to hang her absence on,
no hallway hook.
Just exquisite dust, and aftermath.

INSIDE OUT ON THE EQUINOX

Outside, the distant pulse of traffic
on the West Side Highway imitates
an ocean's peculiar monotony—rhythmic
and persistent. Along the Drive, park-side trees
seem to beseech from memory
a little late-afternoon warmth. Carelessly,
a pigeon leaves the sill.

She left in February, a month ago.

Turning from the window, he imagines
a furious entropy at work: Bookshelves
cave under the weight of their volumes,
the spines of old novels crack and split. A portrait
yanks out the hook that holds its frame.
On the canvas, pure gesso reappears.
A worthless kilim disintegrates beneath his feet,
forcing him into the corner, where the easy chair—
their Throne of Sex—reacts, at last, to years
of sweat by unupholstering itself
and swallowing the tacks. From the kitchen
come the soft groans of iron pans decohering
into molten heaps, and the sigh of family china
unfiring itself, turning wet and heavy
and ready again
for the wheel.
From the bedroom: the ripping
and rending of sheets.

Two movers arrive to cart off the rest. Goodwill bags
her clothes. The super shows up in coveralls
and finds behind the dresser a pair of crotchless
purple panties, three dust-caked pennies, and a smooth
black stone from Mexico. This last, the man pockets.
Paying the help and tipping the super, he
asks them to leave the hallway door ajar,
just in case.

ASKED

He asks me how I came to this place and this work.
—Philip Levine, "Angel Butcher"

So, he asks me how I came to this place,
this work, and I consider telling him snidely
that it was my father's desire
combined with my mother's consent,
that conjuring a life begins with horny
groping at the drive-in and that a life, once
conceived, ought not to ponder its origin,
but I don't.

I am a working man. I've known the nausea
that comes from breathing diesel fuel at six
o'clock in the morning, and enduring years
of glacial dread beneath the owner's clock.
For me, hard labor felt like house arrest,
broken only by wild fits of desire
and long episodes of self-medication,
until I aged out of the labor pool, released
on my own recognizance and lofted
by sympathetic winds to this very desk,
to serve.

I answer him now because I did somehow
come to this place and this work, *meant* to come,
knew all along I'd come, even when the gas ran out
in the wrong neighborhood and wished-upon stars
blinked out. Even when the rules changed and I
stopped looking twice at pretty women.

WHAT I SAW

Please, Medicine Man, I feel a pain. [. . .]
Put on, I beg you, charms made of feathers,
now it's time to help one of your own. [. . .]
Send your second soul beyond the mountains, beyond time.
Tell me what you saw, I will wait.

—Czesław Miłosz, "I Sleep a Lot"

Have I returned in time, Sir?
Such a headwind on the way back!
And add to that the battering demands
of flight—the updrafts,
the thirst.

You've been drumming in my absence.
That stretched hide is worn,
I can tell.

Here on the altar, beside the lodge,
I will place my faithful well-worn pipe.
Claw and skull sit side by side: amulets
to lure the Spirits—like your pen and ink.

Enjoy the scent of elk within this pouch
I've made for you. Breathe deeply of it,
have any girl you want.

The coals feel warm beneath the ash.

Blow on them, old man.
I bring no news, just solace: beyond
the mountains, more of this,
beyond Time, the same,
just seamless worlds ahead.

AT MY WORST

I am the bird who will not fly,
who shivers in the eaves
and cowers near the house.

I am the climber who turns back,
who suddenly pukes green
when he glimpses the thin peak.

I am the horse culled from the herd,
the one the donkeys bray
at from across the fence.

I am the self-forgotten shoot
that listens for the spring,
emboldened by the dark.

I am the betrayer of God,
of men, of countless gifts
directed toward me.

I am the subway con artist,
dressed in cleric's clothing,
my audience the pews.

I am the dog who bares its teeth,
who bites the kindest hand,
who shits where it wants.

I am the worm with no questions,
the lazy hermit crab,
cursed in its unearned shell.

I am the snake that strikes full-length
and the toad who wants his love—
his deadly venom—known.

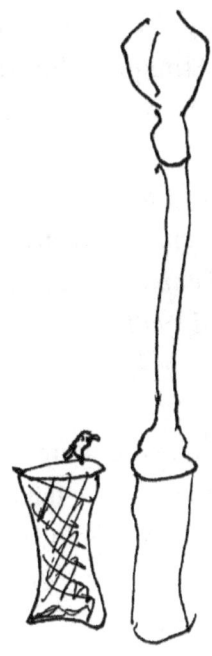

OLD RIP AWAKES

Just dozing, dear,
he mumbles, lying back
beneath the towering oak.
Jug in hand, belly up,
the drunken, no-good, useless goat
is going to dream the years along,
upon the paths of time,
two decades gone. Ivy interlaced
with briars, winters spoiled with mud.
Shrill voices from the caves:
the Rights of Humankind! Wars
the length of famine run and thus
such perfumed nonsense
from the top: Good versus Evil.
Hogwash! Stinkpot! Blunderbuss
and toad! The devil's iron goad.

Oop-doopety-boop,
the rhyme-time skill reawakes
atop the hill and finds dead ivy
in my beard. Nothing of my name
is heard.

Townsfolk line the route
and wave their flags—fail utterly
to get what's really going on.
Perfect weather! Not a drop!
But such a reservoir

of human ingenuity! Look how far
the ape has come!
(Richer, at the very least.)

Join ranks, you celebrants,
drink hearty.
But let this old man through.

LETTER TO MY GRANDFATHER

I have a photograph of us, you seated,
me astride your knee, beneath an elm,
in 1943. The drive to Westfield, NJ, seemed endless
from where we lived, in Cambridge, MA,
but worth it. At your table, we ate bacon
and real butter. Children were seen, not heard.

I've kept some hardbound books of yours:
Plato, Aristotle, Homer, all of Emerson and Proust,
and the Russians—your favorites. I will pass
them on to kin. You stood me on your ornate desk
and lit a fire. I could hear the carnival from there.

You outlived Roosevelt and lived to see
Truman win. You missed Korea, the Interstates,
Integration, and 'Nam. After that, it's been regional wars
and assassinations. No one seems to have learned
all that much. The moon isn't made of cheese,
but you knew that. We got embroiled in empire
and then dropped the ball.

You had a mistress, eh? Your secretary! (And perhaps
her sister, too? My father hinted.) I read your novel,
the one my mother wanted burned. We'll talk.
I'll have more to say than I did back then.

New York City streets are crowded still. Market's up
and down. Television stole the night, small farms
are gone, and everything is super lit. Orwell got it right
about Big Brother, but Huxley hit the deeper truth:
We would succumb like sheep to the lure of ease.
Robots don't mind the work, but they don't seem
so funny anymore.

I met a man today who couldn't tell that his tree
had died. What happens when it doesn't rain and we
have to leave?

By the way, there is no life on Mars.

BELLINI'S ST. FRANCIS IN THE DESERT

Yellow luminescence, as unforgiving
as madness, bathes all other colors
on the canvas. In the foreground,
poor Francis, transfixed.
A sway-backed donkey in the middle distance
pricks up its ears: It seems to get
the message, too.

Way off in the back, a castle on a hill,
a church, a village, a moat perhaps. Winding
streets. Human insignificance.
There's the shepherd with his flock—a touch
too symbolic, but nonetheless serving
as margin between field and kingdom.

Francis has been lifted from his meditations
and now stands stiff as a pillar and stranded
on dry rock. Outstretched arms, upturned palms.
Stigmata. His Bible shut behind him
and the implication of a cave. Witless, a human
skull waits empty eyed atop Francis's desk.
Am I perplexed by this vision, non-Christian me?
Is it clear to my twenty-first-century eye
why this old painting unsettles me so? Ah!
I notice now that water flowed here once.
See the bone-dry spout? Smell the brittle ivy?
Light a match and we will all explode.

ACADEMIA

I planted sunflower seeds in a special
pot this spring, but a resident squirrel
decided I'd done it all wrong, and now,
in July, I notice sturdy sunflowers
diversifying in all the pots, among
marigolds and petunias, without
complaint (that I can discern) from any
of the parties involved. But we will see.
At their roots, they may have formed committees,
the way professors do in colleges,
tasked by some dutiful Provost to suss
out precisely and then capitalize
the Tics and Tumors, Triggers and Traumas
that inevitably arise when one
race of students rubs elbows with another.
But I doubt it. In just such a way
do only humans manage
to ensure the maintenance of *difference*,
and call the process a celebration
of *diversity*.

But the difference between flowering souls
is not the point. Look at them all, focused
more deeply than any thought could
ever hope to be—fully lacking intent
yet driven and blessed by a desire
to grow, grow, and without prejudice, grow.

Look at us, on the other hand, embroiled
within that steaming, lid-rattling slow cooker
called Sophistry, the Art of Clever
Lying, an art hatched at prestigious schools
and raised to adulthood by politicians,
under the banner of Democracy.
We the People, whose inner complaint must
surely be that we're too miserably the same.

TO AN ANGRY FEMINIST POET FRIEND

Fuck the gulls and the fog
they live in. Diddle something else.
Sit on this awhile, or suck it,
come fetch this bone.

You live by the sea, where the waves
drown out the memory of your father's
voice,
and the wind muffles the sickening
thud of his fist on your face.
Hurricanes distract you from revenge,
and three children yank your sleeves,
while your ambitious husband pursues
an artsy buck off-island.

What is moving you tonight? What damp
spasmodic tug? Come on, tell me,
who would you devour
if you could? Or kill, if the insurance claims
went through? Or feed with poetry, if I
appeared to you in a dream?

LONGING, OR CALL IT WHAT YOU WILL

How can I capture this old-man longing?
Why should I even try?
A flame doesn't really leap downwards,
nor an ocean actually float on the sky. What wind
is so limber it suckles itself? The earth
isn't going to give birth from its tombs.
Clover adores the potted violets out back,
but God is a poor excuse for that.

A disease of felt images, dear Keats, an itch
too deep to warrant a scratch, a middle joy
so warm it shivers me.

Call it the ninth symphony of a lingering cat:
a cave door scraping open onto the earliest art,
inviting my inevitable going, airing my knowing
how the stone will slide shut behind me
and seal me in a rapture even fire fears,
yet only fire can find within.

DARKNESS WAKING UP FROM A DREAM

Who is it, knocking about out there?
Maybe the moon, drunk and wobbly
and threatening diminishment again?
Or did thunder stumble into the backyard
looking for periphery?
What sense does anything sensible make?
Surely, Momentum had to start somewhere,
but it's gotten out of control.
See! See there how the dawn sneaks
into the woods, so damn intent on stealing
silhouettes?

FORECAST

There the poet sits, under his umbrella,
thinking, perhaps, of higher-order things.
The tentacles of his thought, with their reach,
escape the bony cage of his skull,

aided in their meanderings, this hot
July afternoon, by a pungent whiff
of marigold served on a gentle breeze,
and moistened lightly with humid molecules

of whatever oxygen there still is,
as Canadian wildfire smoke smudges
the North American continent, blotting
out the sun and, tonight, the moon and stars.

Homage is such a necessary act.
In what other fashion, through what other
medium, and to which divinity
must he turn his attention now, when faced

with his (and our) impending erasure?
He wonders anew about prophesy.
How to divine deeper truth without relying
on data. How to trust that when your skin

crawls, the old boogeyman might be nearby.
How to decipher the kind of alarm
that comes from one's bodily zones, not one's
all-knowing, perhaps medicated, brain.

Ground is everything to the hidden seed.
Earth abides, and in concert with ionized Air,
produces lightning—the source of Fire—
while the seed waits in the dark for Water.

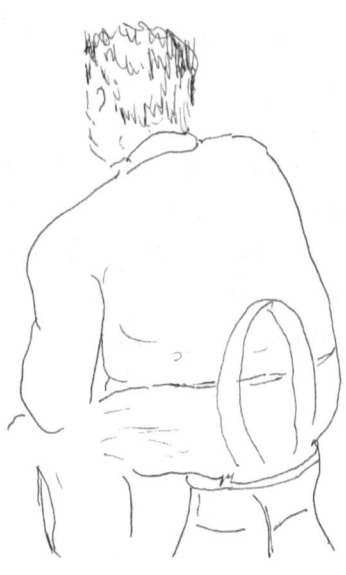

DESPAIR IN A DRY SEASON, NOW

If I knew who or how to ask for help,
I would certainly pivot that way now
and after clearing my throat and taking
a deep breath, after perhaps loosening
my neck muscles, improving my posture,
shaking loose the tension in my wrists
and hands, and maybe even walking in place
with a few jerky knee lifts before settling
down into a stance suggestive
(but looser)
of a soldier at attention—my feet
a few inches apart—I might kneel down
and bring my palms
together to signal supplication.

If I did pray, though, where would I look, up
or down? Or would I look, or could I bear
to close my eyes so as not to look, afraid
of missing something new happening now,
a hopeful sign, like the way that chickadee
just left the feeder peg and suddenly
without hesitation or fear landed
on a thin dogwood branch ten feet away,
landed so delicately that the branch
didn't even shiver in response—
a stunt that seems, every time I see it,
new, and I see it each time with such
wonder, such awe and wonder and surprise—
would that be help enough for now?

EVOLUTION

I

As I evolve, I become more aware
of my animal self. Right now, for instance,
as I bring this red nut to my mouth,
I can feel how my top lip labors to scoop
in the morsel, how, in concert with my tongue,
it shifts the nut slightly for my teeth to chew.
I notice also the mindless detachment
with which I'm half observing two little humans
who've squatted in front of my bench to chalk
nonsensical designs on the rough surface
of the promenade in Riverside Park. While I reflect
recursively, I feel unusually sensate today,
word-sated, content to absorb the nut's salty taste,
admire the reach of overarching locusts, and abhor
without rage the way a hovering helicopter's
whap-whap-whap shatters the air that carries
on it the scent of honeysuckle.
Fingering another nut from the pink palm
of my hand, my some-sort-of-other-thumb
tucks in to protect the rest of the handful
from spilling in my lap, and I feel my thoughts
slowly fading away, until I am what I most
properly am: old and newly a chimp again,
just taking it in,
                    all this.

II

O, blah, blah, blah, I deserve just to sit
and regard myself seeing what it is that I see.
I have worked hard, as my ancestors did
and my progeny will, to make sense
of what makes no sense at all. From my earliest days,
I struggled with the dictate that I/we must die.
I wrinkled pain into pleasure, stole gifts
from thin air—whiffs of Meaning puffed my way
by the prophetic winds that maul and caress
the world and spread fire even into the sea,
                    all this.

III

These days, I blow through brick walls,
as if through fog. Molecules, after all,
even those composing brick,
are made distinguishable only by the space
in between them,
which can be huge—barn-door huge—if you jettison
what your parents intended you to be.
Out of love, I know, out of love,
but misery, too.
For they, too, knew what lay ahead:
                    all this.

IV

Take heart: Even the stars have tricks to teach.
The Pleaides, for instance, Orion's
famously fuzzy companion, the star
cluster which precedes and conditions
the Hunter's unambiguous arrival
each year. Stare hard at the Seven Sisters
(the name by which the cluster is also known),
stare, stare until your eyes ache from trying
to clarify the image directly.
Isn't it maddening that we can only
resolve the deepest mysteries by gazing
somewhere off-center, even off-target,
like a slant rhyme or parable, gazing
not quite *at*
                all this?

MOTHER

Can she feel my eyes on her?
It seems she can. Whatever busyness
she was engaged in has suddenly
ceased: her perfect stillness betrayed
by her now-undulating web.

There. The web has grown quiet again.
I imagine her clinging with aching arms,
praying perhaps that my gaze will return
to my laptop keyboard, which, of course,
it does, as I hunt for and peck
the letters *d*, *o*, *e*, and *s*.

Taking advantage of my sudden
inattentiveness, she balls up a little closer
to the single rung of the wooden footstool
under which she's made her house,
in this, my house.

And if she were to begin humming
from her snug position, having deduced
that I have grown into a harmless being,
might she soon break into song,
as I am trying to do? And might it be
a lullaby?

MY OBSESSIONS

Endings as beginnings

The mysterious nature of experienced time

Coincidence and serendipity

The phases of the moon

The seasonal arcs of the sun

What to make of cloud shapes

New grass

Women

Unearthed grief

Death

SPECIES

It's the way we pronounce the word
that gives us away. Could an elephant
produce such a derisive sound?
Would even a hippo feel at ease
with the sibilance, would the snake, with
such a hiss?

Species: human contempt mouthed
in a bucket of spit.

Does it occur to the crocodile
that the river differs from its banks?
Or to the giraffe that its neck is tall?
Does the chimpanzee think of thunder
as a god, or the painted turtle ever
wonder where the frogs have gone?

DREAD

Legless, it sidewinds into the desert
of my mind, though I feel it lower down—
in the bowels, it seems. Yes, the bowels.

It makes little sense to speak to a snake,
but I've learned to ask what it wants of me
even though all it ever says is *you're*

done. Which makes me laugh because what Dread
means to say, I think, is *done for*, as in
your goose is cooked, you're dead, you've bought the farm,

which I know not to be true, but still, Dread
is not a thought, it's a deep-down-feeling
and in that sense not as dismissible

as thought, so you either take it as real
or take a pill to expel it as false-flagging
of the neuronal kind—mental.

Caesar certainly encountered Dread when
a blind man warned him to beware the ides.
Once voiced, betrayal seems inevitable.

There it is, the snake whispers, *you're* not *done.*
I will make sure you're here for all the fun.
Do bring some water, and maybe a gun.

THE ANIMIST'S VIEW

For days, I've meant to whack that big-leaf weed.
Tried pulling it up once, but it didn't give.
That was weeks ago. Now it's four feet tall,
waving with impunity in a breeze kicked up
by some heat-maddened conductor in the sky,
or so I imagine while sitting in my screened-in office
with its view of our backyard
and, over the fence, our belligerent
neighbor's rotting raised-bed garden.

But then I notice—and this is my gift,
if I have a gift at all—that the tall
weed is flirting like a girl with her granddad,
flirting with the lowest limb of a huge
white pine, a limb I've also been meaning
to cut because it's sagging fenceward
or, as is the case now, reaching out
to the little girl.

In concert, they bend and sway
with a kind of balletic hilarity,
until I can almost feel from here
the delicate caress of pine needle on leaf,
needle poking stem, needle tickling a rib,
breathlessly laughing while tickling,
the girl pulling away and leaning
back in for more, as if without me here

to describe it, they might keep performing
like this, just for themselves, just for the hell of it,
because who needs to talk
while you dance.

MEETING AT THE TREE LINE

I built a small fire in the clearing,
with brush I'd dragged out of the nearby woods.
A dry evening, and from the spot I'd picked
I watched Deneb appear overhead, then
Cygnus entire, its long neck stretched southwest.

A pine twig crackled excitedly, wheezed
and whistled in the agonizing flames.
Pure agony predicts transformation;
the phoenix needs first to suffer the ash.
Ash remembers fire; fire remembers fuel . . .

In just such a backward state of longing
I looked up and gazed without alarm
at two sharp, close-set eyes staring at me
from the darkness beyond the fire: a bear.
The *fact* of a bear. But, of course, a bear.

A bear can sniff a fart from fifty miles,
outrun a mountain lion in a sprint,
chomp through the back door of your SUV.
Patience must suffer hunger to feel sated.
This bear will wait for the fire to die.

IDENTITY, A VILLANELLE

So, let's be the person we want to be.
Whoever we choose, we're sure to be wrong.
We've already changed imperceptibly.

Not even "I am" survives scrutiny.
Nothing alive stays put for too long.
So, let's be the person we want to be.

The Principle's been named Uncertainty,
A twentieth-century science song.
We've already changed imperceptibly.

Attention to Self seems a guarantee
that we'll find a way to truly belong.
So, let's be the person we want to be.

Come celebrate, we're so joyously free,
Even if most of us aren't very strong.
We've already changed imperceptibly.

Identity feels loose and slippery,
But it certainly appeals to the throng.
So, let's be the person we want to be.
We've already changed imperceptibly.

WHAT REMAINS

Those beach stones on the windowsill once lent
weight to my undying love for someone,
but for whom and when? That tinny trinket
from Tibet, still so evocative of poverty
and wisdom, lies untouched
in a small saucer next to a bronze subway
token. A desiccated tree frog squashed flat
in midleap sits in a shard of pottery
from which reservation exactly?

It isn't spring yet, but a balance feels near.
The planet struggles to maintain its tilt,
habituated to seasons, even
when nothing is ever really new. Evidence
of entropy, found in the dust that collects
on surfaces and mixes with my own
sloughed-off skin
is easily ragged or feathered away.

But Medicine of the kind on my sill
begs to be crushed into powder
and hung from the neck in a pouch,
or melted down and shaped to fit
the wrist or finger until rubbed smooth
by time.

How else to contain, to honor and name,
unknowable volume,
unbearable resonance,
unspeakable desire.

WHEN YOU'RE FREE

It should have rained today,
this first full day of fall,
but deadlocked clouds
adjourned at dusk
and mist took over in the field.

Drawn by the change, and fully
mindful of its seductive lure,
still I was unprepared for you,
you within the moon,
your crystal spirit poking
through the passing purple haze,
your soul's eye sailing
in a sad slow dream.

I saw you stir and wake to life
and fall asleep again. And then again,
there was no moon, just me:
a misty field with me grown smaller
in it, waiting for the mist to clear
and leave you free to dance.

The mist will wrap your light
and hold us in it,
when you're free to dance.

A LATE SEPARATION

For me, it seems so long ago, just as
rockets were really becoming a thing,
that my life launched not seaward like a ship
but skyward into the miraculous
blue scheme that Wordsworth called Intimations.
Life would begin with inexpressible
clarity, wend its way through prodigious
bouts of banal certainty, and end with . . .

There comes a time in any long-lived life
when it dawns on you slowly that the drip
you suddenly hear is the drip you've *been*
hearing: that you don't matter anymore.
Not to the world, for sure, but not even
to your loved ones, who for their survival
have abandoned the need to imagine
you alive.

Your son will have found the peace you never
could, and your daughter will have found the mate
you weren't for her mom. Your parents will pose
perpetually in their wooden frames,
echoing the ghostly sorrow you feel
when you dare to glance at the bathroom mirror.

When that time comes, when your industrious
doings lie in pieces on the launchpad
amidst the rusted debris of failures,

when *that* happens, let go, and surrender
into the buoyancy of old age, relax into orbit,
assured that any surge of neediness
you might still feel is simply the trace burst
of the rocket that delivered you here.

Trust the mechanics: What was will always
and forever have been. Teach. And steer for
that weirdly magnetic realm where you just
might be welcomed again, naked, newborn,
and done.

About the Author

Dustin Beall Smith's essays have appeared in *Alaska Quarterly Review*, *The Gettysburg Review*, *Hotel Amerika*, *The Louisville Review*, *New Plains Review*, *The New York Times Magazine*, *The Atlanta Journal-Constitution*, *Backstage*, *River Teeth*, *The Sun*, *Writing on the Edge*, and elsewhere. His honors include a notable mention in *Best American Essays, 2008* and *2009*; the 2007 Katharine Bakeless Nason Prize for nonfiction through Middlebury College's Bread Loaf Writers' Conference; finalist, New Rivers Press 2006–2007 Many Voices Project Prose Prize; fellowships in 1995 and 1996 at the Virginia Center for the Creative Arts; and first-place Labor Press Council Awards for 1982, 1983, and 1984.

In the late '50s and early '60s, Smith helped pioneer sport parachuting in the United States. He later worked as an advance man for Robert Kennedy's senatorial campaign, in 1964, and for the Norman Mailer–Jimmy Breslin mayoral campaign, in 1969. He worked as a key grip in the film industry for twenty-seven years. His book *Key Grip: A Memoir of Endless Consequences* was published by Houghton Mifflin in August 2008.

Smith holds a BA in English and an MFA in creative writing from Columbia University. Starting in 2004, he taught creative writing at Gettysburg College, where he was also the coordinator of the Peer Learning Associates Program, until his retirement in 2021.

For more information, please visit dustinbeallsmith.com.